ANYTHING BUT THE TRUTH

Anything but the Truth

THE CREDIBILITY GAP—

HOW THE NEWS IS MANAGED

IN WASHINGTON

by William McGaffin and Erwin Knoll

G. P. *Putnam's Sons* *New York*

Acknowledgments

The authors wish to thank the following for permission to quote excerpts from their works:
"Can the President Always Tell the Truth?" by Jack Anderson, reprinted by permission of *Parade* magazine. Issue of January 30, 1966. "A Watchdog in Decline" by Robert O. Blanchard, reprinted by permission of the *Columbia Journalism Review*. Issue of summer, 1966. *The Splendid Misery* by Jack Bell, reprinted by permission of Doubleday & Company, Inc. "Press Agent—but Still President" by Ben H. Bagdikian, reprinted by permission of the *Columbia Journalism Review*. Issue of summer, 1965. *The Fourth Branch of Government* by Douglass Cater, reprinted by permission of Houghton Mifflin Company. *Presidential Leadership of Public Opinion* by Elmer E. Cornwell, reprinted by permission of the Indiana University Press. From *Memoirs: 1925–1950*, copyright © 1967, by George F. Kennan, with permission of Atlantic—Little, Brown and Company. *The Invisible Presidency* by Louis W. Koenig, reprinted by permission of Holt, Rinehart and Winston, Inc. *Wilson: The New Freedom* by Arthur S. Link, reprinted by permission of Princeton University Press, © 1956. "Vested Interests of Reporters" by James McCartney, reprinted by permission of *Nieman Reports*. Issue of December, 1963. "What Ails America?" by Hans Morgenthau, reprinted by permission of *The New Republic*, © 1967, Harrison-Blaine of New Jersey, Inc. *American Journalism* by Frank Luther Mott, reprinted by permission of The Macmillan Company, © 1962, The Macmillan Company. Lyle C. Wilson's chapter in *Dateline: Washington*, edited by Cabell Phillips, reprinted by permission of Doubleday & Company, Inc. "The Press, the President and Foreign Policy" by James B. Reston, reprinted by permission of *Foreign Affairs*. Issue of July, 1966. "Letter from Washington" by Richard Rovere, reprinted by permission of *The New Yorker*. Issues of March 18, 1967 and September 23, 1967. *With Kennedy* by Pierre Salinger, reprinted by permission of Doubleday & Company, Inc. *A Thousand Days* by Arthur M. Schlesinger, reprinted by permission of Houghton Mifflin Company. *The Coming of the New Deal* by Arthur M. Schlesinger, reprinted by permission of Houghton Mifflin Company. "The Final Troubled Hours of Adlai Stevenson," *Look* magazine. Issue of November 30, 1965. Reprinted by permission of Harold Matson Company, Inc. Copyright 1965 by Eric Sevareid. Hugh Sidey's column in *Life* magazine. Issue of September 8, 1967. Reprinted by permission of *Life* magazine. "The Government Has the Right to Lie" by Arthur Sylvester, reprinted by permission of the *Saturday Evening Post*. Issue of November 18, 1967. "The Widening 'Credibility Gap,'" reprinted by permission of *Life* magazine. Issue of August 12, 1966.

Preface

Early in 1967 we confided to a colleague in the Washington press corps that we were planning to write a book about the lies told by the government. "Only one book?" he asked. "My God, you could write a book a day." And he proceeded to regale us for more than an hour with his most recent misadventures in the Credibility Gap. That, as it turned out, was a typical reaction. We are indebted to many fellow correspondents and to a surprisingly large number of government officials for assistance in compiling material for this book. For reasons that we must respect, a few of the former and most of the latter asked to remain anonymous.

Among those who searched their memories and their files in our behalf, we are particularly grateful to Ben H. Bagdikian, free-lance magazine writer and commentator on the press; James Deakin, White House correspondent of the St. Louis *Post-Dispatch*; David Kraslow, news editor in the Los Angeles *Times* Washington bureau; Charles Roberts, White House correspondent for *Newsweek*; and Jules Witcover, national political reporter for the Newhouse newspapers. We bear full and final responsibility, of course, for the use we have made of the material they furnished.

Clifton Daniel, managing editor of the New York *Times*, provided the full text of the lecture printed as Appendix B. David Kraslow furnished the letter published as Appendix C, as well as a wealth of published and unpublished material on government deception in connection with the Bay of Pigs, the

Cuban missile crisis, and the intervention in the Dominican Republic.

Portions of Chapter 8 are adapted from an article by Erwin Knoll and Jules Witcover originally published in the *Columbia Journalism Review*. Excerpts from Chapter 1 appeared, in somewhat different form, in the *Progressive*.

This is a book about a crucial problem that confronts Americans in our time of crisis: the problem of government secrecy, deception, and distortion of the news. The problem is crucial because a democracy cannot function—indeed is no longer a democracy—when citizens are denied access to the information they must have in order to form enlightened judgments on the issues and actions over which they exercise ultimate sovereignty.

News management, the Credibility Gap—call it what you will, the problem is a grave and growing one. It is by no means new. Lapses in credibility have occurred in administrations going back to the earliest days of the Republic. More recently, official deceptions have been dramatically exposed in President Eisenhower's U-2 Affair, in President Kennedy's fiasco at the Bay of Pigs, and perhaps most noticeably of all during the Presidency of Lyndon Baines Johnson.

The perils posed by this trend are great, and the need to understand them cannot be exaggerated. The government, the press, and the American people have an urgent responsibility to seek the restoration of candor to the conduct of public affairs. As these pages go to press, President Johnson has declared that he will not seek another term of office. But the problems of official secrecy and deception will not end with his administration, as they did not begin with it. Mr. Johnson's successor, whoever he may be, will face his own Credibility Gap unless a conscious and concerted effort is made to erase the dangerous pattern of secrecy and deception detailed in this book—a pattern that is, by now, all too firmly established.

WILLIAM McGAFFIN
ERWIN KNOLL

Washington, D.C.
April, 1968

Contents

Knowledge will forever govern ignorance, and a people who mean to be their own governors must arm themselves with the power knowledge gives. A popular government without popular information or the means of acquiring it, is but a prologue to a farce or a tragedy or perhaps both.

—James Madison

1. The Gap and How It Grew

"The Credibility Gap"—what a polite, impersonal term! A term with bureaucratic overtones, like "the national debt" or "the balance of payments" or "the nuclear deterrent." A term coined only recently, but one that has passed into the language wherever Americans talk of public affairs. A term whose use is, as Walter Lippmann has observed, "rather like the habit of our Victorian grandparents who spoke of limbs when they were too shy to speak of legs." Newspaper reporters began talking about the Credibility Gap in the mid-1960's when they were too shy to speak of lies—the lies that increasingly, alarmingly, emanate from their government through its official spokesmen, including the President of the United States.

It is a new idea to Americans—the idea that the government lies to them—and one that does not go down easily. It runs counter to the American grain. It does not square with what the civics textbooks say about democracy or what the Founding Fathers said about the people's right to know, the people's need to know. Americans have always recognized that there are exceptions to the rule—that their government would not tell them *everything*. Matters of military security or diplomatic delicacy were tacitly or explicitly acknowledged as exempt from the normal demands of disclosure in an open society. Even Woodrow Wilson, it was acknowledged, was not dealing in absolutes when he pressed for "open covenants openly arrived at." But the developments of recent years differ not only in quantity but also in quality from the historic patterns of disclosure and secrecy. The difference is the Credibility Gap, and it has taken

13

root in the national consciousness. The government has become attuned to falsehood as a routine way of conducting its affairs. Official lies on matters large and small, foreign and domestic, are the daily fare of the Washington press corps, and often they are reported as truth for lack of better information.

Drawing on the experience of half a century, Lippmann commented in 1967: "So far as I know, there has never been a time when the President and the working press distrusted each other so much as they do today. The current conflict has become abnormally acute, and the relations between the Johnson administration and the press are unique, differing not only in degree but in kind from the normal tensions between responsible officials and free journalists. The conflict today has degenerated to the point where there is no longer much pretense that the news is not being manipulated in order to make the Congress, the newspapers, the networks, and the public at large support the President. The only question is supposed to be whether the manipulation works, how successfully the President and his officials and his press officers can operate."

If this were merely a problem for the press corps, there would be no reason for the American people to be interested, let alone concerned. Most reporters are compensated reasonably well for their work and have no claim on the public's sympathy for the occupational obstacles they encounter. Newspapers, magazines, and broadcast media can get along very well—all too well—with incomplete and even inaccurate Washington coverage. The troubling question about the Credibility Gap is how well the nation can get along—indeed, how long it can survive as a democracy—when its citizens are denied the information they need in order to arrive at intelligent decisions about matters of public policy. A persuasive case can be made that the information they now receive is neither sufficient nor reliable.

The situation is rich in paradox. The technology of communications has made formidable strides. Text and pictures—in living color—are transmitted almost instantaneously across the country and around the world. The media, endowed with more than their share of the nation's affluence, are spending more money than ever before to gather and disseminate the news. The correspondents are, by and large, better educated and more adept than those of earlier generations at mastering the complexities of the news. The government itself maintains a huge and growing public information apparatus, replete with armies of publicists and batteries of mimeograph machines and copying devices. The public's level of education has risen significantly, and the capacity for understanding the complexities of national affairs is, while still far from ideal, much greater than it has ever been. Yet it is evident that on the major issues of the time—particularly on the issue of Vietnam—Americans are uninformed (or misinformed) on the essential facts. The lack of facts and the argument over what the facts are have distorted and virtually destroyed the far more urgent debate that could and should be taking place on the difficult questions of national policy that are involved. As the 1968 Presidential campaign got under way, one Republican aspirant for the nation's highest office, Governor George Romney of Michigan, found it possible to charge that he had been "brainwashed" by the Johnson administration into supporting the war. Another, Governor Ronald Reagan of California, contended that the President was deliberately withholding the news that the war was being won. And both were believed by Americans who no longer knew *what* to believe.

In June, 1967, when the United States was accused by Arab leaders of military intervention on the side of Israel in the six-day Middle East war, Arthur J. Goldberg, the American ambassador to the United Nations, found it necessary to offer elaborate inspection opportunities to support the flat (and truthful) American denial—because of the self-serving unreliability of too many official pronouncements. Nonetheless, the Middle East war produced its own new widening of the Credibility Gap—the tragic case of the Navy "communications" ship, the U.S.S. *Liberty*, which was stationed so close to the fighting that Israeli planes and torpedo boats attacked it, killing thirty-four American sailors.

When Congressmen, responding to letters from relatives of the dead sailors, demanded to know why the ship had been so close to the Israeli shore, the Pentagon offered an explanation that the Washington *Post* called "nothing short of ludicrous." It said the position was required so that the *Liberty* could use the moon as a passive reflector for its communications. "How hitting the moon, 238,000 miles away, had anything to do with

changing the position of the ship by a comparatively minuscule
distance was not explained," George C. Wilson wrote in the
Post. "When pressed for an explanation last week, the Pentagon
fell back on 'no comment.' One Defense official, who winced at
his department's claim, quipped that the *Liberty*—to keep up
with the changing position of the moon—'would have had to
sail right across the sands of Sinai.' " In a news release, the
Pentagon asserted that the *Liberty*'s function was "to assure
communications between U.S. government posts in the Middle
East and to assist in relaying information concerning the evacua-
tion of American dependents and other American citizens. . . ."
The truth, which leaked out soon enough, was that the ship was
a spy vessel, equipped with elaborate electronic surveillance
gear and assigned to the National Security Agency, which
specializes in breaking the military codes of other nations. Presumably, the *Liberty* was monitoring Israeli and Arab battle-
field communications. The Pentagon's thin cover stories contributed a new term to the growing vocabulary of government
deception. It was coined by a high Defense Department official
who was overheard stating that the official falsehood about the
Liberty's mission could not be considered a lie, since it had
been formulated at the highest levels of government. It was an
"unlie," the official said.

The government's credibility was cast in doubt again in
January, 1968, in another spy ship incident—one with poten-
tially far more serious consequences than the case of the *Liberty*.
When the U.S.S. *Pueblo* and its eighty-three-man crew were
seized by North Korean vessels on January 23, the administration immediately and emphatically insisted that the ship had
been operating in international waters—"at all stages according
to every indication that we have," Secretary of State Dean Rusk
said. At the United Nations a few days later, Ambassador Goldberg declared that he wanted to "lay to rest—completely to rest—
some intimations that the *Pueblo* had intruded upon the territorial waters [of North Korea] and was sailing away from
territorial waters and that the North Korean ships were in hot
pursuit. This is not the case at all and I shall demonstrate it by
this map. . . . The location of the *Pueblo* was constantly far
away from Korean shores, always away from the twelve-mile

limit until it was taken into Wonsan by the North Korean vessels."

On February 4, however, Rusk and Defense Secretary Robert S. McNamara, who was about to leave the Cabinet, acknowledged that the *Pueblo* had been under radio silence for a ten-day period before she was captured and might have entered North Korean territorial waters. Goldberg and the State Department subsequently explained that their earlier, categorical denials had been intended to apply only to the day the *Pueblo* was seized. "As a technical matter," the Washington *Post* said in an editorial, "the Ambassador and the Department have a point. That is to say, a trained lawyer, with the complete transcript of the Goldberg presentation to the Security Council as well as the maps he used, probably would rule in his favor. So might anybody in the Council chamber at the time who could see the Ambassador pointing to maps as he talked. And so might even the private citizen with a television set who was watching the proceedings closely. But that leaves an awful lot of people who received the very clear impression that Mr. Goldberg was making a much broader claim. . . ." The *Post* added that while it did not believe Goldberg was "trying deliberately to mislead . . . we do think an administration already suspect, rightly or wrongly, on grounds of its credibility has the greater need to worry about its clarity."

President Johnson's Credibility Gap was opened, although no one knew it at the time, on August 11, 1964, when, as a candidate for election to the Presidency that he had inherited the previous November, he addressed himself to the question of the American role in Vietnam. "Some others are eager to enlarge the conflict," he asserted. "They call upon us to take reckless action which might risk the lives of millions and engulf much of Asia, and certainly threaten the peace of the entire world. Moreover, such action would offer no solution at all to the real problem of Vietnam." It is true, as Johnson has repeatedly maintained, that he was not the author of the American involvement in Vietnam, and it is fair to say that he was not the first President to mislead Americans about the nature of the war. The number of United States "military advisers" in South Vietnam was 900 when John F. Kennedy took office, and it had risen to some 16,000 by the time Johnson succeeded him. The fiction of their "advisory" role had been maintained even as they moved increasingly into active combat. Their mission, as the slogan had it, was to help the Vietnamese help themselves. But in 1964 President Johnson's Republican opponent, Senator Barry M. Goldwater of Arizona, was asking, "Why not victory?" and urging that the war be carried to North Vietnam. The President counseled a far more restrained course. It was, Johnson noted on September 28, "an illusion that force or the threat of force can resolve all problems." American military power, he said, "cannot be used to compel and frighten others into following our command." The only consequence of such action "would be constant, rising hostility and deepening tensions." The United States, Johnson warned, could not "demand resolution" of all the world's problems. "In this nuclear age we have concern about the affairs of every continent. This concern does not give us the right or responsibility to order the affairs of all other nations." The President was particularly concerned about the perils in Goldwater's proposal for air warfare against North Vietnam. "Before I start dropping bombs around the country, I would want to think about the consequences of getting American boys into a war with 700 million Chinese," he said.

In the Defense Department, as the President spoke, plans for a massive escalation of the war were well advanced. The case for bombing raids and large numbers of United States combat forces was being actively argued within the administration, but there was no hint of this in Johnson's campaign oratory. At that point, some 190 American lives had been lost in Vietnam, the President said on the stump, "but it is not like the 190,000 we might lose if we escalated the war." On October 21, 1964, he told the American people, "We are not about to send American boys nine or ten thousand miles to do what Asian boys ought to be doing for themselves." (See Appendix E.)

The first major step in escalation—the sustained bombing offensive against North Vietnam—began in February, 1965, three months after the election. The initial attack was on an ammunition dump at Donghoi, just across the seventeenth parallel, and the administration took pains to deny that it constituted an expansion of the war. The raid, it explained, was a "reprisal" for a Vietcong mortar attack on an American barracks at Pleiku in South Vietnam. As the bombing offensive continued in the weeks and months that followed, officials insisted that there had been no change of strategy, only of "tactics." The air war against North Vietnam became the longest reprisal raid in history.

Escalation on the ground began in March, 1965, when the President sent two battalions of Marines to Danang. The troops were dispatched, Secretary of State Dean Rusk explained, "to provide local, close-in security." It was "not their mission to engage in the pacification operations," but merely to protect American installations. Secretary of Defense McNamara offered similar assurances. The Marines, he said, would "patrol within narrow limits of the area and thus should not tangle with the Viet Cong." As the air attacks continued and the American troop commitment doubled and redoubled, reporters in Washington asked whether the war was being escalated. "That's an operational matter, not a policy matter," replied White House Press Secretary George Reedy. He referred the inquiries to the Pentagon, which replied with a minimum of meaningful information.

In May, 1965, two months after the first Marine contingents landed in South Vietnam, an anonymous military spokesman in Saigon acknowledged that the troops were there "to render combat support which includes, if necessary, fighting." A month later, on June 8, this was confirmed by the State Department's official spokesman, Robert J. McCloskey. "American forces will be available for combat support together with South Vietnamese forces as and when necessary," he said. Other State Department officials reported that an order to this effect had gone out to the American military commander, General William C. Westmoreland, "within the past several weeks." By this time such official statements merely confirmed the obvious. Nonetheless, they infuriated the President. A White House statement to the press on June 9 firmly denied that there had been any change in the mission of United States ground forces in Vietnam or that the President had sent any recent order of the kind reported to Westmoreland. Instead, the White House said, Westmoreland had been given "discretionary authority" from the very beginning to use his troops in combat. If this was the case, why had the Secretaries of State and Defense denied that the troops had a combat mission? The White House never said. Neither did Rusk and McNamara.

These were the beginnings of what was to become an undeviating pattern of official concealment and deception about the war. While the United States troop commitment in Vietnam rose into the hundreds of thousands, while casualty totals mounted into the thousands, while great and growing areas of North and South Vietnam were systematically devastated, while the war cast a heavy pall on the President's Great Society at home and on American foreign policy abroad, official spokesmen in Washington and Saigon and at the United Nations in New York continued to disseminate the steady stream of misinformation that will be detailed in Chapter 4. And as controversy over the war mounted at home, the President and his aides added insult to injury by charging that their critics lacked the information needed to form intelligent judgments.

By the fall of 1965 the Credibility Gap was no longer merely a specter conjured up by frustrated reporters and crotchety critics of the administration. The Opinion Research Corporation, in a national poll commissioned by the Columbia Broadcasting System, found that two Americans in three were convinced their government only sometimes told the truth about Vietnam. Thirteen percent believed the government was "almost never" truthful. Historian Henry Steele Commager deplored the "increased trend" in Washington to disguise the truth and blamed it on "the heavy role of the military." Said Commager: "Countries confronted with military problems act this way. They justify it in terms of national security." And he warned that "the habits of deception carry the danger of self-deception; you can begin to believe your own propaganda."

Traditionally, the Washington press corps has been able to enlist certain effective allies in its quest for information that the government wishes, for one reason or another, to withhold. In each administration some officials, motivated by friendship, concern for the public welfare, or simple self-interest, can be counted on to leak information to a favored reporter or to the press at large. The natural workings of the two-party system tend to make the party out of power an ally of the press when it seeks to uncover news that might prove injurious to the ins. And the checks and balances provided by the Constitution have often made the legislative branch an important counterweight to the executive's penchant for suppression. Most significantly, the deep-grained American commitment to the open society and to the people's right to know has tended, in the past, to inhibit federal officials from exercising too blatantly their aptitude for managing the news.

For a variety of reasons, none of these techniques is as efficient today as it once was in assuring the public of access to the facts. By frequent and firm edicts to his subordinates—buttressed, on occasion, by FBI investigations designed to uncover the source of leaks—the President has impressed on all but the most reckless public servants the advisability of maintaining tight secrecy on what he does not wish to have divulged. Washington today, Alan L. Otten has written in the *Wall Street Journal*, is "an exceedingly tight-lipped town, where comparatively little finds its way onto television screens or into print except what and when Lyndon Johnson wants. . . . Well-publicized reports of FBI probes of news leaks, of pointed White House inquiries as to which lower-echelon official talked to particular reporters, of Presidential threats to veto policies prematurely discussed in the press—these have dampened officials' readiness for even the most casual press contacts. Old friends in government suggest reporters call them at home rather than at the office, where their incoming calls are logged; they may not be able to say much anyhow, but this way they're not even suspect. Reporters are told that information is not available, that officials are too busy to talk, that everything about a certain matter must come from the White House (which in turn may say that information is available only at the agencies, putting the reporters on a squirrel run)."

The steady erosion of power of the legislative branch—a process that Congress has abetted by surrendering to the Executive even the constitutional prerogative of declaring war—has made Capitol Hill an ever less likely source of significant government information. Shackled to the shibboleth of "bipartisanship" in foreign policy, increasingly dependent on Presidential patronage, fearful of the wrath of a secrecy-prone administration, legislators of both parties tell little that they have not been authorized to disclose. And there is little that they could tell even if they were so disposed, for the administration no longer feels obliged to deal frankly even with Congress. "Why do they lie to me?" Representative Edith Green of Oregon, a senior Democrat on the House Committee on Labor and Education, exploded one day when she discovered that the federal anti-poverty agency, the Office of Economic Opportunity, had given her wholly misleading figures on the cost of operating Job Corps camps. For more than a two-year period, beginning February, 1966, Secretary Rusk made no public appearance before the Senate Committee on Foreign Relations, though he was re-peatedly invited to do so. The Vietnam war, Rusk explained on one occasion, presents "some very serious and delicate prob-lems" that cannot "always be fully explored or resolved with the Klieg lights and the rest of the world all looking on and listening in." Rusk offered that explanation, the New York *Times* noted, "at a State Department news conference under the floodlights of newsreel cameras."

Truth has fallen casualty to considerations of "national se-curity"—real or imagined—in previous administrations. In 1960 President Eisenhower was caught in a flagrant falsehood about the U-2 photo-espionage plane downed over the Soviet Union. A year later President Kennedy morosely (and privately) re-ferred to his ambassador to the United Nations, Adlai Steven-son, as his "official liar" about United States involvement in the Cuban Bay of Pigs invasion. In 1962 Kennedy's chief lieu-tenants lied about the administration's knowledge of Soviet missiles in Cuba, and one of them later publicly asserted the government's "right to lie" in a national crisis. Even on purely domestic matters the Kennedy administration's record for verac-ity was far from admirable. Six days before the 1962 Congres-sional elections, for example, Secretary of Labor W. Willard Wirtz announced that unemployment had reached a three-year low during October and that the number of unemployed had declined by 2,000,000 since the Kennedy administration had taken office. The Washington *Post* cautioned, in an editorial on November 3, that the claims smacked of election eve partisan-ship. After the election returns were in, Wirtz admitted to James McCartney of the Chicago *Daily News* that his statement had contained "invalid" statistical comparisons because the figures had not been adjusted for seasonal variations. Wirtz had also claimed, before the elections, that "4,500,000 more Americans have jobs than when this administration took office in January of 1961." This total, too, required seasonal adjustment and shrank, after the votes were in, to 1,224,000. Reporters, of course, had no way of independently ascertaining the correct figures; such economic data are available only through the government's formidable statistics-gathering apparatus.

On June 3, 1964, the General Accounting Office reported to Congress that the Kennedy administration had substantially inflated the accomplishments of its highly publicized accelerated public works program. The Comptroller General of the United States reported: "In our examination into the accuracy and reliability of selected information pertaining to the accelerated public works program we found that the reports contained significant overstatements of the number of jobs estimated to be created by accelerated public works projects. We found also that the reports contained overstatements with respect to the number of actual man-months of work created by Community Facilities Administration approved projects already under construction. A comparison of the estimated 21,814 man-months of work reported by the Area Redevelopment Administration for the 190 projects included in this review with the 9,533 on-site man-months actually worked on these projects shows that the estimates were overstated by 12,261 man-months, or about 128 per cent. . . . Our examination also disclosed that the 50,853 on-site man-months reported as actually having been worked on 497 Community Facilities Administration projects were overstated by 23,008 man-months, or about 83 per cent. . . ."

The Johnson administration has engaged in similar juggling of statistics. With appropriate fanfare, the White House announced that personal income in the United States had reached an all-time high in August, 1965. A footnote to the White House release said additional details were available from the Commerce Department. One detail not announced: The rate of farm income had suffered a $1 billion decline. What sets the Johnson administration apart from its predecessors, in fact, is merely that the dissemination of half-truths and untruths has become a matter of day-to-day routine. The President's plans for the coming weekend, the projected size of the federal deficit—no topic is too trivial or too important to be dealt with deceptively. But the truth has been treated most recklessly in official pronouncements about the gravest, most complex, and most controversial issue of the decade, the war in Vietnam. Each new wave of American involvement in Vietnam has washed up the debris of previous prevarication. To many citizens of the United States—and perhaps more of other nations—the war in Vietnam *is* the Credibility Gap.

Hans J. Morgenthau, director of the Center for the Study of American Foreign and Military Policy at the University of Chicago, says the Credibility Gap is the product of the "obvious implausibility" of the government's statements on Vietnam. "The people refuse to believe what the government tells them it is doing and plans to do," Professor Morgenthau wrote in the *New Republic* of October 28, 1967: "As they once credited George Washington with not being able to tell a lie, so they almost take it for granted that President Johnson will not tell the truth. This lack of trust is not limited to official statements on Vietnam; it extends to all matters of public concern. For deception is being practiced not occasionally as a painful necessity dictated by the reason of state, but consistently as a kind of lighthearted sport through which the deceiver enjoys his power. This withering away of the public's trust in government might matter little to a totalitarian regime which can afford to govern through terror and the manipulation of the mass media of communications. Yet a democratic government cannot rule effectively, and in the long run it cannot rule at all, if it is not sustained by at least a modicum of the freely given support of the people and their elected representatives."

In the summer of 1966 half a dozen families in Massillon, Ohio, were interviewed before, during, and immediately after a Presidential press conference that was carried into their homes by the medium of television. In five of the six homes the viewers questioned the accuracy of what they heard, reacting with deep suspicion, in particular, to President Johnson's comments on the situation in Vietnam. "He sends over B-52s at high altitude, and then they claim three hundred enemy killed," said a tool designer. "How do they know? It's a lot of malarkey. Everything Johnson says is to make him and his administration look good. At work we call him 'Honey Lips.'" A housewife commented, "We're not being told the truth about the war. Johnson knows the American people are upset about the casualties.

The real figures would lead to many more demonstrations.
That's why they don't tell us the truth." Said another: "He's
only going to tell me what he wants me to know." Massillon
(population 31,000) was chosen as a representative grass-roots
town by *Life*, which reported these reactions in its issue of
August 12, 1966. "We went to Massillon with no preconceived
ideas," explained Richard Stolley, the magazine's Washington
bureau chief, who headed the team of interviewers. "We
weren't sure there was a story. In Washington everybody talks
about the Credibility Gap, but was this just Capital phrase-
making? It was not."

Life's Massillon survey was a minute sampling, of course, but
there is ample evidence that it accurately reflected a deepening
crisis of confidence. When the American Institute of Public
Opinion (the Gallup Poll) asked Americans in October, 1967,
whether they thought the Johnson administration "is or is not
telling the public all they should know about the Vietnam
war," only 21 percent replied that they thought they were
getting the facts. Seventy percent thought they were not, and
9 percent ventured no opinion. "The prospect of American
citizens in great numbers having to choose whether to believe
their own government or that of an Asian Communist state—
and it's possible things can come to that—is a loathsome prospect, unprecedented, full of dangers," Eric Sevareid commented on CBS News.

President Johnson is understandably sensitive to talk about
the Credibility Gap, although he tries at times to make a joke
of it. "I don't want to appear incredible," he tells reporters
when he tries to duck a news conference question, or "I don't
want to jeopardize my credibility." But privately he complains
that charges of untruthfulness arise from the reporters' personal
dislike for their "cornpone President," as he phrases it, or from
the captiousness of the "Eastern establishment." Johnson's lieu-
tenants contend that the Credibility Gap is just a catchphrase
invented by disgruntled members of the press corps. Yet there
are times when the President and his aides appear to bring a
spirit of zestful competitiveness to the game of public deception.
One such occasion—by no means unique—arose at a televised
news conference on March 9, 1967, when Johnson was asked
whether there was any truth to reports that he was searching

for a successor to Henry Cabot Lodge as United States ambassador in Saigon. "No, there is no truth that I am looking for a successor," the President replied. Lodge, he added, had told him on several occasions that in due time he would leave his post, but there was "no definite date set at this moment for his departure." Less than a week later, Ambassador Ellsworth Bunker was named as Lodge's successor, and the White House press secretary, George Christian, smugly explained to reporters that the President's news conference reply had been "absolutely accurate"—Johnson was not looking for a successor on March 9 because he had already found one.

"Accurate, perhaps, but not truthful," the Chicago *Daily News* protested in an editorial. "In the context of the question, the answer clearly implied that Lodge would stay on. Newsmen were put off the track, the country misled, by a technical escape hatch." The editorial acknowledged that "no great harm was done in this instance," since it mattered little whether the shift of ambassadors was announced one week or the next. But the clearly demonstrated preference for deviousness was disturbing. "If the President, and all the government spokesmen who follow his orders and example, employ the same tricky sidestep on other, more serious matters, what can we believe?" the *Daily News* asked. "How can we know when we're getting the news straight or in such a form that makes it seem to mean the exact opposite of the truth?" The administration, the newspaper concluded, had so far undermined its credibility that only massive doses of straight talk could begin to close the gap. No doses of straight talk, massive or minuscule, were administered.

"Even the little things are guarded ferociously," White House correspondent Hugh Sidey wrote in *Life* magazine on September 8, 1967. "During the Eisenhower years one journalist thought that since payday was such a delightful American institution it would be interesting to chronicle the President's payday. Ike, who never lost his awe of big government, was more than obliging, telling how his paycheck came around from the Treasury Department, how he endorsed it and sent it over to his bank to be put into his personal account, and even a little bit about how he spent it. Several months ago when another writer went to the White House and asked for a story on what Lyndon Johnson did with his $100,000 salary he was met with a horrified expression and an incredulous, 'Are you kidding?' "

Nothing irks Johnson more than to have the name of a prospective Presidential appointee appear in the press before he is ready to make the announcement. Charles Roberts, White House correspondent for *Newsweek* magazine, recalls that in March, 1966, Johnson "was furious when the *Washington Post* reported that he had decided to name Deputy Under Secretary of State U. Alexis Johnson as his ambassador to Japan. After reading the report he barged into a news conference being conducted by Agriculture Secretary Orville Freeman to denounce it. He branded it 'some kid's statement over at the State Department'—a phrase that was changed to 'some*one's* statement' in the sanitized transcript of his remarks put out by the White House. His obvious anger at being scooped by the *Post* made the future of Alex Johnson a forbidden subject at the State Department—until September, when Mr. Johnson, apparently having cooled down, made it official and named him our ambassador to Japan."

Such incidents have occurred time and again. One of the earliest examples came in the fall of 1964, when Johnson was asked, during a news conference at the LBJ ranch, whether he planned to appoint Texas businessman Marvin Watson to the White House staff. "I would like to, but I have no plans whatever," the President replied. "He has other problems, other duties now, and there is not anything in the offing. I see a good deal in the press about it. But if they had taken the same caution you do [by asking the President] they wouldn't have misled their readers." The President's denial was duly reported, and two months later Watson got the job.

James Deakin of the St. Louis *Post-Dispatch* recalls another appointment story. "One sunny day in July, 1965," he says, "the President presided at a ceremony in the Rose Garden. Afterward he invited reporters into his office for an impromptu press conference. In the course of things, I asked him whether he would tell us about his plans for filling the vacancy on the Supreme Court that had been created by the appointment of Justice Goldberg as UN ambassador. Johnson replied flatly that he had not even begun to consider the matter. He did not say, 'I have no comment on that,' or 'I can't tell you anything about that,' or 'I'm not ready to make an announcement on that.' He did not use any of the many phrases available to a President who does not want to answer a question but does not want to mislead the public either. Instead, he said he had not even begun to consider the matter. The next day, he announced the appointment of Abe Fortas to succeed Goldberg."

The President, Deakin concludes, just can't leave well enough alone. "There is no constitutional or legal requirement that a President answer reporters' questions. There are many times when he is well advised not to. But Johnson, it seems, just can't resist the old impulse. He has to play the old shell game. He has to see whether his hand is still quicker than the public eye. The result is that he often misleads the White House correspondents and, through them, the American people."

From such experiences, White House correspondents have formulated what they call the Oshkosh Rule. It holds, in brief, that a Presidential decision will be reversed or at least deferred if it is publicized in advance. Johnson himself proclaimed the rule in the fall of 1966. "The day will come," he said at a news conference, "when regularly employed speculators will find out that their speculations are just pure speculation and nothing else because we don't appoint men on that basis. . . . When you see on the ticker that Oshkosh says that Bob Pierpoint may be named Chairman of the Joint Chiefs of Staff," Johnson continued, looking at Robert C. Pierpoint of CBS News, "you don't necessarily need to give much credence to it because the very fact that it is on there is the best indication that it is not likely to happen."

The President, the Washington *Post* editorialized on September 15, 1967, "ought to get over this annoyance" at press disclosure of his designated appointees. "Such conjectures may take the fine edge of surprise off his own announcements. They may occasionally embarrass him or someone who fancies himself a stronger candidate for a job than he really is. But they serve a useful purpose. No matter how complete an investigation the Federal Bureau of Investigation and the Civil Service may run on a man being considered for appointment, the whole community will do the job better and more cheaply, if given a chance. The appointee, sooner or later, must be exposed to the Senate and to the community as a whole. It is better to elicit the worst that Congress and the community has to say of a nominee before he is nominated than to invite the criticism after the fact. . . . So the press, when it does its best to discover possible nominees for federal posts, is not only fulfilling its public responsibility and duty to its readers, it is also performing for the President a service no one else can perform for him. And it ought to continue to do it, no matter how much he resents it."

But resent it he does, and even more formidable than his proclivity for making news is his zeal for denying it, postponing it, even *un*making it when his decisions are threatened by unauthorized publication. "Premature disclosure reduces his options," Bill D. Moyers, the former White House press secretary, once explained. "Fundamental to his operations and way of life is surprise, which keeps his foes off balance. He wants to retain the advantage of calling his own signals and deciding his own timing." Roberts of *Newsweek* observes less charitably that "the President, in fact, seems to have an Alice in Wonderland concept of the news. Like the Queen of Hearts, nothing is so until he says it's so. And if anyone in government says something is so before Mr. Johnson says it, he risks the fate of the Queen's courtiers."

The scope of the Oshkosh Rule extends beyond the matter of Presidential appointments and touches the most solemn affairs of state. In effect, the rule gives every Washington correspondent a potential veto over national policy: If he writes about it in advance, it is likely to be changed. A typical episode involved Philip Potter, the Washington bureau chief of the Baltimore *Sun*, and it occasioned a break in his long-standing friendship with the President. Potter told the essential details in the *Sun* in January, 1967: "After days of hard digging and talks with many responsible people a year ago," he wrote, "this correspondent disclosed that the President was prepared at a Cabinet meeting to announce a new Food for Peace program taking into account the fact that agricultural surpluses had disappeared and the government would have to acquire food on the market to continue its war on hunger. On reading the article, the President directed that the mimeographed handouts officially disclosing the plan be burned; the plans for public announcement were canceled. The steps were eventually taken, but in a piecemeal fashion. Thus, it could never be said that the *Sun's* article was an accurate forecast. The President felt that an option had been foreclosed and he had been betrayed."

James B. Reston, associate editor of the New York *Times*, has recorded a similar experience. "I once saw the speech President Johnson was going to make at the twentieth anniversary celebration of the founding of the United Nations and printed his plans for ending the financial crisis that was going on in the U.N. at that time. He was furious. He called in the Secretary of State the very night of publication, ordered the speech rewritten to eliminate the reported plans and made a different speech," Reston wrote in *Foreign Affairs*. He concluded that "if you learn that the President is going to do something on Friday and print it on Tuesday, this is likely to be regarded as an impertinence and a presumption which the President will punish by changing his plans."

Perhaps the most blatant instance of *un*making the news involved a political campaign trip "from Boston to Austin" that Johnson had planned just before election day in 1966 and immediately after his seven-nation tour of the Pacific. During the President's visit to Asia, White House aides in Washington, as well as in the touring Presidential party, spread the word that he would visit as many as fifteen states in four days. Advance men and Secret Service agents were dispatched around the country to prepare for the campaign swing. Hopeful Democratic candidates were advised that Johnson would put in an appearance in their behalf. Inevitably, some news stories got into print—and when the President returned from the Pacific, he canceled the trip. What's more, he declared that plans for a campaign trip had never existed, except in the feverish imagination of the press corps. "We don't have any plans, so when you don't have plans, you don't cancel plans," Johnson told the White House correspondents—and the nation. "The people of this country ought to know that all these canceled plans primarily involve the imagination of people who phrase sentences and write columns, and have to report what they hope or what they imagine." Even the staid Associated Press was moved to mild sarcasm that afternoon. It reported: "Leading Democrats from coast to coast busied themselves today unplanning plans for unplanned campaign visits by President Johnson. Really caught short was Boston's Police Commissioner Edmund L.

McNamara, who had 1,100 uniformed men standing by to protect the President on an unplanned appearance planned for today. Faces fell as far South as Memphis, as far North as Chicago and as far West as Los Angeles. . . ." The President later confided to intimates that he had deliberately withheld word of his change of plans from Moyers, who was then winding up his tour of duty at the White House. "Bill would have leaked it to the press," Johnson explained.

Every Washington correspondent has his own favorite examples of the Credibility Gap and his own favorite definition. Henry L. Trewhitt once defined it in the Baltimore *Sun* as "the degree of refusal by the public to accept at face value what the government says and does." Such refusal comes slowly and is based on hard experience, but there has been no lack of experience in recent years. An early lesson was provided in Johnson's first Presidential press conference on December 7, 1963, when he was asked about the size of the federal budget he would submit to Congress the following January. The President gravely implied that the budget could not be kept below $100 billion. President Kennedy's last budget had come to $98.8 billion, Johnson pointed out, and he would have to add about $3.5 billion to cover built-in cost increases. The prospect of substantial budget increases was reinforced later that month by high (and anonymous) administration sources at a briefing for correspondents at the vacation White House in Texas. The reporters were taken in; they believed what they were told and wrote it. The public was prepared, weeks ahead of time, for the first peacetime budget to exceed $100 billion. The budget that was sent to Congress came to $97.7 billion, and Johnson was praised for a remarkable achievement in economizing. The White House correspondents thought it was a remarkable achievement, too, but in their view economizing was the least of it.

"Under President Johnson's leadership," Jack Anderson wrote in the January 30, 1966, issue of *Parade* magazine, "many government departments have issued announcements that tend to mold the facts as the administration would like them to appear. For example, when the Ranger-6 spacecraft failed in its mission to photograph the moon, the public was told failure was due to a minor malfunction. But a report classified 'secret' said an investigation disclosed 'weaknesses . . . so extensive that in combination they suggest that the present hardware . . . is unlikely to perform successfully. . . .'" Another hardware failure—and a disastrous one—was the Apollo I moon capsule fire in January, 1967, that claimed the lives of three astronauts. The National Aeronautics and Space Administration, sensitive to charges of mismanagement and perhaps malfeasance in the Apollo program, placed every conceivable obstacle in the path of reporters trying to ascertain the facts. In its 1967 report, the Freedom of Information Committee of the American Society of Newspaper Editors charged that "NASA information not only was late and sparse, but some of it was deliberately misleading, some of it inaccurate. Although the agency knew within five minutes, it took two hours for reporters to learn that all three astronauts were dead."

George Reedy was still the White House press secretary when the Los Angeles *Times* reported on good authority that President Johnson was preparing to ask Congress for a $4 billion reduction in excise taxes. Reedy scoffed at the figure and declared it bore "no relationship" to any decision that had been made. The total reduction eventually proposed by the President, as it turned out, was $3.964 billion. Johnson himself denounced the Washington *Star* for reporting—erroneously, he said—that he would propose a 3 percent average pay increase for federal employees. The pay raise proposal followed shortly after the denunciation; it averaged 3 percent.

On January 22, 1965, two days after the Johnson inauguration, a reporter asked Reedy whether the President had executed an agreement with Vice-President Hubert H. Humphrey about the procedure to be followed in the event that the President became disabled. (The Constitution had not yet been amended to provide for this eventuality.) "No, we just haven't gotten to that yet," the press secretary replied. A few days later Johnson was hospitalized for treatment of a respiratory infection, and the question came up again. Yes, Reedy said, Johnson and Humphrey did have a disability agreement. In fact, he added, they executed it "sometime before the inauguration." The President's health was in the news again in October, 1965, when Johnson underwent surgery for removal of his gall-bladder. Before entering the hospital, he announced to the press that "a thorough examination showed this to be the only trouble." After the operation, however, the surgeons disclosed that they had also removed a kidney stone. Their curiosity aroused, reporters asked whether there was anything else they had not been told. Just another stone which had not been removed, Johnson's personal physician replied. It was lodged in the left kidney, and the doctors had known about it "for some years."

A catalog of such deceptions, major and minor, could be extended over many pages. Some are, indeed, no more than little white lies—but even little white lies loom large when they are uttered by the President of the United States. The credibility problem has become the topic of a special Washington brand of black humor. It is said that the old Chesapeake & Ohio Canal, which runs from Washington to the mountains of Maryland, is bounded by the Cumberland Gap at one end and the Credibility Gap at the other. Before he left the White House press office to become publisher of the Long Island newspaper *Newsday*, Moyers quipped at a private dinner that "the crisis of credibility has gotten so out of hand that we don't believe our own leaks." Not long ago White House correspondents devised what they called the LBJ Credibility Test. It went like this: "You don't have to worry about the Credibility Gap when the President smooths down the hair on the back of his head; you don't have to worry about it when he strokes the side of his nose; you don't have to worry about it when he rubs his hands; but when he starts moving his lips, look out!"

If the rule is overstated, it has its practical applications nonetheless. Many reporters find it prudent to assume that today's denial will turn into tomorrow's confirmed news and to prepare themselves accordingly. This was what happened, for example, at the vacation White House in Texas over the New Year's holiday weekend in 1967. When the deputy press secretary, Robert H. Fleming, insisted that no announcement was imminent about the proposed supersonic transport plane, a few careful newspapermen began boning up on the SST. Their wariness was rewarded the very next day, when the Federal Aviation Agency announced that Boeing had been selected as the contractor to build the airframe for the huge airliner. Even while that news was being released in Washington, however, the

President was telling a press conference in Texas that "we don't have any definite date" for the decision on the SST. It was only the latest instance of news manipulation on the jet transport project—an enterprise that will eventually cost the nation's taxpayers up to $5 billion. At the very outset, Johnson had secretly assigned a DX priority to the SST—a classification usually reserved for defense and space programs affecting the national security. "The suspicion must arise in many minds," the New York *Times* commented when it learned of the secret DX priority, "that Mr. Johnson took this course because he wanted to avoid a vigorous public debate about the wisdom of the controversial supersonic transport project." Congress and the nation, the *Times* concluded, "should have been allowed a direct voice in deciding whether to put the giant transport ahead of the War on Poverty and the associated effort to give the Negro full equality."

The effort to avoid vigorous public debate on controversial issues—to create an artificial consensus by closing the channels of informed discussion—is certainly one motive for the secrecy and mendacity that characterize the day-to-day conduct of public affairs in the Johnson administration. This, in effect, is what the President's aides mean when they emphasize the importance of "keeping his options open" on policy decisions. An open option, in this sense, is one that has not been foreclosed by the mobilization of public opinion in a democracy. This is not to suggest that the President's decisions—even those arrived at in secrecy or shrouded in deception—are invariably wrong, but right or wrong, they are produced by a process that diminishes the freedom of citizens to take part in the decision-making process.

It may be argued, for example, that the actions the President has taken on a number of occasions to curb inflationary price increases in major industries are justified by the highest motives of national economic stability. This makes it all the more troublesome, however, that extraordinary efforts have been made to hide the federal intervention from public scrutiny. A case in point is the attempt of aluminum manufacturers in the fall of 1965 to raise their prices. Johnson, concerned about inflationary consequences of such a move, arranged for an announcement that the government would dispose of 200,000 tons of its stockpiled aluminum on the open market. The action produced the desired effect: It forced a prompt price rollback. But White House aides, acting under the President's instructions, categorically denied any inference that the threat to dump aluminum had forced the industry to back down. In reply to reporters' questions, White House spokesmen insisted that there was "no connection whatsoever" between the two actions. Later, when the emergency had passed, the President privately boasted about the role he had played in the affair and confided that he had personally intervened with a vice-president of Alcoa.

In the face of such experience, George Christian found it possible to tell a nationwide radio audience in mid-1967 that Johnson is "a very candid man," who is "rather open in his discussions with the press and with the public." In a televised interview on December 31, 1967, Christian said: "The question of the Credibility Gap is something that puzzles me as much as it does anyone. This has happened to other Presidents. It is, in a political sense, a smart thing to do, to discredit your President." Christian denied that he had ever deliberately misled a reporter, though he acknowledged that "there are mistakes on both sides." Johnson himself told a group of college students at the White House on February 12, 1968, "I read a lot about the Credibility Gap, and I know we have one because there are instances when we don't understand the implications of all we say and sometimes the people who hear it don't understand it." In fact, many officials seem genuinely unaware of the dimensions of the credibility problem. Yet lying—or at least the withholding of truth—has become almost second nature to them in the daily performance of their duties. One cannot be certain that the Pentagon spokesman who issued the cover story about the U.S.S. *Liberty* was conscious of the fact that he was putting out a deception in the name of the government of the United States. When the Prime Minister of Singapore, Lee Kuan Yew, announced in the summer of 1965 that a CIA agent had offered him a $3,300,000 bribe five years before, the State Department automatically issued a stiff denial. Unfortunately, Lee produced proof—a letter of apology signed by none other than Dean Rusk. Understandably embarrassed, the department admitted that

Lee was right and explained that its spokesman had been unaware of the facts. It did not explain why Rusk allowed the
denial to be issued.

"This city is awash in lies and deceptions of many kinds,"
Richard H. Rovere wrote in his "Letter from Washington" in
the *New Yorker* of March 18, 1967, "and the mere fact that a
State Department official says the Department has the evidence
to prove that it is telling the truth does not, of course, mean
that such evidence exists. Nor would it necessarily mean, in the
event that what he said turned out to be false, that the man was
himself a liar. It would not be the first time that the truth has
been kept from or misrepresented to high government officials
by other high government officials. In 1960, the U-2 affair, and
in 1961, after the Bay of Pigs, a number of respected spokesmen
were caught in lies that were the product not of their own
mendacity but of their having been deliberately misinformed or
left uninformed." If high government officials cannot count on
the candor of their colleagues, what chance do the press and the
public have?

The essential fact about the current information crisis in the
capital is not that the press is more critical of the Johnson administration than it has been of any other (it is not), nor is it
that this administration is more resentful of such criticism (it is,
but the Kennedy administration gave it close competition). The
essential fact is that the information war has been escalated,
on the government's part, by the use of unprecedented techniques of news suppression and outright falsification. Never in
the memory of senior Washington correspondents has it been so
difficult to ascertain the truth about major decisions and developments within the government.

The press, of course, is not exclusively dependent on official
handouts (although it behaves all too often as if it were). In
virtually every case cited in this chapter, reporters eventually
ascertained the facts, and they were published. As a rule, however, publication came long after the facts had lost their
urgency—and after government decisions had been made without the benefit of informed public discussion. This is the most
dangerous aspect of the Credibility Gap. Another peril lies in
the persistent undermining of public confidence in the established institutions of the nation's political life. As much as the

Vietnam war or the urban crisis or any other specific problem in American life, the Credibility Gap contributes to the spreading disaffection and alienation among thoughtful citizens. Increasingly they seem incapable of the act of faith required to believe in America when America's government can't be believed.

J. R. Wiggins, the editor of the Washington *Post,* has observed that "a government that too readily rationalizes its right to lie in a crisis will never lack for either lies or crises." Washington has a plentiful supply of both.

2. The Vanishing Press Conference

Lyndon Baines Johnson has not been the first President afflicted with a Credibility Gap, though that term has become a household word in his administration. John Fitzgerald Kennedy was certainly not the first to practice the fine art of news management, though that phrase came into the language during his brief tenure in the White House. In fact, Presidential credibility has been stretched—and occasionally shredded—since the earliest days of the Republic, and the Founding Fathers displayed no mean talent as news managers. If their methods were primitive by today's sophisticated standards—well, those were simpler times.

It was easier in those days for politicians to find willing collaborators in the press—editors who worked closely with them and saw nothing unethical about accepting rewards ranging from private loans to government jobs or public printing contracts. The nation's early history abounds in examples of such mutually profitable arrangements. It also offers illustrations of the pitfalls and problems that even then beset the government in its dealings with the press. George Washington, for instance, invited trouble when he assured superb play for one of his speeches in a Philadelphia newspaper by giving it the only copy of the text. The papers he shut out described the illustrious Father of Our Country as "pusillanimous," "treacherous," "mischievous," and "inefficient."

Thomas Jefferson, whose passionate advocacy of a free and unfettered press is unmatched among the Presidents, occasionally found it difficult to put his principles into practice. He made one newspaper, the *National Intelligencer*, the mouthpiece for his administration, giving it a virtual monopoly on news. Other papers reacted by accusing him of keeping a mistress, trying to seduce a friend's wife, padding his expense accounts, and being an atheist.

Samuel Harrison Smith established the *National Intelligencer* in the new village of Washington on October 31, 1800, acting on the invitation of Jefferson, who was then running for the Presidency. It was the first important paper in the new capital, but it was not the first that owed its existence to Jefferson. The first, started by Philip Freneau in Philadelphia on October 31, 1791, was a semiweekly, the *National Gazette*. Jefferson, who was Secretary of State at the time, took care of the editor by putting him on the State Department payroll as a translator.

Jefferson's attempts at news management were hardly unique in that era of highly partisan journalism. He found it necessary to establish the *National Gazette* as a spokesman for his Republican Party because his Federalist rival, Alexander Hamilton, already had his own propaganda sheet, the semiweekly *Gazette of the United States*. John Fenno, who founded it in 1789 when New York was the capital of the United States, frankly stated in his first issue that the paper's mission would be to "hold up the people's own government in a favorable point of light." Carrying contributions from Hamilton, John Adams, and other leading Federalists, he contended that it was "the office of patriotism, by every exertion, to endear the general government to the people."

But endearing the general government to the people was hardly every editor's professional goal. Freneau, Jefferson's protégé, charged in the *National Gazette* that Washington wanted to be King of the United States—an accusation that prompted Washington to assert that he would rather be in his grave than "in my present situation" and to regret that he had not followed out his original intention to resign from the Presidency. A few weeks after his Farewell Address, he may have been sorry that he had let Hamilton talk him into deleting a section denouncing the press for its abuse of him. For the *Aurora*, an opposition Republican newspaper, attacked the retiring President as a man who had "debauched," "deceived," and exerted an "improper influence" on the nation. "Let his conduct then be an example to future ages," it fumed. "Let it serve to be a warning that no man may be an idol. . . ."

The right of a free press to report critically on the activities of its government was a major issue in Jefferson's campaign for the Presidency in 1800. His target was the Alien and Sedition Acts of 1798, enacted by the Federalist Congress to empower President John Adams to deport aliens and imprison editors who wrote "false, scandalous and malicious" statements. As President, Jefferson pardoned everyone who had been convicted during the Adams administration under what he called this "unauthorized act of Congress." Yet Jefferson found little joy in dealing with an unfettered press. Once he proposed, only half in jest, that newspapers should be divided into four sections: "Truths," which would be the smallest, he thought; "Probabilities"; "Possibilities"; and "Lies," which he said would be the largest part. He prided himself, however, on never contradicting "the thousands of calumnies so industriously propagated against myself." Toward the end of his second term he disclosed that this had been part of a deliberate and earnest test. "I have lent myself willingly as the subject of a great experiment," he wrote in 1807, to prove that an administration conducting itself with integrity and common understanding "cannot be battered down even by the falsehoods of a licentious press." He had demonstrated, he believed, that "the press is impotent when it abandons itself to falsehood" and that there was even less danger to an administration such as his from newspapers which confined themselves to the "legal and wholesome limits of truth." So he had suffered the abuse, without contradicting the lies, to demonstrate to the world "the falsehood of the pretext that freedom of the press is incompatible with ordinary government." He retained deep into his old age the conviction that a free press is "the only security of all," as he told Lafayette in a letter written at Monticello on November 4, 1823. "The force of public opinion cannot be resisted, when permitted freely to be expressed. The agitation it produces must be submitted to. It is necessary to keep the waters pure." [1]

It was not the Jeffersonian philosophy of liberty, however, but rather the Jeffersonian practice of press subsidies that pro-

[1] Paul Leicester Ford, ed., *The Writings of Thomas Jefferson* (New York, Putnam, 1905), Vol. XII, p. 322.

vided leading newspapers of that era with their security. On the other hand, the election of a new President could mean the end of the charmed existence which the favored paper had led under his predecessor. Jefferson's *National Intelligencer* managed to retain its priority position for a quarter of a century. In 1830, however, it was replaced as the Presidential mouthpiece by the Washington *Globe*, established by friends of President Andrew Jackson and subsidized by $50,000 a year in government printing contracts. "Old Andy" named the paper's three top executives, dictated ideas which they rewrote into sparkling editorials, and used them as a kitchen Cabinet, which sometimes exercised even more power than his official Cabinet. He extended his influence with the fourth estate still further by appointing a host of newspapermen from other papers to government jobs.

"Jefferson had been an idealist who had never quite understood the rough-and-tumble journalism of the times," Frank Luther Mott concludes in *American Journalism*.[2] Jackson, on the other hand, was "thoroughly practical in his relations to the press," he says, "taking the papers as he found them, molding them, and using them. . . . He certainly had no great reverence for the abstract principle of freedom of the press."

In 1846, the golden tap of federal funds which Jackson and others had used to subsidize their favorite newspapers began to close. Government printing contracts were placed under a competitive bidding system. The tap was sealed shut in 1860, when the Government Printing Office was established. By this time, however, the newspapers were becoming more prosperous, from advertising and mass circulation revenue, and no longer had to rely on the largess of officeholders. With financial independence, they became more influential than ever, and were courted by ambitious politicians. Joseph Medill of the Chicago *Tribune* played a large part in the nomination and election of Abraham Lincoln. During the period when the *Tribune* was building up the Lincoln boom, Lincoln used to frequent the newspaper's offices. After he had become President, Lincoln read the newspapers as carefully as a Johnson, a Kennedy, or a Franklin Roosevelt and was always accessible to their representatives. He also tried his hand, with no little success, at

2 Frank Luther Mott, *American Journalism* (New York, Macmillan, 1950), p. 180.

managing the news. He had a problem, during his 1864 campaign for reelection, with two of the nation's most prominent newspapers, James Gordon Bennett's New York *Herald* and Horace Greeley's New York *Tribune*. The *Herald* had been hostile toward Lincoln throughout the four years of the Civil War. Late in the Presidential reelection campaign, however, it endorsed his candidacy. Greeley, too, had been less than enthusiastic about Lincoln until a couple of months before the election, when he swung over to his support. Lincoln, it is believed, induced Bennett to change his mind by offering to send him to Paris as United States ambassador and won Greeley over by promising to take him into his Cabinet as Postmaster General. Lincoln had a way with young reporters, too. After his election, the Associated Press appointed twenty-five-year-old Henry Villard to be the first reporter assigned full time to cover the President-elect. Villard, however, was so excited as the special train was leaving Illinois for Washington that he forgot to take notes on Lincoln's departure speech. But he was able to file a story from the first telegraph station because Lincoln obligingly wrote it out for him in pencil on the train.

In the administrations between Lincoln's and Grover Cleveland's, the Washington press corps gradually developed in number and, as the Presidents ruefully discovered, in its capacity for intruding into their private lives. This is a common complaint with Presidents, but few have voiced it with as much cause as Cleveland. During his 1884 campaign he was accused in newspaper stories of being the father of an illegitimate son. Two years later, when the bachelor President was married in the White House, he tried to keep the wedding private and off limits to the press. The reporters, however, had other plans, and there was no elaborate Secret Service network to get in their way. First, they surrounded the White House, from which they had been barred, announcing that they did not intend to let the newlyweds escape without them. Cleveland and his bride succeeded in boarding a special train that carried them to a honeymoon camp in Deer Park, Maryland. But the next morning, when the President arose at ten o'clock, he looked out on a lawn full of reporters who had managed to follow him. Cleveland's response was anything but Jeffersonian. First, he fired off a protest to the New York *Evening Post*. Then, a few months later, in the midst of a speech at Harvard, he looked at the two long rows of reporters sitting in front of him and impulsively let loose a memorable attack. "The silly, mean and cowardly lies that every day are found in the columns of certain newspapers," he rumbled, "violate every instinct of American manliness, and in ghoulish glee desecrate every sacred relation of private life."

By 1893, when Cleveland took office for the second time, there were more than 150 correspondents in Washington. The President held no press conferences (the practice was introduced when Theodore Roosevelt's administration began in 1901), and he was not generally accessible to the press. Cleveland refused to be the guest of honor at dinners of the journalists' Gridiron Club, and he once ordered a photographer not to send pictures of him to the New York *World* or the New York *Journal.* He sometimes wrote his own press releases, however, for distribution by his secretary on Sunday evenings, and he talked freely on occasion to his two favorite correspondents, Francis A. Richardson of the Baltimore *Sun* and Francis E. Leupp of the New York *Evening Post.*

It was a far different story with William McKinley. Many of his friends were newspapermen, whom he had first met when he served in Congress. On occasion, he would call in several correspondents to receive an authorized statement from him. And he had a rather neat talent for news management, a knack reminiscent of the techniques of an earlier era. Instead of appointing his campaign manager to be Postmaster General, he chose an editor, Charles Emory Smith of the Philadelphia *Press*, and Smith, in turn, named editors, possibly 3,000 or more, to be postmasters.

When Theodore Roosevelt decided to initiate the first casual question-and-answer press conference ever conducted by a President, he fitted it into the late afternoon hour when his barber came to the President's office to give him his predinner shave. The news conference, like the shave, was a virtuoso performance before a small handful of reporters. When questions offended the President, he would push the straightedge razor aside and pace up and down, lather covering his face, while he rebuked the offending reporter for displaying such ignorance or impudence. But Roosevelt endeared himself **to** the White House correspondents by bringing them in from the outdoors, where they had been compelled to wait, rain or shine, to interview Presidential callers, and installing them in the first White House press room.

Roosevelt also helped the reporters—and himself—by directing his secretary in 1901 to take on the additional duty of functioning, in effect, as press secretary. The position was not formalized until 1929, when Herbert Hoover brought George Akerson to the White House from the Commerce Department and gave him the official title of press secretary. Akerson, in assuming exclusive responsibility for the President's public relations, instituted the practice of holding his own meetings with the White House reporters twice a day. But it was Theodore Roosevelt's secretary, William Loeb, Jr., who acted as the first White House press secretary in everything but name. Before Roosevelt, as Elmer E. Cornwell, Jr., notes in *Presidential Leadership of Public Opinion*,[3] Presidents rarely believed that reporters "must be catered to or wooed." Roosevelt, with Loeb's assistance, set a model for those who came after him of "using the news media rather than being used by them."

Loeb had no background in journalism. He had worked principally as a stenographer and secretary to various politicians in Albany, New York, including Roosevelt, whom he came to know well during his time as governor of New York. Loeb's work, however, put him into contact with many newspapermen, and he was credited with having a good grasp on their problems. To the press, Louis W. Koenig has written in *The Invisible Presidency*,[4] Loeb was a "sympathetic collaborator" and "gentle pacificator" of bruised feelings. "The kindly secretary issued statements to reporters and conducted press conferences in which he was customarily helpful, although, when necessary, he could be as bland and discreet as a polished diplomat." Loeb's briefings took care of the public demand for information about the private life of Roosevelt and his family. In addition, he was "the equivalent of press secretary to the entire executive branch," according to Koenig. Loeb was the first of a long line of White House press secretaries that has included such memo-

3 Elmer E. Cornwell, Jr., *Presidential Leadership of Public Opinion* (Bloomington, Indiana University Press, 1965), p. 15.

4 Louis W. Koenig, *The Invisible Presidency* (New York, Rinehart, 1960), pp. 173, 176.

rable practitioners as Joseph P. Tumulty (like Loeb, doing the job without the title), who served Woodrow Wilson, and Stephen Early, who performed brilliantly as Franklin D. Roosevelt's spokesman during twelve years of Roosevelt's Presidency.

Theodore Roosevelt, who started it all, had a habit of showering exclusive stories on his favorite correspondents while dealing with ingenious variety with his press critics. One surprised reporter who assailed the Roosevelt railroad policies found himself invited to dinner at the White House and later was sent to Europe to study rail problems for the President. Others were relegated to the Ananias Club or faced with Presidential pressure on their employers for their replacement. They were also subject to the hazard that Loeb, acting on Roosevelt's instructions, might blacklist them with government agencies and deprive them of access to the news.

Roosevelt's heated exchanges with the press twice reached the stage of litigation. In 1909, the last year of his Presidency, he did what no President had dared since the Sedition Act cases in the Adams administration: In a moment of anger he had his Attorney General file criminal libel suits against Joseph Pulitzer of the New York *World* and Delavan Smith of the Indianapolis *News.* The Roosevelt temper had been triggered by published innuendos that a corrupt profit of many millions had been made by an American syndicate when the United States had bought the rights to the Panama Canal. Roosevelt lost the case, but he won another which developed three years later during his 1912 Bull Moose campaign for the Presidency. Determined to squelch gossip that was circulating in the press about his drinking habits, he singled out a Michigan Republican weekly, *Iron Ore,* and sued it for $10,000 in damages because it had reported that Roosevelt was habitually drinking to excess during the campaign. He not only offered the testimony of an impressive string of character witnesses, but also took the stand to swear to his temperance. When the defendant agreed to print a correction and apologize, Roosevelt reduced his claim to nominal damages, and was awarded a verdict of six cents and costs.

William Howard Taft, who followed Roosevelt into the White House, was ill at ease with reporters and held few general press conferences. Arthur Wallace Dunn has recorded in *From Harrison to Harding* [5] that one correspondent overheard Taft plaintively ask his secretary before a news conference, "Must I see those men again? Didn't I see them just the other day?" But Taft did have a couple of close friends in the press corps—Gus J. Karger, a correspondent for the Cincinnati *Times-Star*, which was owned by the President's brother, and William W. Price of the Washington *Star*. Taft saved some of his best stories for them.

When Woodrow Wilson succeeded Taft in 1913, he entered office with high hopes of dealing frankly and effectively with the press and with ambitious plans for development of the news conference. He is generally credited with originating the modern Presidential press conference, held regularly and open to all accredited correspondents. Meeting with reporters twice a week, at the outset, Wilson announced that he wanted to establish a close relationship with them; he would take them into his confidence and he hoped that they, in turn, would tell him what the country was thinking. In keeping with his professorial background, Wilson viewed the press conference as a kind of academic seminar; his painstaking preparation for a meeting with the press followed the procedure he had employed in preparing for a classroom lecture at Princeton. But like other visions Wilson brought to the Presidency, his plan for perfect press relations was frustrated. The trouble lay partly in his temperament; Wilson was not comfortable in a press conference, and he could not overcome an attitude of condescension toward the reporters. He was shocked and disillusioned by the aggressive questioning of the 200 correspondents who crowded into his conferences. He resented their claim that the public had a legitimate right to be informed of details of his personal life and was particularly infuriated by wedding rumors published about his three daughters.

He tried to give the impression of frankness, however, and to achieve this effect, Professor Arthur S. Link writes in *Wilson: The New Freedom*,[6] he often resorted to evasion by giving

[5] Arthur Wallace Dunn, *From Harrison to Harding* (New York, Putnam, 1923), Vol. II, p. 110.

[6] Arthur S. Link, *Wilson: The New Freedom* (Princeton, Princeton University Press, 1956), pp. 80–82.

answers that were technically true but actually false. This was a habit that Colonel Edward M. House, his adviser-diarist, called "grazing the truth." According to House: "The President said he thought that lying was justified in some instances, particularly where it involved the honor of a woman. . . . He thought it was also justified where it related to matters of public policy . . . and in answers to questions about foreign policy." Professor Link quotes "one of the best reporters of the time" as having written that it was "impossible to rely" on anything Wilson said. "I do not mean that he lied," said the reporter. "I mean that he took such an intellectual pleasure in stating a thing so as to give an opposite impression to the fact, though he kept strictly to the truth, that one had to be constantly on the alert to keep from being misled." But there was "often little difference between the half-truth and the lie," Link comments, "and sometimes Wilson resorted to outright prevarication when he thought the public interests demanded dissimulation."

An example of "grazing the truth" was recounted by L. Ames Brown in *Harper's Weekly* for November 1, 1913. Attorney General James Clark McReynolds had submitted to the Cabinet a plan to hobble the components of the former tobacco trust by a punitive tax, and Wilson had advised the Attorney General to discuss the matter with Senate leaders. But when correspondents asked the President what he thought of McReynolds' tobacco tax plan, Wilson replied that as far as he knew, McReynolds had no tobacco tax plan. Afterward Wilson explained that he had regarded McReynolds' proposal as a "suggestion," not a "plan." Such episodes undoubtedly helped lay the groundwork for the suspicion and hostility Wilson encountered in the press corps during his last years in the White House. Wilson's tactics, Link notes, "also help to explain the cold contempt that men like Theodore Roosevelt, Henry Cabot Lodge, Elihu Root and William Howard Taft felt toward him. Lodge, for example, fell victim to one of Wilson's half-truths during the campaign of 1916 and ever afterward was convinced that his earlier doubts as to the Democratic leader's honesty were valid."

The reporters aggravated the situation by misquoting the President from time to time. On several occasions they published information which Wilson thought he had given to them in confidence. As relations between the press and the President deteriorated, Wilson refused to let White House reporters attribute important statements to him, insisting instead that his words be described as coming from an "official spokesman." When the Germans sank the *Lusitania* in 1915, he decided to stop the news conferences altogether to prevent foreign correspondents from leaking information to various embassies in Washington. He never resumed them on a regular basis, although he held a few sessions after the war. "Some men of brilliant ability were in the group," Wilson said of the correspondents after he left the White House, "but I soon discovered that the interest of the majority was in the personal and trivial rather than in principles and policies."

Warren G. Harding was a newspaperman himself—he published the Marion (Ohio) *Star*—and his election ushered in a cordial but brief era of good feeling between the President and the press. Harding would drop in at the National Press Club for a game of hearts at a nickel a point, and the reporters went to the White House twice a week in a resumption of the press conference schedule originally attempted by Wilson. The President talked freely in response to spontaneous questions, and all went well until one day, nine months after the beginning of his administration, when he created a diplomatic uproar with a *faux pas*. "Does the four-power treaty under consideration at the Naval Arms Limitation conference contain a pledge of protection of the main Japanese islands?" he was asked. "It does not," Harding answered in effect, relying on a faulty memory when caught off guard by the question. The Presidential *gaffe* sent shock waves across the Pacific. It took a formal correction issued by the White House, plus some soothing diplomacy by Secretary of State Charles Evans Hughes, to calm down the government of imperial Japan. After that, Hughes prevailed upon Harding to have all questions written and submitted fifteen minutes in advance of a press conference. Unwittingly, the bumbling Harding had set in motion a trend that was to reduce the effectiveness of the press conference for the next two administrations. The White House reporters were handicapped under Calvin Coolidge and Herbert Hoover, as they had been under Harding, by a continuation of the Harding rule that questions be submitted in writing and in advance.

Coolidge had an annoying habit of looking through the reporters' questions, answering only those he wanted to answer, and throwing the rest away. "In memory I can see Coolidge riffling through the pile of written questions, deciding which he would answer," Richard L. Strout, Washington correspondent of the *Christian Science Monitor*, recalls. "On one occasion, a dozen correspondents asked the same question: Would Coolidge be a candidate in 1928? Coolidge looked at the first question and put it aside. He looked at the next and the next, putting them all aside, until he came to a question he decided to answer. 'I have here a question on the condition of the children in Poland,' he announced dryly. 'The condition of the children in Poland is as follows. . . .' After talking on this for several minutes, he concluded, 'That's all the questions.' "

Coolidge's reputation as "Silent Cal" was largely a myth created by the correspondents. He talked at length to reporters, and the frequency of his contacts with the press was beyond reproach. He held 520 news conferences in fewer than six years, for an average of well over 7 a month. Unfortunately, their quality did not match their quantity. Coolidge was colorless, dealt in trivia, and never permitted the reporters to quote him, even indirectly. Like Wilson, he required his remarks to be attributed to a fictitious White House spokesman.

When Herbert Hoover moved into the White House in 1929, he enjoyed a high popularity with the Washington press corps. As Secretary of Commerce under Harding and Coolidge, he had been a good friend, whose door was open to reporters seeking a straight inside account of what was going on in the government. It came as a disappointment, therefore, when he announced he would continue the routine of written questions submitted twenty-four hours in advance of a press conference and would, like Coolidge, simply ignore any questions he did not wish to answer. As President, he felt he had to be more guarded than as a Cabinet member, since he was talking from the White House on the record. With the onset of the Depression, he grew increasingly irate over press criticism. The reporters, in turn, chafed over his suggestion, which they refused to follow, that they should exercise self-censorship or submit stories about the Depression for White House clearance before publication. Hoover tried to punish correspondents who found fault with him, and he withheld more and more information, some of it of far-reaching importance.

The New Deal produced by Franklin D. Roosevelt's arrival in Washington in 1933 applied not only to the nation's battered economy but to the battered press relations in the capital. "I am told that what I am about to do will become impossible," Roosevelt said at his first press conference. "But I am going to try it. We are not going to have any more written questions." For the first time since the Harding *gaffe* on Japan, reporters could engage in the kind of toe-to-toe, face-to-face dialogue that makes a Presidential press conference the significant channel of communication it is supposed to be. Roosevelt took on his questioners with a wit as jaunty as the long cigarette holder he had stuck in a corner of his mouth, and he answered almost every question with ready and exact information. In restoring the open press conference, FDR went against the advice of key advisers. He did so well, however, that the 200 reporters who crowded into his office for the first session applauded when it was over.

From the start, Roosevelt showed himself to be a master at wooing the press. He shook hands with all 200 who were there on that first day, calling many by their first names. From then on, he treated the reporters as his unofficial special assistants in the conduct of the government. He would confide in them, exchange quips with them, and boost their egos by making them feel that they were active participants in great events. By nature a genial man, Roosevelt obviously enjoyed the give-and-take of a mass press conference. He also had a shrewd appreciation of the chance it gave him to mold public opinion. He pleased the correspondents by announcing his conferences in advance, and he held them often—twice a week before the war, once a week on the average during the war. In a little more than three terms, he held 998 press conferences. He was probably the first President who really knew a good news story and how to break it. He called the reporters the Class and would often instruct them in how he thought they should do their job. "If I were going to write a story," he would say, in preface to an answer.

FDR had four different categories of information. The first

three, adopted from the Hoover administration, consisted of occasional special items for direct quotation, background information which could be used but not attributed to him, and off-the-record remarks which were strictly confidential and not for publication. The fourth category, which he originated, was information for indirect quotation which could be attributed to him. Like other Presidents, he often used the background briefing as a device to float a trial balloon which could later be shot down, if necessary. And he used the off-the-record technique, as it is often used today, to tie reporters' hands and stop them from printing something which they probably would have found out on their own sooner or later.

Roosevelt obviously was using the reporters and managing the news. But he also was keeping the reporters well informed and helping them carry out their mission of enlightening the public to the greatest extent possible. Every President has a honeymoon period with the nation's newspapers when he enters the White House, and Roosevelt's lasted for the unusually long period of about two years. His popularity began to slip, both with the Washington correspondents and their home offices, partly because of mounting doubts about the New Deal, partly because of his habit of administering rough rebukes from time to time to questioners who irked him. A growing number of reporters became critical when he started a special club of ignominy for reporters who displeased him. Instead of the Ananias Club of Cousin Teddy, he consigned reportorial offenders to a Dunce Cap Club. It began in a moment of pique after repeated questions about his third-term intentions had begun to get under his skin. "Go off in the corner and put on a dunce cap," the President would say. One day during World War II, he awarded a German Iron Cross to John O'Donnell of the New York *Daily News*, whom he accused of giving comfort to the Nazis. And in October, 1944, he caused raised eyebrows with his response to a question about what bets he had made on his election to a fourth term. "You know what the answer is?" he asked, cupping his hands to his mouth. "None of your damned business."

Despite such episodes, Roosevelt is fondly remembered as a "newspaperman's President." His strength in dealing with the working press lay, as James E. Pollard observed in *The Presidents and the Press*,[7] in the fact that he found common ground with the correspondents. "He understood their needs and their problems." The president of the National Press Club told Roosevelt on one occasion when he was visiting the club, "You have made historic news, and you have served it up hot and steaming."

The Roosevelt example, Arthur M. Schlesinger, Jr., has pointed out in *The Coming of the New Deal*,[8] produced an open-door policy throughout the administration, with Cabinet members and agency heads generally holding regular news conferences of their own. Washington became the kind of news center it had never been before. Washington correspondents thoroughly agree with Schlesinger's view of the great contribution Roosevelt made to a more effective type of press conference: "By according the press the privilege of regular interrogation, Roosevelt established the Presidential press conference in a quasi-constitutional status as the American equivalent of the parliamentary question period—a status which future Presidents could downgrade to their peril."

Harry S. Truman understood the importance of the Roosevelt type of press conference, as a vehicle both for informing the public and for keeping the President posted. The President should meet with the reporters once a week to find out "what's on the public's mind," he said. He had a record attendance up to then of 348 correspondents at his first White House press conference on April 17, 1945. He was noticeably humble in demeanor in that first conference and, according to Richard Strout of the *Christian Science Monitor*, "seemed to have so much to be humble about." Before long, however, humbleness gave way, many thought, to overconfidence.

Truman reduced the press conference schedule to one a week but kept most of the Roosevelt innovations. To provide more room for the larger numbers who were trying to crowd into the President's Oval Office, he moved the conferences next door to the Indian Treaty Room on the fourth floor of the old State Department Building, where the correspondents could sit

[7] James E. Pollard, *The Presidents and the Press* (New York, Macmillan, 1947), p. 839.

[8] Arthur M. Schlesinger, Jr., *The Coming of the New Deal* (Boston, Houghton Mifflin, 1959), p. 562.

and take notes when they were not popping up to seek Presidential recognition for a question. Truman obviously enjoyed tilting with the press. The Chief Executive would often interrupt a reporter halfway through a question, sometimes with ridicule, sometimes with an abrupt, angry reply, followed by a disarming smile. If the conference were not moving at a brisk enough pace to suit him, he would have some teasing comments about this as well. But he never developed the sure touch of FDR. Truman's habit of shooting from the hip with a rapid-fire answer resulted on one occasion in a crisis that surpassed Harding's slip on the arms limitation treaty. It was in November, 1950, the Chinese Communists had just entered the war in Korea, and the situation had taken on a new gravity. In response to a question, Truman said that the use of the atom bomb was "always under consideration." This vague answer, which he did not attempt to clarify, gave the impression that the President was considering the use of the bomb in the Korean war. In the worldwide repercussions that followed, Prime Minister Clement Attlee hastily flew over from London to seek clarification of the President's intentions and to emphasize the British view of the need for restraint. The uproar did not die down until two clarifying statements had been issued. "We kept on hand, as a sort of first aid kit, a boxful of 'clarifications,' " Dean Acheson, Truman's Secretary of State, wrote in a national magazine in 1959. This was necessary, he said, because "we learned from all mistakes but one—the fast answer in that nightmare of Presidents, the press conference."

Truman also got himself into trouble at times by uncritically repeating the phrasing of a reporter's question. At a press conference in 1948 a correspondent asked: "Mr. President, do you think the Capitol Hill spy scare is a red herring to divert public attention from inflation?" Truman's unthinking use of the same "red herring" phrase in the affirmative reply he gave the reporter provided his critics with a whip to beat him with in the months ahead. They said this showed that he was soft on the issue of Communist infiltration of the government. Truman became more noncommittal after some of these experiences, and his conferences were held less frequently; but he did not panic and revert to the written question routine, as Harding had done. He clearly felt that the press conference served an important purpose and that it was essential for it to be continued. He held a total of well over 300 during his time in the White House.

Dwight D. Eisenhower was assisted in his press relations by one of the most capable press secretaries ever to hold the job, James C. Hagerty, formerly a political correspondent for the New York *Times*. Hagerty could do nothing, however, about his boss' low boiling point or the tangled syntax of his replies to reporters' questions. Yet Eisenhower would often give completely candid answers to the most searching questions. The Washington press corps will long remember the way he handled a historic press conference on August 1, 1956. (See Appendix A.) It was his first formal meeting with the press since June 9, when he had been rushed to Walter Reed, the Army hospital, for an emergency abdominal operation, precipitated by an attack of ileitis. The conference began at 10:30 A.M., and the 311 correspondents who jammed into the Indian Treaty Room had begun lining up an hour ahead of time in the long corridor outside. Few reporters had seen Eisenhower since his operation, and others had had only a fleeting contact. The country was anxious to know the state of the President's health. His recovery was taking longer than had been expected, and there had been reports that he was suffering from a continuing dysentery. People wondered whether he still felt up to running for reelection and, even if he did, whether he should in view of the heart attack he had suffered in September, 1955, followed by this major operation less than a year later. The Republican Party naturally was not eager to let this popular hero withdraw from his candidacy. The report GOP Congressional leaders carried from a meeting with him on July 10 was that his second-term decision remained unchanged. But the reporters wanted to hear it from the President himself. Looking thinner than before the operation, slower in step and less robust of voice, Ike spent thirty-two minutes with the press that Wednesday morning on the first day of August and answered thirty-seven questions. *Life* magazine later commented that the conference was remarkable for its frankness—"perhaps the frankest, most searching interview since Wilson inaugurated regular conferences in 1913."

A correspondent who joined in the questioning on that day

is one of the authors of this book. William McGaffin of the Chicago *Daily News* told Eisenhower that during his convalescence in Gettysburg, he had gone around the town and asked the President's friends and neighbors how they felt about his running again. "Well, they all love you, as you know, and they said they are going to vote for you," McGaffin said; "but really they wished that you wouldn't run again because they feel you have done enough for the nation, you have made so many sacrifices and, sir, they are afraid that you won't last out, they are afraid you won't live for another four years." It was, said the New York *Times*, a "seemingly harsh question," but nevertheless it was "the great imponderable of the campaign" and was "put most kindly."

"Well, sir, I would tell you, frankly, I don't think it is too important to the individual how his end comes, and certainly he can't dictate the time," Eisenhower replied.

"What we are talking about here is the importance to the country, and it happens that at this moment the Republican party apparently thinks I am still important to them and to the country. And since I believe so much in the Republican party, and I believe that it needed rebuilding so badly, an effort which I have been making, as you well know, I said I would continue to try.

"But this is a decision that the American people are going to have to face. I am flattered by what you tell me about my friends and neighbors at Gettysburg, but I have made up my mind this is the thing I should try, and we will see what the American people have to say about it. . . ."

Eisenhower took that one in his stride. The following year, however, McGaffin learned at firsthand how the President could respond to a barbed question. It was the spring of 1957, and the principal national issue had become Eisenhower's battle with Congress over the budget. He was asking Congress to appropriate $71.8 billion to run the government in the coming year—at that point, the largest peacetime budget in history. Eisenhower's Congressional critics were demanding substantial cuts. He quite properly pointed out that Congress could achieve some economies if it desired. But was it not possible for Eisenhower to make some economies, too? With this thought in mind, McGaffin put the following question at a White House press conference on March 27, 1957:

"Mr. President, do you feel that there are any economies that you can make in the Executive Branch of the government to help cut government spending?" Eisenhower listened attentively, and all was going well up to this point. "For instance, would you be willing to do without that pair of helicopters that have been proposed for getting you out to the golf course a little faster than you can make it in a car?"

This triggered a public display of the explosive temper that had often been seen in private by staff workers who had riled the President. With flushed face and an angry stare, he snapped, "Well, I don't think much of the question because no helicopters have been procured for me to go to a golf course."

"Well—" McGaffin began, getting to his feet again. But Eisenhower cut him off with an icy "Thank you, that is all," and turning his back on the questioner, he signaled a correspondent in another part of the room to ask the next question. Eisenhower's momentary flash of anger appeared to many at the conference "to be as great as he has ever displayed before newsmen," the New York *Times* remarked the next day. "Eisenhower obviously regarded the McGaffin question as unfair," Jack Bell, the veteran Associated Press correspondent wrote in *The Splendid Misery*.[9] It remained, nevertheless, a "perfectly legitimate inquiry," Bell said. "The helicopters had been purchased; there were reports the Chief Executive would use them to reach Burning Tree Golf Course. . . ."

There was little camaraderie between Eisenhower and the correspondents. He remained an aloof figure, more at home in the company of their publishers. He seldom recognized reporters by name at press conferences but would single them out as "the man with the glasses" or "the one with red hair." Yet it was during his time in the White House that giant steps were taken to modernize the press conference. This was the work of Jim Hagerty, who served as press secretary with great expertise and devotion for the eight years that Eisenhower was President. If there were complaints about Hagerty, they stemmed from his approach to his job. He acknowledged that his principal responsibility, as he saw it, was to make the boss look good. He

9 Jack Bell, *The Splendid Misery* (Garden City, Doubleday, 1960), p. 293.

also had an annoying habit of refusing to let reporters talk to any of the White House staff unless they first got his permission, which was often hard to get.

Sensing the potential that television held for Eisenhower, Hagerty persuaded him to carry the White House press conference a radical step further and put it on newsreel film. Live TV coverage was not permitted, but Hagerty released the film for later broadcast after checking it for whatever editing might be required. The networks first brought their cameras into a press conference in January, 1955. This was after the development of a new high-speed film which made it possible to film the conference with little more than normal lighting, instead of the huge, blinding lights that had been required before. But Hagerty did not endear himself to some of the "pencil pushers" in the press corps when he won Eisenhower's approval for this. They complained that the conferences tended to become cut-and-dried, with the President resorting more and more to generalizations. They objected, too, to the showboating which some of the correspondents could not resist practicing in front of the cameras to let the public know who they were and to remind the boss they were on the job. They were encouraged in this by a Hagerty rule which required them, before asking the President a question, to identify themselves by name and organization. Hagerty simply ignored the jibes and wisecracks and reminded the newspapermen that television was here to stay.

He tried to warm up Eisenhower's relations with the press by having the President give a series of small black-tie stag dinners for ranking members of the corps toward the end of the second term. These were dropped, however, after it became apparent that their chief accomplishment was to antagonize the great majority of the working press which had been excluded from them. Eisenhower was criticized for many aspects of his news policy, including his failure to have press conferences more often. But he did carry on the tradition of exposing himself to all the specialists in the press corps, not just the White House regulars, through 200 formal press conferences, announced in advance.

When John F. Kennedy succeeded to the Presidency, the frost which had settled on relations between the press and the White House during the Eisenhower years melted overnight.

Kennedy had a large number of friends in the press, cultivated during his time in the Senate and the House, and he wasted no time in exploiting them. Columnist Joseph Alsop, who was giving a party at his Georgetown home, responded to a ring of the doorbell late on the night of the 1961 inauguration. "My God, it's the President," he exclaimed as he opened the door. Kennedy, who had been President for barely twelve hours, had finished the rounds of the inaugural balls and decided to wind up the night with a surprise appearance at the party his Georgetown neighbor was giving.

Reporters suddenly found that they had access to the White House inner circle. Not for years had so many been invited to the White House for lunch or dinner. Their imagination had been caught by Kennedy's youth, his style, and the tone of the New Frontier, which he was launching with such stirring phrases. When they saw what an accessible President he was going to be and how well he could handle himself in a press conference, they had additional reasons for liking him. The press could and did fault him for not holding conferences more often. There were only fifty-eight in his 1,000 days. But he honored the custom fixed by Roosevelt of announcing them in advance, so that any reporter who wished could attend. He moved them from the cramped quarters of the Indian Treaty Room to the spacious new State Department auditorium on Twenty-third Street, where he took the daring step of letting the television networks broadcast them live, instead of requiring them to be filmed for later broadcasting.

The greatest difference, however, between Kennedy and Eisenhower conferences was in the quality of the answers Kennedy supplied to questions. He had been a newspaperman for a brief period after World War II, and he retained an instinctive knowledge of how a reporter's mind works. Aided by this and by some thorough preparatory briefing organized by his press secretary, Pierre Salinger, he would go into a press conference with a good idea of what he was going to be asked and what he was going to say in reply. The press conferences usually were held at four o'clock in the afternoon. The previous afternoon Salinger would call a conference in his office of the information chiefs from State, Defense, NASA, AEC, and USIA. "Each would produce the hot issues of his department," Salinger told the authors of this book in an interview after he left the White House, "and we would make up a list of about a hundred questions." The next morning, Salinger breakfasted at the White House with the President, the Vice-President, the Secretary of State, the Secretary of Defense, and the Presidential special assistants, McGeorge Bundy, Theodore Sorensen, Mike Feldman, and Walter Heller. "I sat opposite Kennedy and started asking him the questions we had evolved. He would reply, 'I can handle this,' or, 'I need a little more information on this.' I would come away with about a half dozen items, would call the relevant department, and tell them that I wanted more information on this in a couple of hours." Sorensen, Bundy, and Salinger would then go to Kennedy's bedroom at about three o'clock, just after he got up from his nap, and while he bathed and dressed, they would bring him up-to-date. "Then we would go over to the State Department, arriving there about ten minutes to four, and would go into a little room off the auditorium. Right up to the time of the conference, people at State brought us bulletins from the wire services. When the President walked into his press conference, he was up-to-date."

If Kennedy was asked a question he had not anticipated, his quick wit could usually pull him through. He was capable of dodging and filibustering at times, but the persistent reporter who remained on his feet and asked a follow-up question could generally obtain an answer. No other President has been so skilled a performer on television. A Harding or Truman type of *gaffe* would have been a calamity on live television, but there was none under Kennedy. He used these TV appearances, of course, to project a favorable image of himself and his administration. Some correspondents complained that he had turned the press conferences into television spectaculars. But they attracted a wide viewing audience, and they did make news.

Kennedy undoubtedly had greater rapport with the press than any President since Roosevelt. But it can be argued—as it often is by President Johnson's associates—that Kennedy laid the groundwork for what was to become Johnson's Credibility Gap. "Truman was generally candid, and Johnson seems a compulsive dissembler," Richard H. Rovere has observed. Kennedy fell somewhere in between. He set the style, if not the magnitude, of government dissimulation about the war in Vietnam. He inaugurated the furious intramural investigations of government news leaks that were to become institutionalized in the Johnson administration. Newspaper criticism irked him almost as much as it does Johnson. In public, Kennedy joked that he was "reading more but enjoying it less." In private, he was capable of telephoning reporters—or their editors—to complain about stories that displeased him, or of peevishly canceling his subscription to the New York *Herald Tribune,* or of asking the publisher of the New York *Times* to transfer a correspondent (David Halberstam) out of Vietnam.

Salinger was always suspected of planting questions with friendly reporters. The practice is akin to cheating on an examination, for it is easy for a President to have just the right answer when he knows in advance exactly what the question is going to be. Salinger, however, insisted during the interview previously mentioned that over the thirty-five-month period covered by the Kennedy Presidency, he "probably planted only six or seven questions out of some fifteen hundred asked." His rationale was that he had to make sure that the President was asked a question on an important topic he wanted to talk about. "There were so many occasions in the early press conferences when Kennedy was prepared to discuss an important matter and he was never asked the question which would let him do it. Part of the problem is that you only have a half-hour press conference. Part of it, also, is that most reporters, in my opinion, don't do their homework for a press conference." Jim Hagerty had a different way of doing it for an Eisenhower press conference. He would sometimes call reporters in before a conference and tell them that he thought Eisenhower was ready to answer questions on such and such subjects. He would also, sometimes, at his own daily briefing suggest to a questioner that he seek the answer from the President at the next press conference.

In the administration of Lyndon B. Johnson, question planting has become a regular way of life. On one occasion, August 25, 1965, questions were even planted openly before a press conference by the then White House press secretary, Bill D. Moyers, and his assistant, Joseph Laitin. One question, which a correspondent asked as requested, gave Johnson an opportunity to hold forth on the need for a settlement in the steel contract talks. Another obliging questioner cooperated by enabling the President to picture in the worst possible light the House Republicans who had criticized his position on Vietnam the previous day. "Old timers in the White House press room can't remember anything like the activity immediately preceding the August 25th conference," Rowland Evans and Robert Novak commented later in their syndicated column. The resulting conference, they said, "was very nearly as carefully staged as a Broadway play." A few months later, in a January, 1966, interview on WETA-TV, Washington's educational television outlet, Moyers acknowledged that he had planted questions and defended the practice, as Salinger had, on the ground that he wanted to be certain that the questions the President had on his mind "did get asked." The White House press office has followed a somewhat less ambitious policy since the 1965 episode. It now operates more discreetly and, according to one insider's estimate, never tries to plant more than four questions before a Presidential press conference or the daily briefing of the press secretary. "We always used to plant about four questions before a press conference," this source said. "Where Johnson went wrong was when he decided that if we were going to plant four, why not eight or more—why not control the entire press conference?"

Of even greater concern than question planting is the fact that the formal Presidential press conference which served Presidents, press, and the nation for more than thirty years has all but disappeared under Johnson. He has held conferences more frequently than Kennedy—114 in the first four years of his Presidency—but the great majority of these have not fallen into the category of the traditional, Roosevelt type of press conference, announced in advance so that all might attend. The President promised in a press conference at the LBJ ranch on March 20, 1965, that he would "try to follow the standing practice of holding at least one press conference a month of the nature which you describe as ample advance notice, covered by all media. . . ." The promise has not been kept. Instead, he has substituted, for the most part, the surprise press conference which he perfected during his days as Majority Leader of the Senate. By calling a small group of reporters into his office on little or no advance notice, he assures himself of a captive audience, the White House regular correspondents. This permits him to do most of the talking, with few and mostly friendly questions. By declining to give advance notice of a day or two before a press conference, as his four predecessors used to do, he not only reduces sharply the numbers who attend, but also reduces greatly the chances that he will have to answer the kinds of penetrating, sometimes embarrassing questions which cropped up regularly in the press conferences of his predecessors. He does this by shutting out the correspondents who cover the Pentagon, the Treasury, Justice, State, and a wide variety of other beats—the correspondents who have the specialized knowledge to ask searching questions and need not worry about offending White House news contacts.

The Freedom of Information Committee of Sigma Delta Chi, the national professional journalism society, declared in a November, 1967, report that "President Johnson's continued refusal to conduct regular press conferences with some reasonable advance notice continues to be a major problem. His style of press conferences makes it impossible for any but the White House regulars to be present, and it makes it unlikely that he will face any pattern of consistent hard questioning on any subject. He has it well organized for 'a White House snow job,' even though it is doubtful if he is as successful in accomplishing his purpose as he was a year or more ago."

On the relatively rare occasions when Johnson has held a press conference with all the journalistic specialists present, he has often declined to recognize for a question anyone except the White House regulars and a few outsiders who could be counted on to ask the types of questions he favors. This happened, for example, at a formal televised press conference in the East Room of the White House in the spring of 1967. Robert J. Donovan, Washington bureau chief of the Los Angeles *Times,* tried repeatedly, but unsuccessfully, to gain Presidential recognition to ask a question. Afterward Donovan confided that he had hoped to query the President about a matter that the others were carefully avoiding: the Johnson-Robert Kennedy feud. Was it true that LBJ had broken with Kennedy and ordered him not to come back to the White House? What about the reports that their feud was adversely affecting U.S. foreign policy? These were legitimate questions at the time, but a correspondent who was prepared to ask them was never given the chance.

The Presidential press conference used to provide the American people with the equivalent of question hour in the British House of Commons. Correspondents, acting on behalf of the people, were able to meet the President regularly and ask him every conceivable question. As Donovan has observed, it was a "unique institution," "attracted great interest throughout the world," and "impressed political scientists as a new element of strength in American democracy." Johnson, however, has favored a much more restricted kind of press conference—one that entails safer questions and gives him a chance, away from the telltale eye of the TV camera, to complain about the stories which he says "misrepresent" his position and to rebuke reporters who do not toe the line.

Historian Arthur Schlesinger, Jr., has warned that future Presidents who downgraded the Roosevelt type of press conference would do so "to their peril." There is no doubt in the minds of most Washington correspondents that Johnson's downgrading of the press conference has helped bring on what has become one of his most serious problems—the Credibility Gap.

3. Falsehoods and Foreign Affairs

A strange and melancholy phenomenon has characterized the conduct of American foreign policy in the 1960's: Repeatedly the government of the United States has been caught in the act of telling lies to its citizens and to the world. Not euphemisms or exaggerations, not the deft distortions and slick simplifications that constitute the fine art of propaganda, but deliberate and flagrant lies. Three successive national administrations have made the device of outright deception their method of choice in dealing with foreign affairs crises.

"Good diplomats abhor outright lying," Murrey Marder, the diplomatic correspondent of the Washington *Post*, has observed. "They regard it as a sign of amateurism. Centuries of experience have gone into building up a pattern of acceptable circumlocution. There is a Chinese tale of a proud but mediocre chess-playing diplomat who one day lost three chess games in a row. A friend asked how he had done. The diplomat replied, 'Well, I didn't win the first game, and my opponent didn't lose the second. As to the third game, I asked him to agree to a draw, but he wouldn't.' "

There is more to the answer of Marder's Chinese diplomat than mere avoidance, by a technicality, of the act of lying. His careful, self-protective phrasing left the way open for a discerning listener to conclude the truth—that he had lost all three games. Had he claimed victory, however, only an on-the-spot observer of the contest would have been able to contradict him.

In dealing with the major foreign crises of recent years, the government has often strayed from the path of "acceptable

circumlocution" into the thicket of utter untruth. The practice
has foreclosed the possibility of rational and informed debate
on policy decisions that are literally matters of life and death.
What's more, it has confronted citizens with an embarrassing
and painful dilemma as they attempt to evaluate their nation's
course of conduct in world affairs. Neither the conventional
wisdom nor the experience even of sophisticated Americans has
prepared them for the unhappy realization that their government is lying.

David Kraslow, a seasoned reporter for the Los Angeles
Times, opened a dispatch from Santo Domingo with these
anguished words when he was reporting on the United States'
intervention in the Dominican Republic in the spring of 1965:
"For one who grew up believing that when the U.S. government
said something, that was it, the past two weeks in Santo Domingo came as another in a series of awakenings." Kraslow
cited his disillusioning experiences and concluded: "If government officials want to argue that deliberately misleading the
public is justified under certain conditions, they must be
willing to chance undermining the confidence of citizens in
the word of their government. They must be willing to pay the
price of a nation of cynics. Government by consent cannot have
it both ways. There can be no consent where there is no confidence, and there can be no confidence when the people are
not sure their own officials are leveling with them. Perhaps it
is a naïve view, but one might reason that if a policy has to be
nurtured through deception it is not a policy worth nurturing.
Not for the United States."

Murrey Marder, whose reporting from the State Department
played a prominent part in bringing the term "Credibility
Gap" into the language, defined it in December, 1965, as "a
perceptibly growing disquiet, misgiving, or skepticism about
the candor or validity of official declarations"—especially those
concerning the war in Vietnam. Shortly after Marder's article
appeared, Arthur Goldberg, the United States ambassador to
the United Nations, acknowledged that there was official concern about a "crisis of confidence" in the Johnson administration's Vietnam policy. "We have a great problem here maintaining our credibility," Goldberg said.

There was bitter irony in the admission, for credibility has been the keystone of American foreign policy for a decade. The nation's military security has rested on the credibility of its nuclear deterrent. Foreign affairs, as top officials of the administration have asserted time and again, have been guided by the need to maintain the credibility of commitments to its allies and clients. Yet the government's credibility has been systematically undermined—and perhaps destroyed—by the government itself.

The distinction between propaganda and lying is real and significant, though it is often overlooked. Propaganda—or, if one prefers, hucksterism—is deemed an essential weapon by every modern government. No state—no other human institution, for that matter—can reasonably be expected to refrain from casting its conduct in the most favorable light possible. But the resort to propaganda based on outright falsehood has, until recently, been the exclusive preserve of totalitarian states. Hitler's Germany and Stalin's Russia exploited the technique of the big lie. Even the fierce ideological struggle of the early cold war years did not make the big lie palatable to citizens of the United States.

The Korean "police action," which is often compared to the Vietnam war, produced no credibility gap for President Truman. There was no dearth of propaganda, to be sure. Even the basic rationale for United States intervention—the North Korean invasion of South Korea—has been challenged by some responsible observers. George F. Kennan, director of the State Department's Policy Planning Staff in the late 1940's, has stated in his *Memoirs: 1925–1950* [10] that Korea "was, finally a civil conflict, not an international one; and the term 'aggression' in the usual international sense was as misplaced here as it was to be later in the case of Vietnam." The notion that the Korean war was a United Nations undertaking was also, at best, an enthusiastic exaggeration fostered by the government of the United States. But not even the most severe American critics of the Korean war suggested then—or have suggested since—that their government embarked on a deliberate attempt to lie to its citizens or to the world about the war.

For many Americans, one of the first rude realizations that

---

10 George F. Kennan, *Memoirs: 1925–1950* (Boston, Little, Brown, 1967), p. 490.

their government was capable of deliberate deception came early in May, 1960, after a high-altitude jet plane with the convenient headline name "U-2" was downed near Sverdlovsk in the central Soviet Union. The Russians, whose credibility was, for the best of reasons, virtually nonexistent, claimed they had shot down an American spy plane. On May 5 the National Aeronautics and Space Administration announced that one of its weather research planes was missing on a "meteorological observation flight" in Turkey. It was conceivable, NASA suggested, that the pilot had blacked out from lack of oxygen and that the uncontrolled aircraft had drifted over Soviet territory. It seemed as if another Russian outrage had been perpetrated—especially since President Eisenhower had assured reporters at a news conference the year before that he had "personally" issued orders prohibiting provocative flights over the USSR. On May 6 the State Department's official spokesman, Lincoln White, declared that there was "absolutely no—N-O—deliberate attempt to violate Soviet air space . . . [and] never has been."

The next day Premier Nikita Khrushchev told the Supreme Soviet that the U-2 pilot, Francis Gary Powers, had been captured alive and had confessed his intelligence mission. Within a few hours the State Department was lamely admitting that "in endeavoring to obtain information now concealed behind the Iron Curtain, a flight over Soviet territory was probably undertaken by an unarmed civilian U-2 plane." Such flights, it quickly transpired, had been undertaken by pilots of the Central Intelligence Agency for the past four years.

The full consequences of the U-2 episode will never be known. It caused cancelation of an East-West summit conference that was to begin in Paris on May 16 and of a visit President Eisenhower was to make to the Soviet Union in June. It demolished the "spirit of Camp David" and plunged the United States and the Soviet Union back into the cold war. Most serious, perhaps, was its effect as a major assault on American credibility. After leaving the Presidency in 1961, Eisenhower often confided to reporters that he regarded the lies about the U-2 as the most regrettable experience of his administration. In the political campaign year of 1960, leading Democrats were, of course, outspokenly critical of the Republican administration's handling of the U-2 affair. Prominent among the critics were the junior Senator from Massachusetts, John F. Kennedy, and the Democratic Presidential nominee of 1952 and 1956, Adlai Stevenson. Less than a year later, President Kennedy and his ambassador to the United Nations, Adlai Stevenson, were to take part in a deception that made the U-2 case look like a little white lie—the Bay of Pigs invasion of Cuba.

On April 7, 1961, Arthur M. Schlesinger, Jr., reports in his Kennedy biography, *A Thousand Days*,[11] the President told him that "the integrity and credibility of Adlai Stevenson constitute one of our great national assets. I don't want anything to be done which might jeopardize that." According to Schlesinger, Kennedy wanted Stevenson kept fully informed on the plans for the American-sponsored invasion of Cuba so that "nothing said at the U.N. should be less than the truth, even if it could not be the full truth." On April 15, after American-trained pilots in American planes bombed Cuban airfields, Stevenson told an emergency session of the UN Political Committee: "These two planes, to the best of our knowledge, were Castro's own air force planes and, according to the pilots, they took off from Castro's own air force fields." This was the CIA's cover story, and it began coming apart a few hours later. Stevenson, it was soon plain, had been kept in the dark by his government and had lied to the world. So had the United States Information Agency, which broadcast the deception, and the entire public information machinery of the administration.

Press coverage (or the lack of it) of the Bay of Pigs fiasco and the preparations leading up to it is still a matter of heated controversy among reporters and editors, as well as among government officials. The handling of the story raised the most fundamental issues of free and truthful reporting of news involving the "national interest." Schlesinger, who as a White House aide helped peddle the CIA's cover story and persuaded editors to suppress or soft-pedal accounts of preparations for the invasion, says that "in retrospect I have wondered whether, if the press had behaved irresponsibly, it would not have spared the country a disaster."

In a remarkable address to the World Press Institute in St. Paul on June 1, 1966, Clifton Daniel, the managing editor of

11 Arthur M. Schlesinger, Jr., *A Thousand Days* (Boston, Houghton Mifflin, 1965), p. 271.

the New York *Times*, gave a detailed account of the internal turmoil that beset his newspaper with regard to preinvasion coverage of the Bay of Pigs. (See Appendix B.) He told how editors argued about a dispatch by Latin American correspondent Tad Szulc reporting on the CIA-directed buildup, and how they ultimately played down the story and deleted references to the invasion's imminence. "My own view," Daniel concluded, "is that the Bay of Pigs operation might well have been cancelled and the country would have been saved enormous embarrassment if the New York *Times* and other newspapers had been more diligent in the performance of their duty—their duty to keep the public informed on matters vitally affecting our national honor and prestige, not to mention our national security."

David Kraslow was covering Washington for the Miami *Herald* in the summer of 1960, when his editors asked him to check into indications that federal authorities had an extraordinary interest in a Cuban exiles' camp near Homestead, Florida. "By mid or late September," Kraslow later recalled in a letter to Clifton Daniel, "after several weeks of checking at State, the White House, the FBI and elsewhere, I had the answer—and more.

"Although troubled, I wrote a 1,500-word story revealing the CIA's involvement in the Homestead camp and in the broader effort to recruit Cuban exiles, the Justice Department's unhappiness over the brazen violation of the neutrality act by a government agency, and the pressure on Eisenhower from Bill Rogers [the Attorney General] and Hoover [the director of the FBI] to force the CIA to move its training operation out of the country. I knew nothing, of course, at that time about any invasion of Cuba. That plan was not to jell until much later. My first information was that the exiles would be deposited in Cuba by the CIA after their training to undertake guerrilla warfare against Castro. Then I was advised the exiles would be employed in large-scale hit-and-run raids." (See Appendix C.)

Kraslow's story never appeared. He had resolved his doubts "in favor of the basic principle of disclosure in a free society," but his editors concluded, after much deliberation, that they might be tampering with national security. They sought guidance from government officials, and Kraslow, accompanied by his bureau chief, Edwin A. Lahey, put the problem of publication to CIA Director Allen W. Dulles. Here is Kraslow's account: "Dulles replied that if the *Herald* published the kind of story Lahey and I had related to him, it would be most harmful to the national interest. That's about how he said it. He made no specific request that the story be suppressed. It was after this word was relayed to Miami that I was told definitely my story would not run."

The available evidence indicates that President Kennedy himself was far from certain about the proper role of the press in the Bay of Pigs disaster. He refused to entertain questions about it at his first news conference after the invasion attempt. "I do not think that any useful national purpose would be served by my going further into the Cuban question this morning," Kennedy said. (See Appendix D.) Pierre Salinger recounts in *With Kennedy* [12] that the President was furious the next morning when newspapers criticized his refusal to discuss the subject. "What could I have said that would have helped the situation at all?" Salinger quotes Kennedy asking. "That we took the beating of our lives? That the CIA and the Pentagon are stupid? What purpose do they think it would serve to put that on the record? We're going to have to straighten all this out, and soon. The publishers have to understand that we're never more than a miscalculation away from war and that there are things we are doing that we just can't talk about."

There are obvious answers, of course, to Kennedy's rhetorical questions. If we are, indeed, never more than a miscalculation away from war, the fact that "the CIA and the Pentagon are stupid" would seem to be urgent news for the public to have. If we are doing things we just can't talk about, Americans certainly need to know when these things result in the "beating of our lives."

A week after the Bay of Pigs invasion, Kennedy called on members of the American Newspaper Publishers Association "to re-examine their own responsibilities." In a time of cold war, he suggested, newspapermen must exercise some of the same restraints they would show in a shooting war. "Every newspaper," Kennedy said, "now asks itself with respect to every story, 'Is it news?' All I suggest is that you add the question: 'Is

[12] Pierre Salinger, *With Kennedy* (Garden City, Doubleday, 1966), pp. 154–55.

it in the interest of national security?'" His administration, Kennedy added, would "cooperate wholeheartedly" if the press were to agree on voluntary measures to prevent publication of material endangering the national security. But only two weeks later, according to Clifton Daniel, the President told Turner Catledge, then managing editor of the New York *Times,* "If you had printed more about the operation [the Cuban invasion plan] you would have saved us from a colossal mistake." That was still Kennedy's view more than a year later, Daniel said in his World Press Institute address. On September 13, 1962, Daniel added, the President told Orvil Dryfoos, then publisher of the *Times,* "I wish you had run everything on Cuba . . . I am just sorry you didn't tell it at the time."

Salinger, who worries that newspapers may print "things better for the enemy not to know about," has questioned Daniel's account and suggested that Kennedy had no regrets about suppression of the preinvasion stories. But the late President's brother Senator Robert F. Kennedy told members of the American Society of Newspaper Editors in the spring of 1967: "Clearly, publication of U.S. battle plans in time of war would irresponsibly imperil success and endanger American lives. On the other hand, President Kennedy once said that wider press discussion of plans to invade Cuba—known to many reporters and patriotically withheld—might have avoided the Bay of Pigs. . . . In looking back over crises from Berlin and the Bay of Pigs to the Gulf of Tonkin, or even over the past fifteen years, I can think of few examples where disclosure of large policy considerations damaged the country, and many instances where public discussion and debate led to more thoughtful and informed decisions."

Whatever the Kennedy conclusions on the Bay of Pigs, they did not deter the administration from taking the course of suppression and deception again during the Cuban missile crisis of October, 1962. James B. Reston of the *Times* ascertained that U.S. intelligence had confirmed the presence of Soviet missiles in Cuba, but a weekend call from the President to Orvil Dryfoos kept the story out of print until Kennedy himself broke the news to the nation on Monday evening. David Kraslow was on that story, too, for the Miami *Herald.* On Friday, October 19, his editors asked him to check a report in a syndicated column that the presence of missiles and Soviet Il-28 bombers had been established in Cuba. Kraslow called Assistant Defense Secretary Arthur Sylvester, and this is what happened: "He said no one else had queried him on the column. I told him my editors were pressing for some kind of guidance on whether to use the column. He said he would see about it.

"That evening a Pentagon news officer telephoned me at home with the answer (which Sylvester told me that weekend was cleared with McNamara). That answer was the lie that has rankled ever since—the one paragraph mimeographed statement that the Pentagon had no information on the presence of offensive Soviet weapons in Cuba. I wrote a story to that effect which ran on page one of the *Herald* the following morning—five days after the Pentagon had advised the President of the missiles and two days before the President went on television. The *Herald* and many other newspapers . . . were suckered by a lie."

Much later, after he left government service, Sylvester told Kraslow that his query could have been handled in one of three ways: The official spokesman could have refused to comment; he could have issued the untruthful denial; or he could have taken the reporter into his confidence, confirming the facts but requesting that they be withheld from publication for reasons of national security. In retrospect, Sylvester said, he believed that the third would have been the wisest course. But in the fall of 1962 he chose to take refuge in a deception.

Most government lies are like that: dry, terse, bureaucratic denials that what is happening is happening. The big, bold, imaginative untruth is a rare exception—but President Johnson is an exceptional President. On June 17, 1965, in a fervent effort to justify the American military intervention in the Dominican Republic, Johnson told a news conference that "some 1,500 innocent people were murdered and shot and their heads cut off." This might have been florid hyperbole, but it was clearly meant to be taken literally. It made fine newspaper copy. The true figure, when it was finally ascertained was not 1,500 or 150 or even 15—in fact, there was no evidence that any heads had been cut off—and most of the atrocities committed in the Dominican revolt were the work, not of the rebels, but of the junta which the United States secretly supported.

(Part of Johnson's credibility problem may be attributable to the fact that he has never grown accustomed to having his every public utterance recorded by stenographers and preserved for posterity. In Congress, where Johnson long held sway, it is customary for members to "revise and extend" their remarks before they are published in the *Congressional Record.* Consequently, the official *Record* often bears little resemblance to what was actually said on the floor. Attempts are made from time to time to "sanitize" an official White House transcript, but by the time this is done, the President's actual words have usually been reported.)

Almost from its inception on April 23, 1965, the Dominican revolt was the subject of an extraordinary exercise in news manipulation by the government of the United States. On April 27, the right-wing military junta hastily organized to oppose the rebels asked Washington to intervene on the ground that the rebel movement was dominated by Communists. There were grave doubts that this was, indeed, the case at the time, but Washington was disposed to intervene. As one of its representatives later was to reveal, it merely advised the junta to revise its request: to ask for U.S. troops to protect the lives of American citizens. The junta duly complied on the afternoon of April 28, and that evening President Johnson took to the airwaves to announce that he had ordered 400 Marines into the Dominican Republic "in order to give protection to hundreds of Americans who are still in the Dominican Republic and to escort them safely back to this country." Within the next day or two, Washington correspondents reported that fear of a Communist coup in the Dominican Republic had prompted the intervention. These reports were denied by government officials speaking on a background basis. This is the public record from that point:

On April 29, State Department spokesman Robert McCloskey was asked whether there was a danger of a Communist take-over in the Dominican Republic. He replied that it was too early to make an assessment, but that Communists were obviously "participating."

On April 30, the State Department affirmed that the Marines' specific mission was to "protect United States and foreign citizens whose lives are in danger." At the White House, Press Secretary George Reedy used similar language.

On May 1, the word from the State Department was that "the sole mission of U.S. troops in the Dominican Republic is to protect and evacuate U.S. and other foreign nationals . . . and not in any way to take sides in the internal conflict."

On May 2, the President went back on the air and told the American people: "The revolutionary movement took a tragic turn. Communist leaders, many of them trained in Cuba, seeing a chance to increase disorder, to gain a foothold, joined the revolution. They took increasing control."

On May 4, Johnson told a group of Congressmen that on the day of the initial U.S. intervention—April 28—"our intelligence indicated that two of the prime leaders in the rebel forces were men with a long history of Communist association and insurrections." By the end of that first night, the President added, word had been received that "there were eight of those who were in the rebel movement that had been trained by Communist movements."

In Washington, lists of "known Communists" allegedly involved in the rebel cause were hastily compiled and leaked to obliging reporters from mysterious and unspecified sources. Subsequent scrutiny of the lists showed that they included the names of adolescents and the recently deceased, as well as duplications caused by aberrant spelling. In at least one instance, Johnson personally called a reporter and urged him to go see the President's friend Abe Fortas (who was later named an Associate Justice of the Supreme Court) to obtain a copy of the list.

Senator J. W. Fulbright of Arkansas, whose Foreign Relations Committee eventually took secret testimony on the Dominican intervention from administration witnesses, concluded that "U.S. policy was marred by a lack of candor and by misinformation. . . . The United States did not intervene primarily to save American lives; it intervened to prevent what it conceived to be a Communist takeover."

American correspondents on the scene in the Dominican Republic were exposed to maddening contradictions between official U.S. pronouncements and their actual observation of events. While the often repeated official line was one of strict neutrality between the rebels and the military junta, reporters observed that American troops and antirebel Dominican soldiers and police were jointly manning checkpoints and, in some instances, jointly returning rebel fire; that Dominicans were arrested by the U.S. military and turned over to antirebel authorities; that American officials were determined to treat the junta as the "legal" government. Lieutenant General Bruce Palmer, the commander of all U.S. ground forces in the Dominican Republic, exploded the myth of American "neutrality" when he referred, in a May 7 statement to his troops, to "the revolution of April 23, between the Communists and the government of the Dominican Republic."

In June, 1966, Murrey Marder wrote in the *Progressive*, "the administration pointed with pride to the free election held in the Dominican Republic, implying that the election was evidence to justify everything said or done in the Dominican Republic by the United States. But what it did not wipe clean was the unnecessary damage done to U.S. credibility in the interim."

For reporters who covered the Dominican story, there was an unsavory postscript. In July, 1965, Thomas Mann, who was then Undersecretary of State, appeared before the Senate Foreign Relations Committee in secret session to complain about "slanted reporting" of the intervention. He charged that American correspondents had been biased in favor of Juan D. Bosch, the former Dominican President in whose name the rebellion was undertaken. Mann, who played a principal role in charting U.S. policy during the rebellion, said he used the word "slanted" advisedly. What bothered him, he told the Senators, was "that the image of the United States was greatly damaged throughout the hemisphere and throughout the world by assertions and insinuations that United States government officials were lying about what the facts were, and I was shocked."

Mann singled out reporters for the New York *Times* and the Washington *Post* for criticism and hinted that he had talked to their editors about having them reassigned. (They weren't.) "I think what happened," he said, "is that a small group, a relatively small group, became emotionally committed to Bosch, and I think they went down there looking for facts which would support their preconceptions. I do not indict newspapers or the press in general for this, but I think it did us a great deal of harm, and I think, I hope, the newspapers themselves are aware of this." Mann's testimony has never been made public, but the Los Angeles *Times* managed to obtain a transcript and report its contents. Ironically, his comments to the committee provided confirmation of the very facts he accused the reporters of "slanting." Mann admitted in his testimony that the United States had secretly given support to the military junta and confirmed that Washington had asked the junta to request U.S. military intervention to protect Americans—a fact that officials had denied when it was reported in the press.

In Washington, cries of "misinformation" emanate from the administration most loudly and most frequently when the least information is being made available. In recent years, as access to the news has become more and more limited, the volume of official complaints about unreliable reporting has risen sharply. The problem has been particularly acute for correspondents covering foreign affairs, for the federal freeze now extends down to the lower levels of the State Department, where reporters have often received their most valuable guidance. In the July, 1966, issue of *Foreign Affairs*, James Reston noted that "there has been a decline . . . in the relations between the experts in the State Department and the reporters. The reason for this is that the experts know the President likes to dominate public announcements and are afraid that they might disclose something that would detonate his temper. And since the most useful information comes, not from the top leaders, but from the men who brief the leaders, this chokes down a very valuable stream of information."

When crisis flared in the Middle East in the spring of 1967, President Johnson issued a flat directive to all members of his administration to discuss no aspect of the situation with the press. Reporters found that even their best-established sources were intimidated by the Presidential order. While Israel and the Arab states moved toward a conflict that easily might have involved the United States in a world war, Americans were left in the dark on the President's thinking and the government's plans. Correspondents were forced to rely on secondhand accounts of Congressional briefings—accounts that were obviously subject to misinterpretation. The President grew angry, and his press secretary, George Christian, complained publicly about "inaccurate reporting." But no effort was made to set the record straight or to furnish a basis for accurate reports. One official at a strictly off-the-record briefing said he would discuss the situation in the Middle East "up to a month ago."

What little useful information became available to the American people came, paradoxically, from foreign sources. When the President flew to Ottawa in May to discuss the Middle East crisis with Canadian Prime Minister Lester Pearson, he and his aides declined to give any but the most perfunctory account of the conference. But one of Pearson's aides briefed the Canadian press, and the visiting correspondents from the United States were allowed to listen in. The next day Pearson gave a full report to his Parliament, and Americans found out what their President's meeting with the Prime Minister had been about.

A few days later, British Prime Minister Harold Wilson visited Washington, met with Johnson at the height of the Middle East crisis, and held an informative press conference. "President Johnson has found himself a smashing press secretary," Mary McGrory thrilled in the Washington *Star*. "His name is Harold Wilson. He is 50 years old, has wavy hair, a smooth face and pale blue eyes. His diction is excellent, and his vocabulary is admirable. He is extremely adroit. Wilson is a British subject, which raises some difficulties. He also has a full-time job as prime minister of his country, which raises more. But if his government has no policy against moonlighting, perhaps he could be induced to commute, so American reporters could find out what's going on in their country. Johnson has played the Arab-Israeli crisis so cool that it was possible to think it was nonexistent. But Wilson confirmed that the crisis is alive and dangerous. He told the press more about what is being done about it than the White House, State Department and Pentagon combined."

The President failed to share Miss McGrory's enthusiasm; in fact, he took a dim view of the Prime Minister's performance. Johnson's preference, often stated and always implied, is to keep 'em guessing, to keep his options open, to play his hand close to the chest. It is a game he plays with consummate skill, but with unfortunate consequences, for those who are kept guessing are not only his adversaries—be they Congressmen, foreign leaders, price raisers, or inquisitive reporters—but also the people of the United States. And while they are kept guessing, they are in no position to form intelligent judgments on their nation's policies.

In the field of foreign policy, the President's penchant for secrecy takes on an added layer of rationalization: The possibility of behind-the-scenes negotiations must be preserved; the passions of the public must be restrained; the experts must be permitted to function free of external pressure. It is a tempting line of argument, one that has enticed other Presidents and holds a permanent allure for diplomats. But it is incompatible with democracy. Robert F. Kennedy summed up the case admirably when he told the nation's newspaper editors:

"There is always a tendency in government to confuse secrecy with security. Most of our historic involvement in world affairs has taken place in time of war, when secrecy was imperative. We are only slowly adjusting to the reality of continuing conflict and responsibility; and accommodating that reality to the necessities of democratic government. The power to conduct foreign affairs is freed from many of the normal checks of congressional and judicial authority. Much of this is unavoidable. However, we should not add an equal freedom from the check of public opinion. I think history demonstrates that increased revelation of the issues which engage the councils of government will frequently lead to greater public understanding and support. And even where the President feels compelled to take an unpopular decision he will act with fuller comprehension. It may be uncomfortable, but it is not the purpose of democracy to ensure the comfort of its leaders."

4. The Saigon Follies

The management of military news has been a problem since the infancy of the Republic. "The first misfortune of the Revolutionary War," Thomas Jefferson wrote, "induced a motion to suppress or garble the account of it. It was rejected with indignation." Such Jeffersonian candor is as obsolete in Vietnam as the flintlock musket. The precedents for official obfuscation were laid down long before President Johnson began to escalate the war. In a secret cable back in 1962, the State Department directed U.S. commanders in Vietnam to keep reporters from covering missions that might produce adverse publicity. "AMBASSADOR HAS OVER-ALL AUTHORITY FOR HANDLING OF NEWSMEN, INSOFAR AS U.S. IS CONCERNED," the cable advised. "HE WILL MAKE DECISIONS AS TO WHEN NEWSMEN PERMITTED TO GO ON ANY MISSIONS WITH U.S. PERSONNEL . . . CORRESPONDENTS SHOULD NOT BE TAKEN ON MISSIONS WHOSE NATURE SUCH THAT UNDESIRABLE DISPATCHES WOULD BE HIGHLY PROBABLE." In those days, when the United States military role in Vietnam was purely "advisory," American reporters—and the American people— were to be shielded from the news that U.S. forces were directing combat missions against the Vietcong. "WE RECOGNIZE IT NATURAL THAT AMERICAN NEWSMEN WILL CONCENTRATE ON ACTIVITIES OF AMERICANS," the State Department cable noted. "IT IS NOT—REPEAT NOT—IN OUR INTEREST, HOWEVER, TO HAVE STORIES INDICATING THAT AMERICANS ARE LEADING AND DIRECTING COMBAT MISSIONS AGAINST VIET CONG . . . SENSATIONAL PRESS STORIES ABOUT CHILDREN WHO BECOME UNFORTUNATE VICTIMS

OF MILITARY OPERATIONS ARE CLEARLY INIMICAL TO THE NA-
TIONAL INTEREST."

"Clearly inimical to the national interest" is the way military
and civilian officials have viewed all reporting from and about
Vietnam that deviates from the comforting fictions of government handouts. The attitude extends all the way to the White
House, which appears content to base even its crucial decisions
on the euphoric estimates of subordinates eager to furnish only
good news. The same attitude prevails in Saigon, where the
daily military briefing for correspondents is known, not very
affectionately, as the Saigon Follies or the Five O'Clock Funnies.
There begins the process of deception that is amplified and
orchestrated in the official pronouncements that emanate from
the Pentagon, the State Department, and the White House. But
the correspondents in Saigon face an even more frustrating
situation than do those reporters who write about the war from
Washington. At home, what we are told merely contradicts what
we *believe* to be the truth; there, it flies in the face of what they
have *seen*. It has not been unheard of, Warren Rogers noted in
the May 2, 1967, issue of *Look* magazine, for correspondents to
be told at the Saigon briefing "that the American unit they just
saw chopped up in a merciless ambush had suffered only 'light
casualties.' "

Casualty counts are only one aspect—and by no means the
most significant—of the massive misinformation effort that the
government of the United States has mounted in the 1960's in
and about Vietnam. The statistics assume importance, however,
because the Pentagon has made them the prime index of how
the war is going. The kill ratio, demonstrating that four or six
or eight or ten North Vietnamese or Vietcong die for every
American soldier killed in action, is offered as the rationale for
the mounting toll of American lives, and so every military
encounter produces its incredibly precise count of the enemy
dead. Yet correspondents in Saigon who question the totals or
point to inconsistencies risk being chided by military spokesmen for "acting like certified public accountants."

U.S. Army and Marine Corps reports on enemy casualties,
Tom Buckley wrote from Saigon in the New York *Times* of
August 4, 1967, "are no longer taken seriously by observers
who have visited battlefields and talked with survivors." Such

skepticism is shared by virtually every American correspondent in Saigon. "Without exception I have found a radical variation between body count noted on the field and that announced in Saigon by our high command," a CBS News man told John Ed Pearce of the Louisville *Courier-Journal*. "I don't know why. I recall one battle near Con Thien where the Marines claimed 384 KIA [killed in action]. I talked to every survivor, and the most anyone claimed was 78. Later the official figure was revised to 130 without explanation."

Another Saigon correspondent told the authors of this book: "I don't think you could find one respectable correspondent here who has any faith at all in the enemy body counts reported by the U.S. command. If they wanted to put the information out as informed estimates or educated guesses or something, that would be okay with me. I even think we may be killing as many as we claim to be. But the U.S. command insists that the figures it releases are confirmed body counts, and that just ain't so. As a result, one of the basic measures of how the war is going is a distorted measure. The enemy carries off his dead, just as we do, and there just aren't ever many left around to count. But the commanders know their superiors are going to want some kind of count, so they manufacture one which may or may not be reasonable. Sometime back, small unit commanders, pressed for body counts, coined a phrase for the whole process that came into widespread use—WAG for wild ass guess, which is what most body counts are."

Similar numbers games have been played with every facet of the war that lends itself to quantification—and with some that don't. Writing from Saigon in the Washington *Post* of September 20, 1966, Ward Just noted that the totals of bombing targets reportedly destroyed in North Vietnam "boggle the imagination. Literally thousands of trucks, barges, bridges and the like have been destroyed since the United States resumed bombing last January 31. In the fortnight between August 20 and September 3, American military spokesmen announced that 344 trucks, 133 bridges, 481 barges, 133 railroad cars and two locomotives have been destroyed. As each day the bridges in North Vietnam came falling down, a journalist was moved to inquire how many bridges there were in North Vietnam. How many could there be if they were being destroyed at the rate of 133 a week? It turned out that no one knew how many bridges there were in North Vietnam, only that the North Vietnamese were amazingly adept at repairing damaged ones. . . ."

When Defense Secretary McNamara visited Vietnam in July, 1967—his "ninth coming"—he declared that the success of American military efforts could "perhaps most dramatically be expressed and revealed by the extension of the use of the road net of the country." He spoke on the basis of computations by military statisticians who calculated that 43 percent of the nation's roads were "secure" as of July 7, with 47 percent "marginal" and only 10 percent "closed." A year earlier the figures had been 36 percent secure, 26 percent marginal, and 38 percent closed.

"The actual situation, according to other American military and civilian officials, is less hopeful," R. W. Apple, Jr., of the New York *Times* reported from Saigon. "The official figures, these observers indicate, are subject to many qualifications. First, the classifications are highly subjective. They represent judgments, not facts, and the views of officers in different parts of the country vary. Sometimes the assessments are contradicted. A twenty-mile stretch of Highway 1 northwest of Danang, for example, is labeled secure, but on July 3, a Vietnamese Army convoy was smashed in a Vietcong ambush there. Twenty trucks were destroyed and fourteen others damaged. Second, the military figures apply only to military travel, in which weapons are always carried. Even on 'secure' highways, American soldiers carry loaded M-16s and use jeeps whose floors are covered with sandbags to give some protection against enemy mines. . . . American civilian officials are discouraged from traveling anywhere outside Saigon by road, except to Bienhoa, just north of the capital and the site of an American base. Third, the military flatly refuses to classify any road in the country as safe at night—not even the four-lane, fifteen-mile expressway that links Saigon with Bienhoa. . . . Fourth, the military statistics cover only 1,743 miles of highways—a fraction of the national total—that are considered 'of strategic importance' by the military. . . . The highways that are omitted from the tabulations are for the most part impassable to all military traffic."

That was the word from Saigon, but when McNamara returned to Washington he asserted once again that "perhaps the most dramatic change that I saw that reflects the military situation was the opening of the roads." That was the message that reached most Americans at home.

Press reports from Vietnam, President Johnson has repeatedly told visitors, are at variance with official data—and so the press must be wrong. On October 16, 1967, the New York *Times* reported from Saigon that Ambassador Ellsworth Bunker had been exerting pressure on the government of President Nguyen Van Thieu and Vice-President Nguyen Cao Ky to undertake necessary reforms in the country and to keep in mind the political problems of President Johnson in the United States. A White House official who sees the President daily labeled the *Times* story "atrocious." Was it wrong, he was asked, and he replied: "I don't care if it's right or wrong—even if you have it nailed down, even if you have it laid out in your lap, you don't write that kind of story. It just gives aid and comfort to the North Vietnamese. It proves to them that the South Vietnamese are nothing more than our lackeys."

At a celebrated "background" session with reporters early in February, 1968, Secretary Rusk reacted with similar indignation to questions about a possible failure of U.S. intelligence in connection with the Communist Tet offensive in Vietnam. Why, Rusk demanded, must the press always accentuate the negative? "There gets to be a point," he said, "when the question is, whose side are you on. I'm the Secretary of State, and I'm on our side." When a reporter inquired whether Rusk was suggesting the press was disloyal, the Secretary replied with what the *Wall Street Journal* called "this extraordinary tirade": "None of your papers or your broadcasting apparatuses are worth a damn unless the United States succeeds. They are trivial compared to that question. So I don't know why, to win a Pulitzer Prize, people have to go on probing for things one can bitch about when there are two thousand stories on the same day about things that are more constructive in character."

The notion that it is "atrocious" to report news the government wants to suppress found its chief defender in Arthur Sylvester, the former Assistant Secretary of Defense for Public Affairs, who until his retirement in 1967 was the principal architect of Pentagon news management techniques. He will be remembered as the official who formally proclaimed the government's right to lie. Shortly after the 1962 Cuban missile crisis, when he addressed a dinner meeting of Sigma Delta Chi, the journalism society, in New York, Sylvester declared: "It would seem to be basic, all through history, that a government's right— and by a government I mean a people, since in our country, in my judgment, the people express, have the right to express and do express every two and every four years what government they want—that it's inherent in that government's right, if necessary, to lie to save itself from its going up into a nuclear war. This seems to be basic. Basic."

The remarks, as Sylvester never tired of explaining to Congressional committees, were taken out of context. "But I would like to put them in context," he explained on one such occasion, "because they were in effect a shorthand of a basic point of view, and that is that any nation has the right of survival, self-preservation, particularly in this time when it can be faced almost overnight with a nuclear holocaust. In our country the governmental representatives of this people whom they elect and dispose of have a duty to take whatever means in their judgment or in the judgment of the top people is necessary when that people faces nuclear disaster." His defense of the government's right to lie, Sylvester added, was intended to apply only to the Cuban missile crisis. In practice, however, it governs the Pentagon's information policies from day to day.

"The government has the right to lie," Sylvester reasserted in an article for the *Saturday Evening Post* of November 18, 1967. At the same time, curiously, he denounced "the misinterpretation, misrepresentation and downright lying that tarnish the American news industry, written and electronic." Betraying an unusual conception of the role of the press, Sylvester complained that "newsmen are gabby." He charged that "some itinerant newsmen damaged their country's interest by revealing U.S. Air Force combat planes were flying out of Thailand against North Vietnam at a time when the Thai government threatened to deny us the bases if any publicity developed. Newsmen in Saigon who had been briefed honored the request for silence, only to be beaten by the blabbermouths." The "blabbermouths," of course, were correspondents who believed

Americans had the right to know their government was widening the war in Southeast Asia by using Thailand as a staging area for air attacks on North Vietnam.

It was Sylvester who instituted the Pentagon rule, rescinded only in mid-1967, requiring all Defense officials to report daily on the "substance of each interview and telephone conversation with a media representative." This and other information policies established in the early 1960's, wrote the late Mark Watson of the Baltimore *Sun*, long the dean of Pentagon correspondents, suggested "the policy and performance of Adolf Hitler's propaganda chief, Paul Joseph Goebbels." It was Sylvester, too, who found it prudent to install military officers in key information posts formerly held by civilians. "Military information officers—while often more knowledgeable—are also easier to control since their fitness reports are at stake. They can be transferred without fighting the machinery of civil service," George C. Wilson wrote in the Washington *Post*. Sylvester himself once put it more succinctly: "I can fire them with one phone call."

Military information officers are turned out by the Defense Information School in Indianapolis, an institution whose guiding philosophy was summed up this way by one of its lecturers, Army Captain Gary Werner: "Our task is to prepare the students for their primary obligation, which will be to the people they work for, the executive branch. The public's right to know is not the controlling factor as far as the individual information officer is concerned." Martin F. Nolan, Washington correspondent for the *Reporter* who taught at the Defense Information School as a draftee, said: "The course's main aim is to further goals of the brass and not the public's right to know. The spirit of public relations prevails while democratic ideals get lip service."

These teachings have been generously reflected in the daily performance at the Saigon Follies. It was understandable, therefore, that members of the American corps of correspondents in Saigon were eager to confer with the Assistant Secretary of Defense for Public Affairs when Sylvester scheduled a visit to Vietnam in the summer of 1965. The confrontation took place on July 17 at the home of Barry Zorthian, minister-counselor of the United States Embassy. One of those present, CBS correspondent Morley Safer, later wrote this account for *Dateline 1966*, a publication of the Overseas Press Club of America:

"Zorthian was less relaxed than usual. He was anxious for Sylvester to get an idea of the mood of the news corps. There had been some annoying moments in previous weeks that had directly involved Sylvester's own office. In the first B-52 raids, Pentagon releases were in direct contradiction to what had actually happened on the ground in Vietnam. Also, those of us involved in broadcasting were anxious to discuss the increasing problems of communication. There was general opening banter, which Sylvester quickly brushed aside. He seemed anxious to take a stand—to say something that would jar us. He did:

" 'I can't understand how you fellows can write what you do while American boys are dying out here,' he began. Then he went on to the effect that American correspondents had a patriotic duty to disseminate only information that made the United States look good. A network television correspondent said, 'Surely, Arthur, you don't expect the American press to be the handmaidens of government.' 'That's exactly what I expect,' came the reply. An agency man raised the problem that had preoccupied Ambassador Taylor and Barry Zorthian— about the credibility of American officials. Responded the Assistant Secretary of Defense for Public Affairs: 'Look, if you think any American official is going to tell you the truth, then you're stupid. Did you hear that?—*stupid.*'

"One of the most respected of all the newsmen in Vietnam— a veteran of World War II, the Indochina War and Korea—suggested that Sylvester was being deliberately provocative. Sylvester replied: 'Look, I don't even have to talk to you people. I know how to deal with you through your editors and publishers back in the States.' At this point, the Hon. Arthur Sylvester put his thumbs in his ears, bulged his eyes, stuck out his tongue and wiggled his fingers. A correspondent for one of the New York papers began a question. He never got beyond the first words. Sylvester interrupted: 'Aw, come on. What does someone in New York care about the war in Vietnam?' "

Predictably, Sylvester denounced this account as "an abusive piece" and a "gem of misrepresentation." Eight other correspondents confirmed Safer's version of the encounter. A few months later, however, when he appeared before the Senate Foreign Relations Committee to testify on Vietnam information policies, Sylvester was in an expansive mood: "It is obvious, and they are the first to say it, that American newsmen in Vietnam need help from their government if they are to report accurately and objectively to the American public. The Department of Defense Public Affairs policy is to provide them with all possible help, both in Vietnam and here in the United States. I believe strongly that we have met the unique public affairs challenge of this war with a dynamic and successful response."

One of Sylvester's last official acts before he retired early in 1967 was to denounce Harrison E. Salisbury, an assistant managing editor of the New York *Times,* as a "Hanoi-picked correspondent" for reporting from North Vietnam that American bombing raids had taken a heavy toll of civilian casualties—a fact that had been energetically suppressed by the White House, the State Department, and the Pentagon. It was another instance of reporting "clearly inimical to national interest"—but true. Ironically, Salisbury's dispatches won rare praise for the United States around the world. The Vatican newspaper, *L'Osservatore Romano,* called the reports from Hanoi "a service to the truth, all the more valuable in that the truth to be ascertained can turn out to be against oneself or, rather, against the presumed benefit of the propaganda cause of one's own country, and is presumably disagreeable." Elsewhere in Europe, newspapers lauded American democracy for permitting the press "to investigate and publish reports that run counter to official statements" and for allowing officials "to openly admit that mistakes have been made."

Anyone who supposed that the Saigon Follies—or their Washington counterpart—would get a new script when Sylvester left the management was doomed to be disappointed. The show goes on. In 1967, as the credibility crisis grew at home, an able and conscientious American correspondent in Vietnam—one who prefers to remain anonymous because "I'm trying to be a reporter here, not a critic or crusader"—set down his private impressions of United States information policies in a letter to the authors of this book. He stressed that he supported the American involvement in Vietnam—"I am by no means a dove"—but that he had become convinced that official misrepresentation was a critical problem. These were among his examples:

"After many months of denials and putting off questions by people here, the Pentagon recently got around to a new version of U.S. plane losses in the war. The new figures were almost double the ones previously put out.

"Often the U.S. Mission here reports cases of alleged Viet Cong terrorism which, since they come from Vietnamese sources, are given out 'on background.' This protects the U.S. Mission as the source of the information, even though the Mission puts it out and it is often wrong. Recently the U.S. spokesman reported—and many stories were printed about—a case in which the VC allegedly used women and children as human shields in an attack on a government battalion. The facts were that no such attack occurred, no one was used as a human shield and the people were killed by misdirected artillery. It should have been just as easy—easier, in fact—for the U.S. Mission to get the truth as it was for reporters.

"The U.S. Command not so long ago put out a directive to information officers telling them to emphasize and promote the role being played by Vietnamese troops in the war. It was also suggested that U.S. GIs should be encouraged to sing the praises of their Vietnamese allies in their letters home. I don't expect the U.S. Military to stand up and say the host army is not worth a damn. But the fact is that it isn't. The Vietnamese have all but completely quit fighting the war and have left it to the Americans. And I don't think it serves the truth, or serves the purpose of informing the public, for the military to undertake a campaign to say otherwise.

"We are almost buried in optimistic statistics here. For example, we get weekly reports on the new records being set by the Chieu Hoi program to lure Viet Cong back to the government. And it is a good program and it is having success. But we have to almost pull teeth to get the facts about desertions in the Vietnamese armed forces, and they are part of the story too. Last year, for example, we were told over and over again about the 20,000 or so Chieu Hois being double the number who came in last year. That's impressive, but so is the fact that more than 100,000 Vietnamese military personnel deserted—not to the enemy, but deserted their units and responsibilities.

"Recently a top economist in the U.S. Aid Mission called correspondents in for a briefing on the acute rice shortage and the record-high price of rice, which was beginning to create serious concern among the people. He candidly admitted that one reason for the briefing was that the correspondents could 'help' the situation, apparently by writing stories to the effect that thousands of tons of U.S. rice were on the way and the problem would soon be licked. Clearly he hoped to use the press to get the message across, which is all right even though we're hardly supposed to be here to perform the information functions of the AID program. But while he wanted help, the official did not want to answer questions about the responsibility for the shortage because the responsibility—quite clearly—lay with inadequate U.S. estimates of the rice needs here and inadequate shipping arrangements to get the stuff here on time.

"There is also a good deal of what I call 'censorship by foot-dragging,' that is, putting off answers to questions until the issue dies down. A case in point was the recent incident in which planes mistakenly bombed a Montagnard village and killed more than eighty people. It took the U.S. Command several days of 'investigating' to determine that they were American planes, though everyone knew perfectly well that they were.

". . . [When] U.S. artillery mistakenly shoots up a village and kills innocent people, it is announced as an 'incident,' regrets are expressed and there is a lot said about Americans giving blood to the wounded, providing medical care, etc. Fine. I can understand that. But when a Viet Cong mine blows up a bus and kills civilians, it is automatically announced as an act of deliberate terrorism. It may be. But I suspect the Viet Cong mines that get buses may be placed in the roads to hit U.S. or Vietnamese military vehicles now and then. And perhaps they have accidents too. This sort of black-and-white approach breeds skepticism and suspicion.

". . . Most of the trouble comes, I think, from the fact that U.S. officialdom has lost its credibility. When they have a good story to tell, it's never good enough. They can't resist embroidering or shading it. They always want to tell you, for example, how many new hamlet schools have been built under the pacification program. But it's next to impossible to get them to say how many of those same schools have already been destroyed by the Viet Cong—or how many of them are being used as military billets instead of as schools.

". . . I think what the Vietnam effort needs, perhaps more than anything else, is a large dose of candor. . . . [This] rundown on the information policies out here is a lot shorter than it might have been. It is a great mess."

The great information mess in Saigon has its striking parallels in Washington. But while correspondents in Vietnam are likely to be preoccupied with casualties, tactics, and logistics—with keeping a daily box score on the war—the Washington press corps confronts the same pattern of confusion, concealment, and deceit on the broad issues of national policy—the issues that, in a democracy, are presumably under the public's purview. How much, for example, has the war in Vietnam cost the American taxpayers? It is unlikely that they will ever really know. The administration that prides itself on its cost effectiveness programs, on "getting the most bang for the buck," has never fully taken the people into its confidence on the cost of the war, though it has repeatedly assured them they can afford it. On September 22, 1966, a reporter put this question to President Johnson at a White House news conference: "Mr. President, sir, we really have not been told how much the war in Vietnam is costing and how much it is costing from day to day. This question has been put to Mr. McNamara early in the year and he said it is almost impossible to tell, and lately U.S. officials said they couldn't quite tell us. Don't you think the American people ought to be told?" The President's reply had a characteristically admonitory tone: "I think that the Congress, through the Appropriations Committee and Authorizations Committee, have had very full details on our expenditures, men, money and material in Vietnam. I would recommend to you some homework. Read the hearings."

The correspondents were baffled. They *had* read the hearings and had found in them none of the information to which the President referred. Nor, for that matter, had the members of the Appropriations and Authorizations committees. When Robert

H. Fleming, the deputy White House press secretary, was asked after the news conference where such information appeared on the public record, he answered: "We do not have the committee record available so that we can cite dates and pages." On Capitol Hill, Representative Melvin R. Laird of Wisconsin, second-ranking Republican on the House Defense Appropriations Subcommittee, questioned Pentagon Comptroller Robert N. Anthony about Vietnam war costs. "When I asked him where the Vietnam cost estimates were that the President referred to in his news conference," Laird later said, Anthony replied: "There is nothing in the hearings that would tell you the cost of the war in Vietnam."

It was several months later—after the fall Congressional elections—that the administration advised Congress that it had inadvertently underestimated the cost of the war by some $10 billion in fiscal 1967. This was the first official acknowledgment that the war was costing at least $20 billion a year. Inadvertent underestimates have been the pattern ever since. By the time President Johnson submitted his proposed federal budget for fiscal 1969, the total for "special Vietnam" costs was officially given at $25.8 billion. At the same time, however, Democratic Senator Stuart Symington of Missouri disclosed that staff members of the Senate Appropriations Committee had calculated the true costs at a total more than $6 billion higher. "The men who compiled these figures are as thorough and experienced as any men in government," Symington said. In a February, 1968, editorial, *Fortune* magazine charged that it was "partly the Treasury's fault that the public was deceived on the true costs of the Vietnam war for more than a year following the 1965 decision to mount a major U.S. military effort." *Fortune* said the Treasury Department must bear "some of the blame for the dissembling, the secrecy, and the last-minute improvision in economic and fiscal matters that have become standard Johnsonian practice."

In the massive confusion of claims and counterclaims about Vietnam, one constant and consistent theme has been the government's assurance that all is going well—although administration spokesmen candidly admit at each point that six months, a year, or two years ago the outlook was far from encouraging. On any day of any week, correspondents can visit the White

House basement office of Walt W. Rostow, President Johnson's special assistant for national security affairs, and receive "on a background basis" handsome full-color charts and graphs depicting the steady upward curve of every conceivable war indicator. For many months, one such indicator was the "Chieu Hoi" statistic, showing the number of Vietcong defectors. It proved, Rostow said, that the United States was winning the war. But when the Chieu Hoi rate suddenly plummeted late in 1967, this, too, was offered as evidence of success. The Vietcong, Rostow explained, were convinced that the war would soon be over and therefore were not bothering to defect.

In November, 1967, the Johnson administration mounted an extraordinary effort to persuade the public that substantial progress was being made in Vietnam. Ambassador Bunker and General Westmoreland were brought back to Washington, and in a series of speeches, interviews, and backgrounders they painted a rosy picture of American accomplishments. Westmoreland, who was soon to request additional U.S. troop commitments, predicted a "phase-down" in two years or less. Bunker reported that more than two-thirds of the South Vietnamese population was under government control. Both repeatedly talked of "steady progress," and Westmoreland made headlines by describing the situation as "very, very encouraging." Two months later, all these claims were shattered by the Communist Tet offensive, which rendered absurd both Bunker's "security" statistics and Westmoreland's predictions of a phase-down.

Even the grim news of the Tet offensive, however, failed to dampen the administration's enthusiasm for cheering assessments. While battles still raged in cities seized by the Vietcong, Johnson proclaimed the Communist effort to have been "a great failure," and administration officials worked overtime dispensing "captured documents" purporting to show that the Vietcong had failed to achieve their objectives. Rostow told reporters that the Communist offensive had brought American victory closer. The only high official who appeared to have learned from past overoptimism was Secretary McNamara, who was about to leave the Defense Department. His last "posture statement," submitted to Congress in January, 1968, was by far the gloomiest assessment he had yet made—at least publicly—of the outlook in

Vietnam. But by that time McNamara was firmly established as a principal architect of the Credibility Gap.

"Mr. Speaker," Congressman Laird observed on the floor of the House, "Secretary McNamara's best known prediction on Vietnam was his statement of October 2, 1963, reporting his judgment that the major part of the U.S. military task can be completed by the end of 1965, although there may be a continuing requirement for a limited number of U.S. training personnel. This is not, however, his only contribution to the Credibility Gap. On November 21, 1963, Secretary McNamara said, 'We are equally encouraged by the prospects for progress in the war against the Viet Cong.' As he spoke, the Viet Cong were rapidly gobbling up great areas of South Vietnam. This he admitted two months later when he said: 'The Viet Cong moved in . . . and had many successes during the period of November and December.' "

As Congressman Laird went on to note, McNamara told the nation on January 27, 1964, that the successor to the Diem government "has considerably more popular support than its predecessor." Two days later that government was overthrown. On April 24, 1964, McNamara expressed the expectation of "dramatic progress" in Vietnam by July or August, and on July 15 he reported an improvement in the morale of the Vietnamese. On August 7, however, General Khanh found it necessary to declare a state of emergency throughout Vietnam. Widespread student rioting followed, and Khanh was forced to resign on August 25.

On May 9, 1965, McNamara appraised the military situation in Vietnam by saying, "In the last eight weeks there has been an improvement." Yet on October 13, 1965, he said that the Vietcong in May and June came close to cutting South Vietnam in half and destroying the regular South Vietnamese military forces. "In that period of time [May–June, 1965]," he declared, the Vietcong "substantially increased their control of the geography of the country." On November 29, 1965, McNamara declared, "We have stopped losing the war." Yet during the period when, according to the Secretary, the war was being lost, he made statements acclaiming "progress" and exuding optimism on no fewer than fourteen separate occasions. "This list of inaccurate prophecies and faulty assessment is far from complete, but it is enough to show why the public is skeptical about administration statements on Vietnam," Congressman Laird concluded.

McNamara's rosy public assessments of the war appear to have continued long beyond the point when he began entertaining private doubts about the prudence of the administration's policies. There were, to be sure, reports from the Pentagon that the Secretary was determined to curb what the *Wall Street Journal* called his "spectacularly over-optimistic forecasts." Frederick Taylor wrote on April 27, 1967, that McNamara "has mended those ways, and voices only cautious predictions about the outlook. Forecasts and predictions are necessarily speculative, however; the habit the Defense boss has yet to break is his careless way with plain hard facts." When McNamara returned from his inspection trip to Vietnam in the summer of 1967, he found it possible to cite "tremendous progress," "dramatic change," and "very substantial improvement." Three weeks later, President Johnson announced that the war would require at least 45,000 more American troops and requested a 10 percent surcharge on income taxes. And less than three months after that, Johnson nominated McNamara to the presidency of the World Bank amid widespread reports that the Secretary was disillusioned about the American strategy in Vietnam and the prospects for bringing the war to an end.

While McNamara was on his summer, 1967, inspection trip to Vietnam, Senator Mike Mansfield of Montana, the Democratic leader, anticipated the tidings the Defense Secretary would bear back to Washington. Mansfield told the Senate:

"And once again, Mr. President, the Secretary of Defense has gone to Saigon to make a first-hand evaluation of the situation. According to the press he has heard and accepted the most encouraging reports of 'progress' toward our 'objectives' in Vietnam. While I do not in any sense question the accuracy or the objectivity of the evaluations which he has received, it must be asked in all frankness what is meant by 'progress' toward our 'objectives' in the context of the present situation in Vietnam? In all frankness, it must be said that these generalizations of progress would be more reassuring if they had not been heard from American leaders in Vietnam at many other times, stretching years into the past. Indeed, I know of no American leader, military or civilian, in Vietnam during the past decade or more who has contended that we were doing anything else except making 'progress' toward our 'objectives.'

"The fact is that reports of progress are strewn, like burned out tanks, all along the road which has led this nation ever more deeply into Vietnam and Southeast Asia during the past decade and a half. They were present when the sole function of American military personnel in Vietnam was that of aid suppliers to the French-commanded Vietnamese loyalist forces. They were present when our military functions in Vietnam evolved into that of trainers and advisers of the South Vietnamese forces, to that of air transporters and supporters, to that of combat bulwarks and, finally, to that of combat substitutes for the South Vietnamese forces.

"The generalization on progress, in short, is the ever-present beat which is to be heard throughout the transition of the American military role from the most remote and invisible rear to the most forward and conspicuous front of the Vietnamese war. It has been present, this promise of progress, as the casualties in our forces in dead and wounded have increased from less than ten a year, to ten a month, to ten a week, to ten a day, to ten an hour of every hour of every day. It has been present as the estimated expenditures of the federal government for Vietnam have increased from a few hundred million a year, to $2 billion, to $12 billion, to the present level of probably not less than $25 billion a year."

The parallel development cited by Mansfield—the steady escalation of the war accompanied by equally steady assurances of progress—accounts for much of the credibility problem over Vietnam. For the propaganda theme itself is hardly unique or even unusual. It is standard procedure for wartime governments to trumpet their successes and suppress news of failures. The problem in the case of Vietnam—the reason why there is a Credibility Gap—is that Americans have become involved in the war slowly, reluctantly, and at each stage under the impression, fostered by official rhetoric, that victory was just around the corner. A citizen relying, for example, on the public utterances made through the years by Secretary of State Rusk, would have every reason to suppose that the nation's military commitment in Vietnam would be both tolerable and transitory. Here is but a small sampling of Rusk's comments on the progress of the war:

On February 1, 1963, "There are some definitely encouraging elements. The ratio of casualties between government and Viet Cong forces, the ratio of arms captured or lost between the two sides, the steady expansion of the strategic-hamlet program, the increasingly effective work of the Montagnards along the border areas—all those indicate some turning in the situation." On February 13, 1963, "The momentum of the Communist drive has been stopped." On April 18, 1963, "The South Vietnamese themselves are fighting their own battle, fighting well." On April 22, 1963, "There is a good basis for encouragement. The Vietnamese are on their way to success and need our help; not just our material help—they need that—but our sympathetic understanding and comradeship." On February 24, 1964, "I think the resources and capabilities are there to get this job done on the present basis of assistance to the Vietnamese so that they themselves can handle this problem primarily with their own effort." On July 1, 1964, "I think they [the Vietcong] have very serious problems—not only in fact, in terms of losses, disruptions, but in terms of morale. So I am not pessimistic about the situation." On August 25, 1966, "We are beginning to see some signs of success of this strategy. The Viet Cong monsoon offensive, which we know from captured documents it was their intention to carry out during the period of May to October, has not materialized because of Westmoreland's tactics of carrying out spoiling operations based on intelligence he has received. . . . The number of defections this year has doubled compared to the past year. No doubt this is a sign of erosion of morale." On January 1, 1967, "I do believe that one basis for optimism is that the other side must surely now understand that they are not going to succeed in seizing South Vietnam by force." On April 16, 1967, "I think we have seen some very favorable signs that we are making headway on the military side, but that does not mean that the war is just about over. . . . I must say that I have been impressed by the doubling of the rate of defectors from the other side." On July 19, 1967, "The other side is hurting, and they are hurting very badly."

The *New Republic* compiled these and other official utterances under the heading "Keep the Faith, Baby."

The optimist-in-chief, of course, has been the President of the United States. In one rare slip, Johnson referred to the war in his 1967 Memorial Day proclamation as a "bloody impasse," but he swiftly moved to correct the record by directing General William C. Westmoreland to dispose of "this 'stalemate' creature." The American military commander in Vietnam was pleased to comply. "The statement that we are in a complete stalemate is complete fiction," he told reporters. "It is completely unrealistic. During the past year tremendous progress has been made."

The Gulf of Tonkin Resolution, approved by both houses of Congress on August 7, 1964, with only two dissenting votes, has often been cited by the President as the legal justification for the massive American military intervention in Vietnam. The resolution declared that "the Congress approves and supports the determination of the President, as Commander in Chief, to take all necessary measures to repel any armed attack against the forces of the United States and to prevent further aggression." It was enacted in an atmosphere of crisis after the first direct collision between the United States and North Vietnam—a naval encounter in the Gulf of Tonkin early in August, 1964—and has been described by Undersecretary of State Nicholas deB. Katzenbach as a "functional equivalent" of a declaration of war against North Vietnam. Yet this important milestone in the escalation of the war is enveloped in a fog of confusion and contradiction. Some members of the Senate Committee on Foreign Relations who steered the resolution to passage, including Chairman Fulbright, have come to hold grave reservations about the events in the Gulf of Tonkin—even to the point of doubting that the attack which triggered the American response actually took place. Fulbright says he regrets "more than anything I have ever done in my life that I was the vehicle that took the resolution to the floor and defended it."

After many months of frustrated efforts to ascertain the full facts about the Gulf of Tonkin incident, Fulbright succeeded in February, 1968, in bringing Secretary McNamara before a closed session of his committee. The censored transcript of Mc-

Namara's seven-hour appearance revealed many apparent discrepancies. McNamara, who had assured Congress and the nation in 1964 that the two American destroyers in the gulf, the U.S.S. *Maddox* and the U.S.S. *C. Turner Joy*, were on "routine patrol" when they were attacked by North Vietnamese vessels, now conceded that they had been assigned to an intelligence mission. In 1964 the Secretary had insisted that the *Maddox* and the *Joy* had not been involved in South Vietnamese raiding operations against North Vietnam that were then taking place. "Our Navy," he said then, "played absolutely no part in, was not associated with, was not aware of any South Vietnamese actions, if there were any. I want to make that very clear to you. The *Maddox* . . . was not informed of, was not aware of, had no knowledge of, and so far as I know today has no knowledge of any South Vietnamese actions in connection with the two islands [of North Vietnam]." But the committee record disclosed in 1968 that Captain John J. Herrick, the commander of the American task force in the Gulf of Tonkin who was aboard the *Maddox*, had specific knowledge of the South Vietnamese operations, indicated that the North Vietnamese thought his patrol was part of the operations, and therefore requested air cover before the attack took place. McNamara said in 1968 that his 1964 statement may have been "ambiguous" and was misunderstood.

The committee record also revealed that Captain Herrick had informed the Pentagon, a few hours before retaliatory strikes were ordered against North Vietnam, that "review of action makes many reported contacts and torpedoes fired appear doubtful. Freak weather effects and over-eager sonar-men may have accounted for many reports. No actual visual sightings by *Maddox* suggests complete evaluation before further action." Commenting on this cable, Fulbright said: "If I had known of that one telegram, if that had been put before me on the sixth of August, I certainly don't believe I would have rushed into action. . . . It never occurred to me that there was the slightest doubt . . . that this attack took place." Democratic Senator Albert Gore of Tennessee told the committee, "I feel the Congress and the country were misled. . . . I know I have been misled."

Established beyond reasonable doubt is the fact that the

administration began drafting the Gulf of Tonkin Resolution long before the Gulf of Tonkin incident took place. Assistant Secretary of State William Bundy told a closed meeting of the Senate Foreign Relations Committee that early drafts were part of "normal contingency planning" for the Vietnam war. Marvin Kalb, the diplomatic correspondent for CBS News, who obtained access to Bundy's secret testimony, reported on November 9, 1967, that "Bundy insists the advance drafts were not checked with the White House nor inspired by it and were taken as a precaution since the President was entering an election campaign and might need such a resolution." But Tom Wicker of the New York *Times* has written that Johnson ordered drafting of the resolution and "had been carrying it around in his pocket for weeks waiting for the moment."

Never in the years of steady escalation of the war has the word "escalation" passed the President's lips—except when it has figured in a scornful denial of "unfounded speculation" that the war was being widened. Only rarely and under the pressure of irrefutable evidence has Johnson conceded that the war was "more far-reaching" than it had been in the past—and such admissions have been coupled with the standard denial of escalation. Richard N. Goodwin, a former assistant to and speechwriter for Presidents Kennedy and Johnson, complains that "we are buried in statements and speeches about negotiations and peace, the defense of freedom and the dangers of Communism, the desire to protect the helpless and compassion for the dying. Much of it is important and sincere and well-meaning. Some is intended to deceive. Some is deliberate lie and distortion." Goodwin adds that "by its nature, war is hostile to truth. Yet with full allowance for necessary uncertainties, I believe there has never been such intense and widespread deception and confusion as that which surrounds this war."

Even more widespread and intense than the deception and confusion that surround the war are the dissimulation and concealment that have clouded all attempts to restore peace. "I will talk to any government, anywhere, any time, without any conditions, and if any doubt our sincerity let them test us," President Johnson asserted on April 27, 1965, and he has used almost identical language time and again to demonstrate his determination to negotiate an end to the Vietnam war. "The dream we share, of course, is peace," the President said aboard the USS *Enterprise* on November 11, 1967, and he issued this "call across the seas to Hanoi": "Now hear this—you force us to fight, but you have only to say the word for our quarrel to be buried beneath the waves." Yet the administration's sincerity has repeatedly been put to the test, and in each instance news of the challenge has been withheld from the American people.

In 1964, we now know, the United States rejected two tangible and specific proposals to initiate peace discussions. In late July, French President Charles de Gaulle called for a Geneva type of conference, and the Soviet Union asked the fourteen nations of the Geneva Conference to reconvene. The Vietcong stated they were "not opposed to the convening of an international conference in order to facilitate the search for a solution." The governments in Hanoi and Peking also endorsed the proposal, and the United Nations Secretary-General, U Thant, reiterated his support for the reconvening of the conference. The official reply of the United States was that "we do not believe in conferences called to ratify terror, so our policy is unchanged." In September, 1964, while Johnson was campaigning for election on a platform of prudent moderation in Vietnam, the administration spurned U Thant's efforts to arrange a meeting between United States and North Vietnamese representatives in Rangoon, Burma, to discuss terms for ending the hostilities. More than a year passed before this episode was officially confirmed. On November 16, 1965, the New York *Times* reported: "The State Department confirmed today a report that a year ago the United States rejected an offer by North Vietnam to have representatives of the two nations meet in Rangoon, Burma, to discuss terms for ending hostilities in Vietnam. Robert J. McCloskey, State Department press officer, said that during that period the United States received reports from numerous third parties who had contact with officials of North Vietnam. On the basis of the total evidence available to us, we did not believe at any time that North Vietnam was prepared for serious peace talks, Mr. McCloskey said."

The government's evaluation of North Vietnam's "seriousness" may well have been correct, though one must wonder how it was arrived at in the absence of discussions. One must wonder, too, about Secretary Rusk's statement on November 15, 1965: "My position has long been known. It is that we should search in every possible way for a peaceful settlement in Vietnam and should be prepared for unconditional discussions with the governments concerned, in large groups or small ones, at any time and any place." The best account we have of the abortive Burma conference is Eric Sevareid's report, in *Look* magazine, of an interview with the late Ambassador Adlai Stevenson:

"In the early autumn of 1964, he [Stevenson] went on, U Thant, the U.N. Secretary General, had privately obtained agreement from authorities in North Vietnam that they would send an emissary to talk with an American emissary, in Rangoon, Burma. Someone in Washington insisted that this attempt be postponed until after the Presidential election. When the election was over, U Thant again pursued the matter; Hanoi was still willing to send its man. But Defense Secretary Robert McNamara, Adlai went on, flatly opposed the attempt. He said the South Vietnamese government would have to be informed and that this would have a demoralizing effect on them; that government was shaky enough as it was. Stevenson told me that U Thant was furious over this failure of his patient efforts, but said nothing publicly.

"Time was passing, the war expanding. The pressures on U Thant, supposedly the Number One peacemaker of the globe, were mounting from all sides within the U.N. So he proposed an outright cease-fire, with a truce line to be drawn across not only Vietnam but neighboring Laos. U Thant then made a remarkable suggestion: United States officials could write the terms of the cease-fire offer, exactly as they saw fit, and he, U Thant, would announce it in exactly those words. Again, so Stevenson said to me, McNamara turned this down, and from Secretary Rusk there was no response, to Stevenson's knowledge."

All these moves were, of course, withheld at the time from the American people, who were, in fact, repeatedly assured by their government that there was no willingness to negotiate on "the other side." Late in February, 1965, U Thant again tried to set up peace discussions and disclosed at a news conference that he had made specific proposals to the United States and to other powers principally involved in the Vietnam question. A New

York *Times* report stated that the "Communist government of North Vietnam has notified the Secretary General that it is receptive to his suggestion for informal negotiations on the Vietnam situation." But the White House replied, "The President has not authorized anyone to participate in negotiations. He has no meaningful proposals before him." A few months later, administration officials privately confessed that if they had agreed to peace talks with Hanoi, it might have toppled the government in Saigon.

During a pause in the bombing raids on North Vietnam in May, 1965, a few weeks after the President had professed his eagerness to "talk to any government, anywhere, any time, without any conditions," Hanoi asked the French government to indicate to the United States its interest in negotiations, withdrawing its previous conditions that there had to be a prior withdrawal of American troops from South Vietnam. This was Rusk's subsequent account to the American people of the North Vietnamese bid: "In May, there was a cessation of bombing which ended after a harsh rejection by the other side of any serious move toward peace."

On February 3, 1967, the Washington *Post* disclosed, in a dispatch from Robert H. Estabrook at the United Nations, that two months earlier, on December 4, a message from Polish Foreign Minister Adam Rapacki had reported Hanoi's willingness to begin talks with the United States at the ambassadorial level in Warsaw. North Vietnam posed no prior conditions for the talks and asked that special representatives be dispatched from Washington to Warsaw. But on December 13 and 14, American bombers conducted the raids near Hanoi that heavily damaged civilian areas, and North Vietnam withdrew its agreement, charging bad faith.

A day before this news broke on February 3, President Johnson was asked at the White House about the possibility of peace negotiations. He replied: "With the information that I have, with the knowledge that is brought to me, I must say that I do not interpret any action that I have observed as being a serious effort to either go to a conference table or to bring the war to an end. . . . I have seen nothing that any of them have said which indicates any seriousness on their part. I am awaiting any offer they might care to make." When he was asked what kind of step would be required on Hanoi's part to bring about a new suspension of the bombing, the President replied, "Just almost any step. As far as we can see, they have not taken any yet."

The next possible opening for an end to the war came during the Tet (lunar new year) cease-fire from February 8 to 11, 1967. President Johnson was under pressure to extend the bombing pause and explore the possibility of negotiations, but he rejected this course. He had, Johnson said, "no alternative but to resume full-scale hostilities" because North Vietnam had taken advantage of the truce for "major supply efforts of their troops in South Vietnam." In fact, no evidence of such "major supply efforts" was ever produced. The official communiqué of the United States command in Saigon on February 12 spoke of vessels "sighted along the coast of North Vietnam"; traffic being loaded "25 and 50 miles north of the demilitarized zone, respectively, or moving South or West toward the DMZ or Mu Gia pass"; trucking and shipping that "occurred in Southern North Vietnam." All this, it must be noted, happened in *North* Vietnam. Raymond R. Coffey of the Chicago *Daily News* cabled from Saigon on February 10 that "for all the road, sea and air traffic sighted in the North, U.S. officials acknowledge that they still do not have any reports of men or materiel moving into the demilitarized zone. . . ." After the truce ended, Coffey reported: "Only light traffic of men and supplies was observed in North Vietnam Monday before resumption of U.S. bombing raids there, U.S. sources said. . . . The spokesman also acknowledged that he has seen no reports of any movement of North Vietnamese men or materiel into South Vietnam since the Tet holiday truce began last Wednesday. The volume of truck and water traffic reported Monday was much lower than the sightings reported during the first two days of the truce, when U.S. military officials had said the North Vietnamese might be trying to move as much as 35,000 tons of materiel under cover of the cease-fire. The traffic in the North had decreased noticeably even in the 48 hours before the truce ended Sunday. The U.S. military here now refuse to say whether the Communists did indeed move 35,000 tons of materiel."

Coffey's article came to the notice of Representative Sidney R. Yates, who had been told—as most Americans had been told— that the North Vietnamese *had* moved 35,000 tons of supplies and equipment into South Vietnam during the truce. The Illinois Democrat asked Secretary Rusk for an explanation and received this reply from William B. Macomber, Jr., the Assistant Secretary of State for Congressional Relations: "The sharp decrease in the remarkable daylight movement toward the South reportedly observed in North Vietnam right after the stand-down ended, but before the resumption of air strikes, appears to indicate that the prolongation of the bombing pause caught the North Vietnamese off guard. It seems to me that otherwise, had they known the pause would continue a little longer, the North Vietnamese would surely have put it to use as much as they did the bombing pause during the cease-fire."

There was a curious footnote to this episode. The Air Force, which routinely issues daily statistics on the volume of cargo airlifted to units in Vietnam, omitted releasing the figures for two days during the Tet truce. When the data finally became available, they showed that a new record had been set for supplies airlifted to American forces in the field. In Washington a State Department spokesman saw no inconsistency between this fact and the charges leveled at North Vietnam. The Communist activity, he explained to reporters, was "clear evidence of their intent to continue their aggressive action," while the United States was merely furthering its goal of combating aggression. Was the actual absence of North Vietnamese resupply activity "just almost any step" designed to encourage a move to the conference table? Americans will never know, just as they will never know about other peace initiatives that may have been offered.

New light was cast on the events of February, 1967, some seven months later by Harry S. Ashmore, the executive vice-president of the Center for the Study of Democratic Institutions at Santa Barbara, California. Ashmore, formerly the Pulitzer Prizewinning editor of the *Arkansas Gazette*, and William C. Baggs, editor of the Miami *News*, had visited Hanoi in January. The following month, Ashmore disclosed, he had with the State Department's knowledge and assistance drafted a "conciliatory" letter to the North Vietnamese government in the hope of initiating peace talks. That effort, Ashmore charged in September, was "effectively and brutally cancelled" by a far harsher letter from President Johnson that reached Hanoi first.

The President's letter was eventually made public by North Vietnam—not by the United States. Ashmore accused the President and the Department of "double-dealing" and an "almost total absence of candor."

The State Department publicly claimed there was "no inconsistency" between the Ashmore and Johnson letters and privately accused Ashmore of "breaking faith" and speaking from wounded pride in revealing the episode. Government officials from the President on down grumbled about private citizens "running around the world trying to win a Nobel Peace Prize" by settling the Vietnam war. They may, indeed, be right in maintaining that such amateur efforts are doomed to failure. But the significance of the Ashmore incident lies in the fact that it has become possible for a citizen to accuse his government of deception and bad faith on the vital issue of war and peace—of "crude duplicity," in Ashmore's words—and to be widely believed. On this issue, as on so many others, the government has used up its credit with the people—credit necessary to assure an American citizen that his government did not, on that very day, receive and reject an opportunity to end the war in Vietnam.

The dilemma for Americans is that in the absence of information they have lost the power to tell their government how they want it to proceed. "Every time that truth is distorted or denied us, we are denied a bit of our liberty," Senator Mark O. Hatfield, the Oregon Republican, has observed. "When government spokesmen misrepresent international situations and misrepresent our national intentions, they effectively greatly narrow alternatives to their policies. Many feel forced then, out of confusion and on the basis of no clear alternative, to endorse current policy. Thus is created the tyranny of the 'big lie'—a tyranny of 'no alternatives,' a tyranny that does not allow Americans the liberty of choice and that does not allow us effective voice in directing our nation's course."

5. Don't Quote Me, but . . .

The scene is the long bar at the National Press Club in Washington.

First Reporter: "A reliable source reported to me this morning that the State Department will soon merge with the U.S. Coast Guard as an economy measure as well as a practical matter."

Second Reporter: "I checked this out with a high-level spokesman at the White House and he denied it."

First Reporter: "How high was your high-level spokesman?"

Second Reporter: "He was a damned sight higher than your reliable source at the State Department."

Third Reporter: "It doesn't make any difference who outranks whom because I just spoke to an informed source at the Pentagon, not for attribution, of course, and he told me off the record that he could not comment on it, which certainly makes one believe there is something to it."

Fourth Reporter: "A government spokesman who backgrounded us this morning said it was his understanding that State was going to merge with Health, Education and Welfare and the U.S. Coast Guard was going to become part of the Library of Congress."

There is more truth than fiction in this parody of the background briefing written by humorist Art Buchwald for the Washington *Post* and other newspapers. The famous Washington backgrounder can produce confused, inaccurate, or slanted reporting. It is readily exploited by government officials eager to launch trial balloons or to promote intramural bureaucratic feuds. The official who agrees to meet with reporters on a background basis knows that his name will not be linked to any stories that result. The reporters agree in advance that the official may remain anonymous in return for whatever information he chooses to provide. These invisible, unofficial contacts between reporters and their news sources have become increasingly important in the struggle to get the news and present it in perspective. Correspondents have discovered that it is often easier to get a busy official to come meet a group of them over lunch in a private dining room than to get into his office for an individual interview. In such *sub rosa* sessions, the official is supposed to talk more freely—and frequently he does—since he knows his remarks will not be attributed to him.

For the official, there are a number of advantages in the use of the background device. When Bill Moyers was White House press secretary, he would sometimes read aloud at such background meetings the latest cables from Ambassador Henry Cabot Lodge to President Johnson, as well as other secret memoranda dealing with Vietnam. His purpose was to outline the alternatives the administration faced to buttress his argument that the course it was following was the soundest and most logical. Early in 1967, during a heated moment in the feud between President Johnson and Senator Robert F. Kennedy, each man found it useful to convey his side of the dispute to the public through not-for-attribution meetings with trusted reporters. When Kennedy returned from a highly publicized visit to Europe in February, he accepted an invitation to confer with the President at the White House. As Johnson later related it, Kennedy offended him by declaring that United States policy had been faltering in Europe ever since the death of his brother, President Kennedy. The Senator insisted, however, that he said nothing of the kind. "All I did was express the views of the Europeans that they felt lonely, ignored, and not clued in to U.S. policy," Kennedy told reporters. Johnson bridled at this and asked his assistant Walt Rostow to get a list of the number of times he, Johnson, had seen European visitors.

In talking privately to reporters, Johnson made no mention of the angriest exchange that had taken place between him and Kennedy. This began with a discussion of a news magazine's report that Kennedy was bringing back a Hanoi peace feeler from his European visit. Kennedy agreed that the report was inaccurate. But he refused Johnson's request that he tell the reporters waiting in the White House lobby that Hanoi had *never* made an overture to talk peace. Kennedy said he could not do that because he did not know it to be a true statement of the facts. Johnson replied, in effect, "Well, I'm telling you it is." Pointing to Rostow, he added, "Walt's telling you it is, too." When he eventually saw the reporters, Kennedy would not go beyond denying that he had brought back a peace feeler. The most sulfurous moment of the Johnson-Kennedy encounter was provoked by the President's displeasure over the Senator's urging of a pause in the bombing of North Vietnam. If Kennedy kept on in this vein, he would not have a political future in six months, Johnson snapped. He declared that Kennedy wanted American boys to fight with their hands tied behind them. At one point, Kennedy threatened to leave. He did not have to sit there and listen to that kind of talk, he told the President.

Ten days after his acrimonious visit to the White House the Senator was the luncheon guest of a background group of sixteen correspondents. Meeting with them in a private room of the Occidental Restaurant on Thursday, February 16, he revealed that Pope Paul VI had told him in Rome that the United States might be winning the war in Vietnam militarily but was losing it politically. He had heard this everywhere in Europe, Kennedy added. He had two other newsworthy items for his hosts. He disclosed that he had decided to make a speech shortly calling for a temporary end of the bombing of North Vietnam as a way of trying to initiate peace talks. Kennedy put this off the record, however; this meant the reporters could not write it. His purpose in telling them, apparently, was to build up interest in the coming speech and ensure the best possible play for it in their papers.

He also revealed that the subsidizing of the National Student Association by the Central Intelligence Agency had been known at the White House level in the Eisenhower, Kennedy, and Johnson administrations. He did not know which official had handled this matter for Eisenhower, but it was McGeorge Bundy who did it for Kennedy and Walt Rostow for Johnson, the Senator reported. This was a significant story, since it refuted the claims of a White House spokesman that Johnson knew nothing about the CIA subsidy until the story broke in the papers. Kennedy agreed that his hosts could write it with attribution to "a former high official in the Kennedy and Johnson administrations." The guest and his hosts parted in an atmosphere of congeniality and goodwill. But the next morning the hosts discovered they had been scooped by two reporters who were not members of their group. The story which they had agreed not to write was prominently displayed in the Boston *Globe* and the Washington *Star*. Martin Nolan, then with the *Globe*, and Mary McGrory, of the *Star*, two of the Senator's favorite reporters, had seen him after his luncheon with the background group. They had reminded him that a year had passed since he had made a proposal that the United States should agree to negotiate with the Vietcong, and they wanted to know what he had to say about the war now. He responded that he would make a speech soon urging a cessation of the bombing—and he gave them permission to print it. Their stories appeared on Friday, February 17.

The next day the Associated Press and United Press International wires carried stories nailing the Johnson administration's connection with the CIA subsidy of the National Student Association and identifying the source as Robert Kennedy himself, rather than just "a former high official in the Kennedy and Johnson administrations." This brought a bitter reaction from members of the Thursday group, who complained to Frank Mankiewicz, Kennedy's press secretary, that they had been "doublecrossed by Kennedy two days in a row." But James Doyle, the Washington bureau chief of the Boston *Globe*, had a different reaction: a newcomer to Washington, Doyle had been urged by his editors to get into some of the background groups. However, Doyle said he had become convinced that these were not a good thing. "There are too many reporters walking around this town with secrets they cannot print because their hands are tied," he said.

Sometimes a backgrounder is used by an administration official to carry out a defensive operation. Toward the end of 1966, Robert Komer, the President's special assistant in charge of pacification operations in Vietnam, began putting out a self-serving line on a not-for-attribution basis. Why had pacification not got off the ground in Vietnam? "The previous programs were sound in concept, but the resources given them were ridiculously small," Komer explained. "Pacification has not gotten under way seriously yet because we have not had enough military forces to establish security and not enough follow-up civilians." He had a feeling, he said, that by the end of 1967 "we might begin to see some quite significant changes."

One of the more noteworthy uses—and abuses—of a backgrounder involved Johnson's attempt to obtain a resolution of support from Congress in advance of the summit meeting of Latin American presidents held at Punta del Este, Uruguay, in April, 1967. Concerned about issuing a "blank check" to the President, the Senate Foreign Relations Committee voted a cautious resolution that fell far short of the mandate Johnson had sought in support of future economic aid for the Alliance for Progress. Late in the afternoon of April 4, White House reporters were summoned into the Fish Room at the Executive Mansion for what they thought would be an information briefing on the President's forthcoming Latin American visit. Instead, they were exposed to an attack on the Senate committee's resolution by Walt Rostow. Rostow's words, the reporters were told, would have to be attributed to "administration sources on Inter-American affairs." The Senate committee's resolution "does not respond to the situation faced by the United States at the summit meeting," the President's special assistant for national security affairs declared. "In the circumstances it is worse than useless." The comment, it was obvious, was being made at Johnson's behest in an effort to reverse the committee's action. Reporters present protested that this was strong language to attribute to "nameless, faceless sources" and urged that the attribution be changed at least to "White House sources." The request was denied, and Rostow's remarks were front-paged the next day as those of "administration sources on Inter-American affairs."

The incident reopened the question of the backgrounder and its abuse. At the Washington *Post* a meeting of the paper's national staff, called by managing editor Benjamin C. Bradlee, produced much soul-searching and a resolve to be far warier of future backgrounders designed to further political purposes rather than to impart information. Editors of the New York

Times came to a similar decision and instructed their reporters that in circumstances when the White House refused to accept responsibility for its statements, the *Times* would merely report that "the White House had no comment." When the White House attempted, a few weeks after the Punta del Este meeting, to issue a statement on the Kennedy Round of trade negotiations without attributing it to the President's negotiators, *Times* correspondent Max Frankel interrupted the briefing to announce his paper's new policy—and the statement was promptly put on the record.

Robert S. McNamara was a fervent practitioner of the background conference, as is Dean Rusk. Pentagon reporters frequently met with Defense Secretary McNamara at three o'clock on Thursday afternoons in Room 3-E-912, a private conference room adjoining the Secretary's office on the elite third-floor E ring. The Secretary walked into the room on the dot of three, and any reporter arriving a minute or two after that encountered a locked door. The Secretary was accompanied by his top troika of press agents, Phil G. Goulding, Richard Fryklund, and Daniel Z. Henkin. Although every reporter present knew the rules by heart, Goulding solemnly restated them each time, as his predecessor, Arthur Sylvester, had done before him: Any information that came out of the session could not be attributed to McNamara (until May, 1967, Goulding decreed that "U.S. officials" must be given as the source), and nothing could be put in direct quotation. Under pressure from press critics, he modified the rules slightly in May and from then on let the source be given as "Defense officials."

For thirty minutes McNamara ran the conference like a stern schoolmaster, nodding or pointing to reporters, who raised their hands to be recognized for questions. Toward the end of the period McNamara would announce, "One more question," and then, "That's all, fellows." The Secretary would get up and leave the room, without waiting for the "thank you" from the press which other officials—even the President—accept as the signal that a news conference is over. The backgrounders enabled McNamara to get a point of view across to the public without acknowledging that it came from him. Among the topics discussed were his disputes with the Joint Chiefs of Staff over such issues as construction of an antiballistic-missile de-

fense network in the United States and the choice of military
and industrial targets to be bombed in North Vietnam, as well
as his arguments with the Air Force over construction of a new
manned bomber, with the Navy over the building of more
nuclear-powered surface ships, and with Congress over such
items as the strategy being pursued in Vietnam and the size of
the U.S. force which could be safely moved out of the NATO
alliance.

At the State Department the background ritual occurs on
Friday afternoons at five o'clock and is something of a social
occasion. "The setting is the lavish spread on the eighth floor
which is ordinarily reserved for formal diplomatic functions,"
Richard Harwood has written in the Washington *Post*. "Secretary of State Dean Rusk presides. Drinks are served and the
atmosphere is easy. The sessions usually last for an hour and
produce ruminations attributed to 'U.S. officials.'" At times,
however, Rusk will caution that something he has said can be
used only as "deep background." This means that the reporter
cannot attribute the information to anyone, not even "U.S.
officials." If the Secretary provides, for example, an analysis of
the latest turn of events in Vietnam, the reporter is required to
write it as his own thinking—a practice known in Washington
as compulsory plagiarism.

Ben Bradlee of the *Post*, who is convinced that "we demean
our profession" by conniving in the not-for-attribution game,
has described the State Department sessions as "very sociable
affairs, old friends gathering once a week over a dry martini or
two." They are followed, Bradlee notes, by "those Saturday
morning stories, regular as clockwork, quoting high government
officials on this or that foreign policy nuance. Everyone in
Washington knows Max Frankel is quoting Dean Rusk—including the Soviet ambassador and the Red Chinese spies.
Everyone, that is, but the readers. Who the hell is conning
whom?"

Harwood's article on backgrounders, published on April 30,
1967, was a rare newspaper disclosure of the existence of the
background sessions at State and the Pentagon. Harwood also
revealed the identity of the "high government official" who had
recently reported to the *Post* that 50,000 more American troops

would be sent to Vietnam soon, causing a further rise in the costs of the war. "A reader might have assumed that the story came from a general or the Secretary of Defense or the President. If so, they were wrong. It came from a banker, William McChesney Martin, chairman of the Federal Reserve Board."

"The fact that Martin was right only accentuates the dilemma," Ben Bradlee later commented. "The reader had a perfect right to know in this instance that the authority was a banker, not a warrior. McGeorge Bundy, who was one of the classiest background briefers of his day, told the American Society of Newspaper Editors [ASNE] recently that when he was in government he used to be able to understand the morning news of Washington most of the time . . . because he knew who was backgrounding whom on what. Now absent from Washington, he said he needed more help and was getting less."

Bundy, a special assistant to Presidents Kennedy and Johnson who left Washington to become president of the Ford Foundation, complained to the 1967 ASNE convention that under the background system "editors always know, the government usually knows, and the public very seldom knows what's going on." This has produced, he said, "the greatest guessing game on earth," and he asked the editors, "Could there be a more startling reversal of the purpose of a free press?" Bill Moyers has also had second thoughts about backgrounders since leaving the White House. Public officials too often use unattributed stories in newspapers "to say what they are afraid to say on the record," Moyers told a New York convention of the American Newspaper Publishers Association. He was speaking now from his new viewpoint as publisher of *Newsday*. "The tendency to use background stories without attribution leaves the reader confused about the source and therefore about the credibility of the information." Acknowledging the existence of a Credibility Gap, Moyers declared, "Let us beware of believing things are going as well as those who hold public office would wish us to believe."

The about-face executed by Bundy and Moyers on the subject of backgrounders struck the Washington *Post* as "fresh and comforting evidence that the government's secrecy rites do not cast a permanent spell, even upon their most ardent practitioners." Nor were they the only prestigious former officials to discover flaws in the background game they once played so enthusiastically. Robert Kennedy, a frequent and resourceful background briefer as Attorney General, delivered to the editors at the concluding dinner of the ASNE convention a thought they could not have expressed better themselves. Government officials could help the task of the newspapers, he said, by reducing the number of briefings held on a background basis. "It is often more out of a lingering habit than necessity that the press is forbidden to mention the source of information intended for publication," he said. "The unfortunate consequence is the inability of an informed reader to make his own evaluation of the reliability, authority, and special interests of the official spokesman; forcing him to discount the news altogether or accept it on faith." As the antibackgrounder bandwagon gathered momentum, even Johnson climbed aboard. *Newsweek* reported the President had snapped to a group of intimates that he did not believe in backgrounders. "And to the astonishment of his audience, he added: 'That's why I fired Moyers and Bundy. They gave too many backgrounders.'" It was this same President who, a few weeks later at the Glassboro summit conference, instructed his aides to deliver a background briefing for the press in handout form. "They were mimeographing leaks, for God's sake," exclaimed James Doyle of the Boston *Globe*.

As a Washington custom, the backgrounder dates back to the time of Herbert Hoover and beyond, but it did not become a systematic practice until World War II. It was begun by General George C. Marshall and Admiral Ernest J. King when, as Army Chief of Staff and Chief of Naval Operations, they carried a heavy responsibility for the conduct of the war. Douglass Cater, now a special assistant to President Johnson, recounts in *The Fourth Branch of Government* [13] how the practice started: "As usual with affairs of the press, it began quite informally, almost haphazardly. Admiral King agreed to meet with a few reporters at a relative's home in Alexandria, Virginia. It was in early November, 1942, a time when continued Japanese sinking of Navy ships was creating a national morale problem. King, though ordinarily a hardbitten and taciturn

13 Douglass Cater, *The Fourth Branch of Government* (New York, Vintage Books, 1965), p. 131.

naval officer, came to enjoy these informal get togethers, and, according to one who attended, 'learned to make use of the press with the skill of a public relations counsel.' An instance of this, King used the background conference to publicize and help nullify what he considered an ill-conceived plan to take General Marshall away from his post as Army Chief of Staff. For his briefings, General Marshall preferred the more austere surroundings of the conference room. But this didn't prevent him from making calculated revelations of great importance. At the time of the landing in North Africa, a noisy political uproar was developing because of General Eisenhower's dealings in Algiers with Admiral Darlan, of the Vichy government. Marshall summoned thirty newspaper and radio men to his office. For nearly an hour he read to the assembled group Eisenhower's dispatches revealing all the details of the delicate diplomatic maneuvering. He had faith that facts would dispel the rumors. It was all off-the-record, but soon the word spread around Washington and the Darlan scandal was cut down to size. Marshall was utterly candid in these briefings, once disclosing to the reporters the Allied battle order in the West. It was for their private information only; the reporters took no notes. After each session they usually compared recollections and prepared confidential memoranda for their editors. No one was expected to use what he learned there for a news story. The purpose of the briefings was largely preventive—to keep the reporter from going off half cocked."

There was at least one occasion, however, when one of these backgrounders produced a story—a sensational one. It came out of a meeting with Marshall on the afternoon of a New Year's Eve and appeared in the papers the next morning, January 1, 1944. The story, as it ran in the Washington *Post*, went like this: "The taking over of the railroads by the Army and the walkout in the steel mills may have prolonged the war against Germany by six months, causing hundreds of thousands of needless casualties. This blunt statement came yesterday from a personage high in the councils of the United States and of the United Nations and who is thoroughly familiar with the struggle confronting the Allies, and who has no anti-labor axe to grind."

Ben W. Gilbert, deputy managing editor of the *Post*, who

recalled the incident twenty-three years later in an article for his paper, explained that "the war had not reached the point where victory appeared assured and the home front was burdened with a series of difficult-to-solve labor disputes." Some of the reporters urged the general to put his statement on the record, since it was not usable without attribution. When he declined, they persuaded him to let them attribute it to a "high personage." The story, Gilbert wrote, was a wartime sensation. "Labor leaders were indignant and demanded to know the name of the 'personage' who was allowed to make such serious charges with the protection of anonymity." When the story went out on the wires, editors, too, demanded to know its source. Finally, a correspondent who was not present at the session, hence was not bound by its rules, publicized the fact that Marshall was the source. William Green, president of the American Federation of Labor, confirmed this and demanded that President Roosevelt reprimand Marshall. Instead of complying, Roosevelt issued a statement saying that he had been "thinking along the same lines." The correspondents were relieved when Marshall agreed to continue the briefings, despite the furor over this one, for they had come to value them for the access to facts and overall policy factors which they provided. They "did not solve all the newsmen's problems, of course," according to the late Lyle C. Wilson, who attended the briefings as Washington bureau chief of the United Press. "But," he wrote in *Dateline: Washington*,[14] "it helped us to avoid going off on tangents of snap judgments, amateur opinion and plain peeve when the facts themselves could not be revealed to a puzzled public."

After the war Washington reporters felt the need for a continuation of the backgrounders on a much more extensive scale to help them understand and write about the complex issues of the cold war. Government officials were quick to cooperate, and since the issues discussed were not the sensitive matters of life and death that occupied them during the war, it was soon decided that the character of the backgrounder should change. Instead of being purely for the self-edification of the correspondents, the information coming out of the backgrounders

---

[14] Cabell Phillips, and others, *Dateline: Washington* (Garden City, Doubleday, 1949), p. 189.

could be printed, it was agreed. The rule governing its use was that the correspondents could not attribute it to anyone. This is what Dean Rusk calls "deep background" but what the Washington press corps knows as the Lindley Rule. It was named for Ernest K. Lindley, then a correspondent for *Newsweek* and now an adviser to Rusk, who says the system served the correspondents well. He recalls that participants were not run-of-the-mill reporters, but columnists, editors, and editorial writers. They did not look for scoops in these private seminars, but for an understanding to help them write more intelligently about the problems of the government in the cold war.

Before long, however, there was a quantum jump in the number of reporters attending backgrounders. For many of the young reporters, it meant a chance to bypass the government press agents with whom they usually had to deal. And the direct contact they had with a normally inaccessible official over lunch or dinner not only provided them with information but also gave them a certain amount of prestige among their fellow correspondents. For the officials, the backgrounder had several appealing features. It was an ideal setting for the anonymous promotion of new policies and projects or for the defense and explanation of old ones that might be in trouble. It offered opportunities to test the reaction of Congress and the public to policy changes under consideration and, if the reaction proved unfavorable, to deny that any new policy was contemplated. In addition, officials could save themselves the time and trouble of a succession of individual interviews by seeing a larger group all at one time. As the backgrounders proliferated, they became more like press conferences held behind closed doors than the scholarly academic seminars they had been at the outset. Many of the reporters who attended them did not have the leeway to follow the Lindley Rule. They had to attribute their information to some source, however vague and fictitious. To meet this need, they invented a wide variety of disguised titles. "A high official has disclosed. . . ." Or a government expert, a qualified source, an authoritative source, and so on. The Lindley Rule, however, is still vigorously enforced by the Overseas Writers Association, one of the oldest and largest background groups.

The backgrounder was used for a variety of purposes in the Truman and Eisenhower administrations. Dean Acheson, while

Undersecretary of State, employed it to stir up public alarm at a time when this was deemed necessary. George Kennan, chairman of the State Department's Policy Planning Board, used it to calm the public. Acheson called in a little group of reporters to alert them to demands the Russians were making against Turkey. This was, he suggested, an indirect form of aggression that had been overlooked in the news. Kennan's purpose, when he held his backgrounder, was to prevent public hysteria after the disclosure by President Truman that the Soviet Union had succeeded in conducting an atomic explosion. But to achieve the effect he intended of playing down the announcement, Kennan deliberately misled the reporters and told them, contrary to the facts, that the timing of the Russian blast was no surprise to United States policy makers.

Secretary of State John Foster Dulles was one of Washington's most skillful and persistent conductors of backgrounders. On one occasion, just before the international meeting called in London to negotiate a Japanese peace treaty, he spread the word that unless the British were willing to make concessions, there was a grave danger that the treaty negotiations would fail. The great pressure this publicity brought on the British helped persuade them to agree to the concessions Dulles was seeking. On another occasion, Dulles spent three days in background sessions with reporters, on an individual and collective basis, to help ensure approval in Congress for a new policy, the Eisenhower Doctrine for the Middle East. He told reporters the details of the policy for publication, without attribution to him, and succeeded in creating a favorable climate for it among the general public. Then he called in the Congressional leaders to present the policy formally and officially. The leaders were "cautious in their reaction," the New York *Times* reported. But the administration's plan had been so widely publicized before they reached the White House that they could "do little more than adopt the new policy as presented," the *Times* observed.

Twice during the Eisenhower administration the public was alerted to the dangerous uses to which a backgrounder can be put. In the spring of 1954 a proposal for United States intervention in support of the hard-pressed French in the war they were fighting in Vietnam was made at a convention in Washington of the American Society of Newspaper Editors. The proposal was made by Vice-President Nixon during a background talk to the editors. American troops must be used, if necessary, to prevent a French defeat, he asserted. Nixon was speaking for a clique within the administration that included Secretary Dulles and Admiral Arthur W. Radford, Chairman of the Joint Chiefs of Staff. His statement was an attempt to promote a policy which had not yet been approved. It met with a negative reaction from the editors and was eventually rejected by President Eisenhower.

A year later, in the spring of 1955, the crisis point had shifted to U.S. relations with Communist China. Tension mounted in the Formosa Straits as mainland guns shelled Nationalist Chinese troops on the offshore islands of Quemoy and Matsu. On Saturday, March 26, a number of major newspapers carried sensational stories about the imminence of war between the United States and China over the offshore islands. A Chinese Communist attack on them was expected in April, it was reported, and the United States was said to be considering an all-out defense. There was no indication in the stories who was responsible for concocting the war scare, but before long Admiral Robert B. Carney, Chief of Naval Operations, was disclosed as the source. He had been the guest of some twenty Washington correspondents at a background dinner held in a private room of the Sheraton-Carlton Hotel. Carney and Radford, the super hawks of their day, were trying to sell the line that a military confrontation with China was inevitable. President Eisenhower, however, had no knowledge of any coming invasion and was shocked when he read the stories that Carney had generated. Three days later the newspapers played an account that completely contradicted the Carney line. A story in the New York *Times* was headlined EISENHOWER SEES NO WAR NOW OVER CHINESE ISLES. These stories, which carried no hint of who had inspired them, were the product of a backgrounder hastily called by the White House press secretary, James Hagerty, to mute the war drums. Later, Eisenhower himself publicly expressed his displeasure over the incident, and Carney left Washington before the year was out to take a job with private industry.

The problems and risks for reporters attending the Dulles'

backgrounders were bluntly stated by historian Arthur M. Schlesinger, Jr., in the March 31, 1953, issue of the *Reporter.* "Washington newspapermen today hardly know whether to believe the Secretary of State, because they do not know if he is speaking to them as reporters or seeking to use them as instruments of psychological warfare," he asserted. "What is the responsibility of a newspaperman when he discovers that some rumored development of policy is really only a psychological warfare trick? Should he print the truth at the risk of wrecking the plans of the Secretary of State? Or should he suppress the truth, betray himself, and deceive the American people?" (It was a dilemma that would haunt Schlesinger in his own White House days as a background briefer for President Kennedy.)

Eisenhower left the background briefing up to Dulles, Hagerty, and other key figures in his administration, doing almost none of it himself, except for an experimental stag dinner or two toward the end of his second term. Kennedy, however, quickly became a major practitioner of the technique. He devoted much time to private sessions with individuals and small groups from the Washington press corps. He also initiated the practice of calling in the White House regulars who accompanied him to Palm Beach over the Christmas holidays and giving them a wide-ranging story on background that included his impressions of the past year, as well as his expectations for the year ahead. Lyndon Johnson followed the same general routine early in his administration, before his press relations deteriorated, but he preferred to have Bill Moyers interview him and then pass the word on at background sessions. Johnson favors seeing reporters singly or in small groups, and top figures in his administration have not been slow to follow his example. The backgrounder clearly has become their favorite means of dispensing information, though the experience has been painful to them at times.

Ben Gilbert of the Washington *Post* is convinced that events will force the identification of a source if the story is sensational enough. "Insiders generally know anyway, and an outsider who knows the right insiders rarely has to work very hard to find out," he says. It is not often that a source is publicly unmasked, but it happened to Robert S. McNamara early in his first year as Defense Secretary. In a closed-door meeting with a small group of reporters he revealed that there was no "missile gap." It was a significant admission, since it refuted Kennedy's campaign charge that the Eisenhower administration had permitted the Russians to outdistance the United States in the production of intercontinental ballistic missiles. It was an embarrassing moment for McNamara when two or three of the reporters printed the story, which he insisted had not been intended for publication, and when he was identified as the source.

There was a similar aftermath to a spectacular story that emerged from a backgrounder held in Saigon in 1966. The gist of the story, which appeared in several major newspapers with correspondents in Vietnam, was that the war would last another five years even with the deployment of 750,000 American troops. This was more than twice the 290,000 men on duty there at the time. No responsible official ever before had talked in such gloomy terms of how many men might be needed or how long the war might last. While government press agents went into action to try to discredit the story, Washington correspondents began probing to find the source. In a matter of hours they were able to inform their readers that the story had come from General Wallace M. Greene, Jr., then the Marine Corps Commandant. Greene was so embarrassed that he called a press conference when he returned to Washington, admitted that he had seen a few American correspondents in Saigon on a background basis, but insisted that he had not made the statement attributed to him. Greene obviously had not anticipated that the story would create such a stir that his identity as the source would be forced into the open. The administration resented the story because it was bad politics in an election year for anyone to suggest that the war could last so long. Greene's purpose in planting the story, according to the privately voiced opinion of Arthur Sylvester, then Assistant Secretary of Defense for Public Affairs, was to try to pressure the White House into sending more Marines to Vietnam.

Backgrounders have become such a deep-grained habit in Washington that Secretary Rusk even holds special ones for the Communist foreign correspondents stationed in the capital. The press corps itself is deeply divided on the merits of the backgrounder. Max Frankel of the New York *Times* says he has found that "most government officials say nothing on background they wouldn't say on the record, if asked." Some correspondents criticize the backgrounder for often producing little information of value, despite the protection afforded the source. Some government officials try to describe the backgrounder as something conceived simply to serve the interests of the press. However, the timidity of the executive branch in its dealings with the press is reflected in the constantly repeated request: "Don't quote me, but—" Members of Congress, on the other hand, rarely resort to the backgrounder. Senator Charles H. Percy of Illinois startled his hosts at a background luncheon one day when they were trying to decide on how to attribute his views. "Why don't you attribute them to me?" he inquired. Legislators have even more to lose than officials of the executive branch if a statement made on the record backfires, for the positions they take must stand the test of the ballot box. But the importance of publicity to their careers apparently outweighs the risks involved in the open press conference and on-the-record pronouncement.

Those Washington correspondents who favor backgrounders agree with their colleague Ben Bagdikian that they can serve a very useful purpose. "There is a great deal of policy, especially diplomatic policy, which the government cannot discuss explicitly because it is in the process of being negotiated," he says, "but it is important for the press to know about it." He maintains, however, that the backgrounder has been badly abused by the Johnson administration. "Instead of employing it for serious long-term purposes, they use it crudely and indiscriminately as a tactical weapon for self-defense," he says. He recalls an occasion when Jack Valenti, then a Presidential special assistant, called a backgrounder to try to knock down a magazine story Bagdikian had written naming the six most important men in Johnson's life. Valenti sought to throw doubt on the story by asserting that Bagdikian had not even talked to anyone in the White House about it. "But I had," says Bagdikian. "I had seen George Reedy." He had typed a list of names on a piece of paper, taken it to Reedy's office, and asked Reedy to tell him which six on it were most important in the Johnson story. Reedy went down the list, circled six names, and neither he nor Bagdikian spoke a name aloud. Bagdikian had deliberately chosen to interview Reedy in this unusual manner so that if Reedy's office were bugged, as he suspected, Reedy would not be embarrassed by anything said within earshot of any eavesdropper.

Historian Bruce Catton has said that American government "wouldn't work" without the backgrounder. Like Bagdikian, he sees it performing an effective service during the formation of policy. Moyers says that the reporter should realize "that a good backgrounder is a work of art, and impose enough self-discipline to avoid making hard news out of soft news." He thinks, however, that public officials "should ask themselves if they can make a statement anonymously, is there any good reason why they can't make it publicly?"

In the judgment of the Washington *Post*, the background practice may have begun innocently enough "as a device for disseminating information and insights for which government officials did not wish to be held strictly responsible." But the backgrounder "has been increasingly abused as it has been increasingly used," the paper declared in an editorial. Someday, the *Post* hopes, it will become apparent "that the service performed by this system, to the participants, is outweighed by the disservice it does the public, and the system will either break down, or be reformed."

Whether the backgrounder will ever be seriously reformed or discontinued is difficult to say. "The government will not move to straighten out the rules," says McGeorge Bundy. "If there is to be reform, it will have to come from the press." The press, if it were to make a concerted effort, could probably put a stop to the backgrounder or at least force constructive changes in its format. But the backgrounder has become an institution, and institutions are not lightly discarded in Washington.

6. The White House Technique

Casting a baleful eye over the White House correspondents assembled in the Cabinet Room to cover a military award ceremony, the President of the United States delivered an impromptu lecture. "There is something about our open society that gives the play to what went wrong instead of what went right," Lyndon Baines Johnson complained. The reproach was a familiar one to the reporters in the room. They had heard it on many previous occasions from the President's lips—often in the earthy tones that mark Johnson's private discourse. They had heard it from the President's press secretaries and from other members of his administration. They had heard it from Johnson's predecessors in the White House, and they had heard it since their earliest newspaper days from sewer commissioners, mayors, and governors. Public officials at every level of government and in every locale have an understandable interest in seeing their accomplishments in print and a natural aversion to having their mistakes or misdeeds published. The more resourceful and less scrupulous among them resort to suppression, concealment, or falsehood to keep bad news from seeing the light of day. But the press has a contrary role in a democracy: to report what went wrong—and what is likely to go wrong tomorrow—while often assuming that what went right will take care of itself. Unlike the town crier of Colonial days, the press cannot confine itself to intoning dutifully from time to time that all is well.

The conflict between press and government is, therefore, a historic and pervasive one. Where it does not exist, the likelihood is that the press is failing to do its job. Invariably, in this century, every national administration has entered office determined to woo the press and ensure that the play is given to what goes right. Inevitably, each President has had to discover that the press will not stay wooed and that the headlines often banner what went wrong. In an open society, founded on the principle that an informed public is the ultimate sovereign, such a state of affairs is more to be rejoiced in than regretted.

If it is true, however, that an adversary relationship between press and government is wholesome or at least essential, it is also true that the conflict has never been so acute and bitter as it is in present-day Washington. James Deakin, the White House correspondent of the St. Louis *Post-Dispatch*, has observed that "the relationship between the Washington press corps and the Johnson administration has settled into a pattern of weary cynicism. To an unhealthy degree, many reporters no longer credit the administration's truthfulness or its good faith. This goes beyond a mere spat; it has sunk deep into the fabric."

The garrison state attitude that has tainted public policy since the beginning of the cold war has also done much to undermine the traditional concept of the open society. In the interest of "national security," facts are withheld—and lies are told—in matters that could not have even the remotest relevance to sensitive military or diplomatic efforts. Officials who testify behind closed doors before Congressional committees freely exercise their powers to sanitize the official transcripts subsequently made public—not only by censoring their own answers, but also by expunging from the record the critical questions that prompted them. Representative Glenard Lipscomb of California was moved to comment on the floor of the House that "there have been far too many occasions when this classification process has been applied in a rather curious and, to me, illogical way. It is difficult to discern, sometimes, whether the Department of Defense is primarily interested in keeping information from the enemy or in keeping it from the American people." Lipscomb, the ranking Republican on the Defense Appropriations Subcommittee, recalls one sanitized transcript of testimony by Defense Secretary Robert S. McNamara. The Pentagon censors left in the record McNamara's explanation of a decision to overrule the Air Force, "but all of my questions about the original classification of the subject, and the answers, were heavily censored," the Congressman says.

Members of the Senate complained during the debate on fiscal 1968 defense appropriations that the secrecy requirements imposed by the Pentagon and the State Department prevented them from making an effective public case for their viewpoints on controversial issues. "The members of the executive branch of the government have gone far out of line in classifying material to which the American people are entitled," said Senator Joseph S. Clark, the Pennsylvania Democrat. Chairman John C. Stennis of the Senate Preparedness Subcommittee said Congress should "insist upon our rights and not be satisfied when the administration sends matters back and declares they are classified." Official secrecy resulted in the muzzling of the administration's supporters, as well as its critics. Chairman Fulbright of the Foreign Relations Committee, who favored curtailment of United States military aid to underdeveloped nations, said that if the facts were known, "it would be difficult for the administration to obtain the money." But Senator John Tower, the Texas Republican, who opposed the reduction, said that unfortunately the best reasons for his viewpoint were classified, "and we cannot talk about this here in an open session of the Senate." As Senator Albert Gore pointed out, "True debate is impossible under such a handicap." The Tennessee Democrat cited one instance when the Pentagon had affixed a secrecy classification to a document describing military aid to an African nation as "general defense equipment to be mutually agreed upon." Said Gore: "Oh, what a secret."

Federal law authorizes three—and only three—security classifications that may be invoked to shield government papers from public view when the national interest is at stake. They are "Confidential," "Secret," and "Top Secret," and the law provides for their use under rigidly controlled conditions to prevent abuse of the process of classification. But inventive bureaucrats have devised scores of unofficial classifications of their own and freely invoke them to avoid the inconvenience and occasional discomfort of public disclosure. Among the many classifications that may be found stamped on official documents in agencies far removed from the realm of national security are these:

LIMITED USE ONLY
FOR OFFICIAL USE ONLY
FOR STAFF USE ONLY
FOR GOVERNMENT USE ONLY
EYES ONLY
NOT FOR PUBLIC INSPECTION
ADMINISTRATIVELY RESTRICTED
NONPUBLIC
NOT FOR PUBLICATION
CONFIDENTIAL TREATMENT
ACCEPTED IN CONFIDENCE
INTERNAL DOCUMENTS

There are many more, but they all mean the same thing: Don't let the word get out.

These are merely the most obvious devices in the government's arsenal of instruments designed to direct and control the flow of information to the public. Others are more subtle—and far more effective. They encompass such mysterious rites as the inspired leak, the off-the-record briefing, the background-only news conference, and others discussed elsewhere in these pages. They include the government's huge public information apparatus, which can be harnessed as efficiently in the cause of distorting the news as in disseminating it. No federal agency today is so small or so obscure as to be without its information office, and the larger and more active departments of government budget millions of dollars each year for the process. The Associated Press found, in an office-by-office survey of government agencies conducted by its Washington bureau in 1967, that 6,858 federal employees are occupied full or part time in the public information effort. The military alone assigns some 3,000 persons to publicity duties, the AP reported, and spends at least $32,000,000 for this purpose. In all, the AP estimated, the government spends about $425,000,000 a year to disseminate its news and views—more than double the combined outlay for news gathering by the two major United States news services, the three large television networks, and the nation's ten biggest newspapers. At that, the AP estimate was on the conservative side. Theodore H. White has recorded, in *The Making of the*

President—1964,[15] how Johnson once told a group of federal agency publicists that "the government was spending almost a billion dollars on people like them and they had better start earning it."

Whether they earn their pay or not, the flacks and the tons of news releases that emanate from their duplicating machines are increasingly indispensable to the reporters trying to cover a large and complex government. But this dependency has made the press extraordinarily vulnerable to misinformation and, what's worse, to the interminable flow of distracting trivia. "Help, I am trapped in a handout factory," one White House correspondent exclaimed after a morning briefing that produced a particularly heavy volume of insignificant releases.

The misinformation process is not confined to efforts to frustrate, bedazzle, or befuddle the press corps. In recent years a more direct approach to the public has been developed—one that raises the gravest questions of public policy in a democracy. Silently and surreptitiously, such arms of government as the Central Intelligence Agency, the Department of Defense, and the United States Information Agency have begun commissioning their own works and subsidizing their publication and dissemination—without disclosing to the American people that they are being exposed to officially sponsored propaganda. Subscribers to the respected journal *Foreign Affairs* who read in 1966 a learned treatise by George Carver defending the Johnson administration's Vietnam policy were not told by the editors— if, indeed, the editors knew—that Carver was employed by the CIA. Americans who bought a book called *The Truth About the Dominican Republic* by *Time* magazine correspondent Jay Mallin had no way of knowing that this was "the truth" according to USIA, which carefully selected the author, paid him, revised his manuscript, and arranged for its commercial publication in the United States. Another Mallin effort, *Terror in Viet Nam*, was also sponsored by USIA.

Senator Fulbright has called USIA's secret book subsidies "most objectionable, entirely contrary to our traditions." In a confrontation with agency officials who appeared before his Senate Foreign Relations Committee, the Senator said: "USIA

---

[15] Theodore H. White, *The Making of the President—1964* (New York, Atheneum, 1965), p. 57.

is not authorized to propagandize the American people. If you'd said that the books were published by USIA, it would be one thing—but not to do so is doubly subversive of our system." But USIA had good reason for engaging in "double subversion," or so its administrators thought. During a House hearing on the agency's $6,000,000-a-year "book development" program, Congressman Lipscomb of California asked USIA Director Leonard Marks, "Why is it wrong to let the American people know when they buy and read the book that it was developed under government sponsorship?" "It minimizes their value," Marks replied, and he went on to explain that "if we say this is our book, then the author is a government employee in effect. It changes the whole status of the author. . . ."

Geoffrey Wolff, the book editor of the Washington *Post*, has written: "There is much evidence that books are used increasingly as engines of propaganda, that highly placed persons are pre-censoring books they find repellent or embarrassing, and that they are commissioning and controlling the writing of books without disclosing the facts of such control. If we believe that truth has a more exclusive claim to our attention than partial truth or falsehood, and if we believe that openness and disclosure of the circumstances surrounding the writing, publishing and marketing of a book are requisites of a free access to ideas, then we must be alarmed at the sham, illegality and indirection that have infected much of what is sold as objective reality."

The special circumstances of government-sponsored authorship are intimately related to the broader problems of government secrecy and news management. The Pentagon and other sensitive agencies have much information under security classification that would be immensely useful, if not indispensable, to authors. When it suits the government's purposes, the classification is lifted for a particular writer's benefit—provided he agrees to let the agency read and edit his entire manuscript before publication. The effect is precensorship, without appeal, review, or opportunity for public discussion and criticism. Under Congressional pressure, USIA was compelled, eventually, to divulge and curtail its book-control operations. No such pressure has been applied to the CIA, and none is likely to be; but it is an open secret in Washington that this agency, too, has widely engaged in the practice of subsidizing publications. The prestigious Anglo-American magazine *Encounter*, it has been established, received support from organizations identified as conduits for CIA funds.

To an increased extent, materials produced by the government to indoctrinate or propagandize foreign audiences are also being disseminated for domestic consumption. A typical case involved Israeli General Moshe Dayan, who traveled to Vietnam at USIA expense to write about the war for the newspaper *Maariv*. The information agency commonly furnishes transportation to foreign journalists who are likely to take a sympathetic view of American policy, but as it turned out, Dayan's articles, highly favorable to the United States position, were published not only abroad but also in the Washington *Post*, whose editors were unaware at the time of his arrangement with USIA.

In a similar vein, Pentagon troop indoctrination materials are made widely available to civilian audiences at home. An example is the film *Why Vietnam*, produced late in 1965 to provide members of the armed forces with "a better understanding of the conflict." By early 1967 more than 1,600 prints of the film were in general circulation at home. Senator Fulbright arranged for a private showing and found *Why Vietnam* to be "a propaganda film" designed to "whip up war fever." It was, he said, "very effective as a piece of persuasion on the American people." It also, he added, played fast and loose with the facts. But the then Deputy Secretary of Defense wrote to Fulbright that it was "customary" to make Defense Department films available for public showing when circumstances permit. "Following troop orientation use," Cyrus Vance wrote, " 'Why Vietnam' was requested by civic organizations and schools throughout the United States. State Superintendents of Education and national education associations were informed of the film and told where it could be obtained for non-profit showing upon request. There has been much public interest in it."

The executive branch can—and will—go to extraordinary lengths and great expense to tell its story to the public, just as it can, under other circumstances, take infinite pains to keep a story from being told. By its very nature, the government holds the power to make news happen and to keep it from happening.

The power is hardly a new one, but it is being exercised more freely—and more recklessly—today than it has ever been before. To what extent this is due to inexorable forces—to cold and hot wars, to the ossification of entrenched bureaucracy, to the infinite complexity of modern government—is a matter of dispute even among those of us who live with the problem from day to day. But to a considerable extent today's crisis in credibility is directly attributable to the personality, philosophy, attitudes, and actions of the incumbent President. I. F. Stone, who keeps a sharp eye on both press and government through his weekly Washington newsletter, once commented, "Johnson sometimes seems to think the Constitution made him not only Commander-in-Chief of the Nation's armed forces but Editor-in-Chief of its newspapers." And Walter Lippmann has observed that the Credibility Gap "is the result of a deliberate policy of artificial manipulation of official news" designed "to create a consensus for the President, to stifle debate about his aims and his policies, to thwart deep probing into what has already happened, what is actually happening, what is going to happen."

Senator Robert F. Kennedy will long remember the whirlwind of activity that was generated at the White House on the day, early in 1967, when he planned to attack the President's Vietnam policy in a speech on the Senate floor. Johnson called a sudden press conference to produce a headline-making announcement: He had received a communication from Soviet Premier Alexei Kosygin, he said, agreeing to negotiations on the problem of antiballistic-missile competition. (On sober reflection, correspondents concluded a few days later that the President had substantially exaggerated the significance of the communication.) In rapid sequence after the news conference, Johnson rushed to the campus of Howard University to deliver a civil rights address and then went on to the United States Office of Education to speak about the state of the nation's schools. On Capitol Hill, Senator Henry Jackson of Washington, an administration stalwart, produced a long letter from the President defending his Vietnam policy. At the State Department, Secretary Rusk dismissed Kennedy's proposals as old stuff, and across the world in Saigon, General Westmoreland, the American military commander, issued his rebuttal—all in time for the morning papers. The object of the carefully orchestrated exercise was to counteract and diminish the effect of Kennedy's speech—and it worked.

The most familiar—though not the most frequent—scene of Johnson's encounters with the press is the great East Room of the White House, where the President's televised news conferences are held. For these occasions the ornate white-and-gilt chamber, normally used for receptions and balls, is virtually transformed. Some 300 straight-backed chairs are arranged, theater-style, facing the black podium adorned with the Presidential seal. Behind it a large blue canvas cloth is stretched to provide a suitable backdrop for the television cameras. At the sides, large directional microphones are poised, out of camera range, to pick up reporters' questions. Immediately in front of the podium, 30 or 40 seats are reserved for the regulars—the correspondents for major newspapers, wire services, networks, and magazines who cover the White House full time and who are likeliest to receive the Presidential nod of recognition.

At the appointed moment, an amplified voice announces, "Ladies and gentlemen, the President of the United States and Mrs. Johnson." The correspondents rise as the Johnsons enter the East Room. The President strides to the podium, and Mrs. Johnson takes a front-row seat. He opens a black, leather-bound loose-leaf notebook as the cameras start rolling. If he has any prepared announcements—they are called voluntaries—he reads them from the notebook. If not, he invites questions, occasionally glancing at the notebook, which contains suggested phrasing of replies to some of the more sensitive questions likely to come up. When thirty minutes have elapsed, the senior wire service correspondent present calls out, "Thank you, Mr. President," and the news conference is over.

These are the news conferences Johnson likes least of all, and though he has pledged on a number of occasions to hold them once a month, that schedule has rarely been observed. In 1967, more than five months elapsed—from March 9 to August 18— between "live" televised news conferences. The President knows that somehow he doesn't come across in the nation's living rooms. He has tinkered frequently with style and format: switching to contact lenses and then back to spectacles; using and then abandoning a huge prompting device that was nicknamed Mother; even giving studied attention to his haircut. In a radical departure from his previous style the President introduced a new device at a televised press conference on November 17, 1967—a lavaliere microphone suspended at tie-clip level from a cord around his neck. It freed him from the podium and allowed him to move about the East Room as he answered questions, gesturing freely and appearing to many viewers far more natural that he normally does on these occasions. The fact is that despite his wealth of experience, Johnson is nervous before the cameras. The patient, polite manner he usually feels compelled to cultivate for the TV screen does not come easy to the President. He much prefers the informal gathering of correspondents in his Oval Office, with cameras and microphones barred, where Johnson can be himself.

Often these sessions are called on just a moment's notice, and only the White House regulars attend. Their faces may not be friendly; but at least they are familiar, and Johnson is less likely to be thrown a curve—a provocative question that probes into controversial issues of policy or politics. If such a question is asked, Johnson feels free to brush it aside and even, on occasion, to rebuke the reporter who posed it.

Still more to the President's liking are small, select background briefings with groups of editors, Washington bureau chiefs, or correspondents. These sessions, at which nothing is said for the record, produce those remarkable exercises in apparent journalistic mind reading in which the President is reported as "known to believe" or "reported to think" something or other. The number of such background discussions has been inordinately high in the Johnson administration—and particularly at times when Johnson's policies, prestige, or poll ratings appear to be slipping.

Despite these varied forms of press contact, weeks sometimes go by when even the White House regulars have no direct access to the President. In these periods the mainstay of their reporting is the briefing conducted twice a day by the President's press secretary. (See Appendix F.) Here are announced Johnson's on-the-record appointments, as well as the routine day-to-day actions of the White House. Here, too, correspondents can pose questions of fact or interpretation, though answers are frequently hard to come by. The President closely studies the transcripts each day; he receives special copies in which staff members have inscribed the names of the reporters asking various questions. But even the transcripts submitted to the President are doctored from time to time—when it is feared that a particular question (or answer) may arouse his ire.

The press secretary's job is perhaps the most demanding after the President's—particularly in the Johnson White House. Sooner or later trouble has developed between Johnson and every man who has held the post. President Eisenhower had only one press secretary during his eight years in office, Kennedy had one during his thousand days, but Johnson was on his fourth by early 1967, after not much more than three years in the Presidency. "When Johnson gets a new press secretary," one White House insider says, "he gives him his head for a while. He tosses him a bone to give to the press—like putting a press pool on Air Force One so that representatives of the press corps can maintain contact with the President between jet stops. The secretary gets to feeling that he has a way with the President that his predecessors did not have. But sooner or later the President decides that he wants to take the job back and run it himself."

Almost from the beginning, Johnson chose to be his own press secretary. In communicative periods—during the 1964 campaign, for example, when he recognized the need for ample public exposure—he saved most of the White House news to dispense personally, although his manner of dispensing it—the President's walking press conferences around the White House lawn, for instance—at times seemed designed more to humble the reporters than to inform them. More frequently, a cloud of secretiveness has descended on the White House, and no press secretary—neither George Christian nor his predecessors, Pierre Salinger, George Reedy, and Bill Moyers—has been able to offer much help to those trying to pierce the murk.

One Wednesday afternoon in May, 1967, during the crisis that led to the six-day war in the Middle East, Christian was asked at the regular White House briefing whether the President had any travel plans for the following day. Reports from Ottawa indicated that Johnson was expected to confer there with Prime Minister Lester B. Pearson about the Middle East situation. "I frankly don't know," Christian said of the possibility of a Canadian trip. "There is a possibility?" a reporter asked. "At this point, I don't think there is," the press secretary replied. Four hours earlier, Secretary of State Rusk had telephoned Pearson in Canada to arrange the Thursday meeting. The Canadian government made the announcement Wednesday night. Most White House correspondents learned of it at seven thirty Thursday morning, when the White House called to tell them to board a jet at Andrews Air Force Base by nine.

Two other incidents on that Wednesday in May give further illustration of the frustrations of coping with White House secrecy. The ambassador of the United Arab Republic, the correspondents discovered, had made an unannounced visit to the White House. As is often the case with Presidential visitors, his name was not included on the public list of appointments. This was the exchange at the afternoon briefing:

Q: "Can you comment in any way on the long conference between the President and the Ambassador of the U.A.R. today?"

CHRISTIAN: "No."

Q: "Did they meet?"

CHRISTIAN: "So far as I know, the Ambassador came by for a farewell call."

Q: "How long was he here?"

CHRISTIAN: "I don't have any idea."

Reporters also asked that day whether the President's long-awaited special message on campaign financing was ready for submission to Congress. Christian said he didn't know. The message was sent to the Capitol the following morning, while the President and the press were winging their way to Canada. Reflecting on these events in the Washington *Post*, White House correspondent Carroll Kilpatrick concluded that Christian was, from Johnson's point of view, the ideal press secretary: "He never talks too much." Kilpatrick added, "Obviously, Christian is acting on the President's orders. But whether he is serving the President's cause is a different matter altogether."

In the summer of 1967, Dan Rather, a White House correspondent for CBS News, learned from a United States Senator that the government was planning to build an anti-infiltration barrier across South Vietnam, just south of the Demilitarized Zone. Rather asked Christian to confirm the story and was told by the press secretary that it was wholly without foundation. The correspondent thereupon dropped the story, but a couple of weeks later his Senatorial source called to say that regardless of any White House denials, the barrier project was definitely under way and would eventually be announced by the Pentagon. Rather was now convinced that the Senator knew what he was talking about. He did not again consult Christian, but went before the cameras on the White House lawn to tape a report on the Senator's disclosure. Soon after he finished, he was summoned by Christian, who asked him what he had been talking about. Rather suggested that Christian find out by tuning on the early evening CBS News program, which was due to be broadcast in about an hour. Disregarding this suggestion, Christian asked if he had by any chance been talking about the barrier, and Rather replied that he had been. Richard Rovere, who reported this episode in the September 23, 1967, issue of the *New Yorker* (identifying Rather only by the pseudonym "Network") gave the following account of what happened next:

"Sounding as if he had no interest higher than a solicitude for Network's reputation—a friendly desire to save Network from needlessly creating a 'credibility gap' of his own—Christian said that anyone who reported the construction of an anti-infiltration barrier in South Vietnam was simply purveying misinformation. He went on to say that the whole idea of a barrier was one that had never at any time been given serious consideration by the Johnson administration. Network, who had never had any reason in the past to suppose that Christian would knowingly mislead him, said that he trusted the source of the information he had just taped, and that he would take his chances with his reputation as a journalist. Christian then asked if it would make any difference to Network if he, Christian, checked his own source again and was able to come back and say categorically, on the highest authority, that there would be no barrier. Knowing that the authority was the President of the United States, and unable to see any possible gain for Mr. Johnson in deceiving anyone on this particular matter, Network said that he supposed it would make a difference.

"Christian thereupon left the office, and in a few minutes returned to say that he had made his new check and was in a position to give Network the categorical and authoritative assurance of which he had spoken. Christian did not say that he had talked with the President, but Network assumed that he had, and therefore phoned his network to ask that the barrier story be killed, which was done. A week ago, less than ten days after the incident in Christian's office, the Secretary of Defense told a news conference in the Pentagon that work had begun on an anti-infiltration barrier across South Vietnam just south of the Demilitarized Zone."

A Presidential press secretary—any President's press secretary—is faced with a major crisis when the President is ill. Even a minor Presidential disability immediately becomes a matter of national concern; the stock market trembles, the entire world watches, and the American public pours out its sympathy. An example from Johnson's medical history illustrates the special problems that confront the press secretary—and the press—in this administration. In October, 1965, when Johnson underwent surgery for removal of his gallbladder, he appeared to enjoy the public attention to the point of wishing to prolong his convalescence. Moyers was taking a week's breather at the time, and Joseph Laitin, then deputy press secretary, was handling the daily press briefings on the President's condition. Laitin consulted often with Johnson's physicians at the Naval Hospital in Bethesda, Maryland, who assured him that the President was making excellent progress. They were eager to get this word out to the public, so Laitin's daily press briefings told of a steady recovery. Johnson, however, began to make irritable remarks about "Dr." Laitin and "Press Secretary" Cain—Dr. James C. Cain, his family physician. When Moyers returned after a week, he told Laitin, "Joe, I've been listening to your briefings, and you've done a great job." Then he went to the Presidential suite to check in with the boss. When he came back downstairs a little later, he reversed his earlier judgment. "Joe," he said, "you did a lousy job." Johnson was annoyed because Laitin was making him well at too swift a pace. Laitin was also blamed for the famous picture of the President's surgical scar, which caused uncomplimentary comment around the world. Laitin had suggested to Johnson that he might pose for photographers on the hospital grounds. They had finished when the President impulsively called out, "Wait a minute. I have something to show you." Then, to the amazement of the photographers, he pulled up his shirt and displayed the incision. Later, when cartoonists and commentators had a field day with the episode, Johnson told Moyers it had been Laitin's idea.

The scar photo made front pages everywhere, of course, but it takes no such stunt to put the President on page one. Johnson has often demonstrated that he is well aware of his office's awesome power to shape the news—and that he can use it to telling effect. A notable example occurred in February, 1966, when critical hearings on Vietnam in the Senate Foreign Relations Committee began to dominate the newspapers and television channels. Overnight the President stole the play by hastily arranging for a "summit meeting" with South Vietnamese leaders in Honolulu. On a number of occasions Johnson has deliberately scheduled news conferences to draw attention from competing events.

Nonetheless, Johnson has been far from satisfied with the performance of the huge government publicity apparatus he commands. From the outset of his administration the government's army of information men has been under the President's close—and often captious—scrutiny. On December 23, 1963, barely a month after succeeding to the Presidency, Johnson directed Salinger to summon the eight or nine key information officers of the government—such men as Arthur Sylvester, then Assistant Secretary of Defense for Public Affairs, and Robert Manning, his counterpart at the State Department—to a meeting at the White House, where Johnson lectured the publicists. This "high-priced talent" that he had inherited from Kennedy was not earning its keep, the President complained; it was not getting his picture on the front page often enough. "You are working for me now," Johnson reminded them. Getting down to specifics, he noted that only one White House story had appeared on the front pages that week—and that was the annual lighting of the national Christmas tree, arranged without any help from them.

Such Dutch-uncle talk has been repeated to the senior information men on subsequent occasions. At one such, on August 27, 1965, Johnson accused the publicists of spending more time cooperating with reporters in search of stories that displeased him than in producing favorable news of his administration.

The sort of thing he had in mind, Johnson said, was the new calculating machine that was increasing efficiency in the Department of Agriculture. The announcement of its installation should have come from the White House rather than from the Agriculture Department, Johnson insisted. If the information specialists could not produce the sort of good news he wanted about his administration, the President warned, he would hire some high school seniors from Johnson City, Texas, to do the job.

It was on this occasion that Johnson laid down the rule that the White House had prior claims to all the news of government, regardless of where it originated. If something was to be announced, the President decreed, the White House was to know about it first. The order gave rise to what quickly became known as the Pedernales Press Service, named for the Texas river that flows through the LBJ ranch. Each Friday the federal agencies were required to send to the White House a digest of upcoming news events that the President might wish to appropriate for issuance through his office. Top federal officials have learned that when big news breaks unexpectedly within their areas of jurisdiction, they must hold it up to let the White House either announce it first or give them a clearance for disclosure. The result, according to one senior Washington correspondent, James Free of the Birmingham *News*, is "tightly controlled, often personalized news . . . on a scale larger than Washington has ever seen before in peacetime."

Johnson also keeps close tabs on day-to-day contacts between the press and high officials of his administration. In February, 1967, Muriel Dobbin disclosed in the Baltimore *Sun* that "at the request of the President, White House special assistants and State and Department of Defense officials down to assistant secretaries have been reporting on their communications with reporters." Christian confirmed that the report was correct. He said he had inherited the practice and did not know how long it had been in operation. The purpose, he explained, was to keep the White House "advised" of the questions being raised by the press, so that it could properly coordinate information. A useful by-product of the process, of course, is that it keeps the President up-to-date on the interests and attitudes of individual correspondents and of the press corps as a whole.

The President, it should be clear by now, is obsessed by the press. He woos it, worries over it, denounces it, and often despises it. "Lyndon, I must hand it to you. You were really fine to them," Mrs. Johnson was overheard saying once after the President had entertained two correspondents at the White House. "Yeah, but they'll still write as they please," the President replied. The fact that reporters, or at least most of them, will still write as they please—despite such blandishments as Texas barbecues, Presidential luncheons, dinners, and receptions, and even swimming parties in the White House pool—is, to Johnson, one of the heaviest burdens of the Presidency. "Johnson doesn't understand the press," one candid member of the President's staff confided. "He doesn't understand that a reporter is not like a Congressman. He can't be bought." Correspondents who covered Johnson in his Senate days have vivid recollections of the "treatment" they were likely to receive after publication of an unfavorable story. "What did I ever do to you?" the furious Majority Leader would ask. Even as President, he remains convinced that personal malice or at least partisan bias must motivate any reporter who writes a story that is not to Johnson's liking. As White House correspondent James Deakin has observed, "Johnson equates dissent with disloyalty and does not understand the function of the press to be a critic in our free society." After an interview with the President, James Cannon and Charles Roberts wrote in *Newsweek* that Johnson "is convinced that what he wants to do is right for the country and he believes that the press, like Congress and the people, should support him. He looks on newspapers, magazines and television as another powerful device to line up public support for the programs of his Great Society or, as he puts it, 'The press is one of the best servants I have.' " But it is often an unfaithful servant, Johnson feels. "Your damn profession, your First Amendment!" he once exploded at two interviewers.

Most Presidents enjoy a honeymoon period with the press when they first enter office, and Johnson was no exception. In the aftermath of the Dallas assassination, the new President was the beneficiary of a shocked public's sympathy. The great Bobby Baker scandal was unfolding on Capitol Hill, but Johnson, who had figured prominently in the daily stories as Baker's Senatorial mentor, was no longer mentioned in the news reports. Most of the press, like most of the public, gave Johnson the benefit of every doubt. The era of good feelings ended, abruptly, with news accounts of an incident at the LBJ ranch. Johnson, spending the Easter holidays in Texas, had invited the correspondents who accompanied him from Washington to the ranch for a relaxed day of sight-seeing. In the course of the day, according to the stories that were written later, the President took the wheel of his cream-colored Lincoln Continental and sped down the highways at eighty and ninety miles an hour. He had, according to *Time* magazine, a "paper cup of Pearl beer within easy sipping distance," and when he tried to pass a car on the crest of a hill he found himself "squarely in the path of an oncoming car." The other motorist veered off the paved surface to the road's shoulder to avoid a collision, and one of the President's passengers groaned, "That's the closest John McCormack has come to the White House yet." (The nation had no Vice-President, and elderly House Speaker McCormack was first in the line of succession.) Three of the four passengers in the President's car were newswomen. One of them, pretty blond Marianne Means of the Hearst newspaper chain, "kept her baby-blue eyes fastened on Johnson," *Time* reported, "and cooed: 'Mr. President, you're fun.'" Some of the other re-porters, however, were not amused. Seth Kantor of the Scripps-Howard newspapers decided he had an obligation to write the story, and accounts in *Time* and *Newsweek* followed. Johnson's reaction was a public denial that he had ever traveled at the speeds clocked by reporters traveling in cars immediately be-hind him. Privately, the President fumed that his hospitality had been abused. He was seconded in this judgment by Betty Beale, the society columnist of the Washington *Star*, who de-clared that reporters had no right to tell all when they were guests of the President.

The press, Johnson says—and apparently believes—is directly responsible for many of his troubles. He has blamed it for im-peding his freedom of action, for undermining public con-fidence in his foreign policies—notably with respect to Vietnam—and even for imperiling the state of the economy. One day in the spring of 1966, prices on the New York Stock Exchange skidded to a $10 billion paper loss after the Associated Press reported that Johnson might soon propose a tax increase if prices kept on rising. The AP's White House correspondent had merely reported what he had heard the President tell a group of White House Fellows. But Johnson angrily accused the AP man of causing the market decline.

When Johnson was criticized for sending Chief Justice Earl Warren, rather than Vice-President Humphrey, to Winston Churchill's funeral—a move the British regarded as a slight—the President contended that the press had manufactured an international incident. "I will bear in mind in connection with any future funerals your very strong feelings in the matter and try to act in accordance with our national interest," he told reporters. When White House invitations to India's Prime Minister Lal Bahadur Shastri and Pakistan's President Ayub Khan were abruptly canceled, Johnson was criticized for an undiplomatic act that upset an entire subcontinent. His explanation at the time was that the volume of Congressional business and the continuing pressures of Vietnam left the President with no time for visitors. Some newspapers suggested, however, that he had canceled the visits out of pique because the two leaders had been critical of American policy in Vietnam. A few weeks later Johnson offered another explanation; he told reporters at a news conference that Ayub and Shastri could not have achieved the main purposes of their scheduled visits because Congress had not yet completed action on the year's foreign aid bill. Charles Roberts of *Newsweek* reported that when he asked Johnson about the postponed visits, the President complained that the press had "speculated" about his reasons. To the President, Roberts noted, "speculate" was a dirty word. "Apparently," he wrote, "the President thinks that the press should print the news in tape-recorder fashion, just as he dictates it, without any unauthorized explanation, interpretation, background or speculation. If that day comes, it should be noted, there will be no need for White House correspondents—the *Federal Register* dutifully reports the President verbatim."

Johnson has complained at length that the White House correspondents are "middlemen" who intrude needlessly between the President and the public, who report what he does not want reported, distort what they report, and ignore what he wants publicized. Occasionally he must look with envy at those foreign governments that operate unhampered by the inconvenience of a free press. In fact, to a remarkable and frightening extent, he has succeeded in emulating their style. A Washington correspondent who completed a tour of duty in Moscow not long ago finds striking similarities between covering the White House and covering the Kremlin. "On neither beat," he notes, "can you believe all you're told—and there's a lot going on behind the scenes that no one will talk about."

7. Friends, Foes, and Faithful Servants

The telephone rang one night in the Washington bureau of United Press International. The wire service editor who picked up the phone was startled to find that the President of the United States was on the other end of the line.

"Hello, Pat, this is Lyndon Johnson," said the President.

"Yes, Mr. President."

"Say, I have here . . . (pause) . . . A101N from Johnson City, Texas, about the homestead, by Kyle Thompson. Let's see . . . (pause) . . . you say in there that there's going to be a fee for the tour. Well, that's not right at all. The idea is to give it to the people."

"Just a minute, Mr. President, and I'll get the story."

"You see what it says. It says 'the home was opened to the public for fee tours.' That isn't right. You see, it's for free. That's the idea. Do you see that?"

"Yes, Mr. President. It looks like they dropped the 'r' in the word 'free.' I guess they omitted it in transmission."

"Well, Pat, it sure does mean just the opposite of what we mean."

"It sure does, Mr. President. I'll fix it."

"Well, we want it to be free."

"Certainly, Mr. President. I'll straighten it out right away."

"I'd appreciate it if you would clean this up for me."

"I certainly will, Mr. President."

"We hope you will take the necessary steps to straighten this out."

"Yes, sir, Mr. President."

"Thank you, Pat."

"Thank you for letting us know, Mr. President."

This example of how closely Lyndon Johnson follows the news carried on the wire service tickers installed behind his desk was printed in the UPI house organ, *UPI Reporter.* It raises an immediate question: If the President's vigilant scrutiny of what is reported about him extends even to catching typographical errors, what happens when correspondents defy his exhaustive efforts to manipulate the news? What happens when they exercise their right to produce critical pieces about him?

"The President and his staff seem to ring like burglar alarms whenever and wherever the name 'Johnson' appears in print or is uttered on the air," Washington correspondent Ben Bagdikian observed in the *Columbia Journalism Review.* "A small item in a West Texas paper mentioned Billie Sol Estes in connection with the President in a three paragraph story on the inside; the editor claims he got a telephone call from the White House in time to kill the item in later editions. One television correspondent was awakened in the middle of the night by the White House, which had heard that he planned to make some critical remarks the next day. A newspaper correspondent wrote a critical morning story and got three telephone calls from the White House before breakfast. The *New York Review of Books,* a medium-highbrow publication, ran a scathing review of Johnson's Vietnam policy and its editors got a phone call from a White House aide suggesting that in the future they have Vietnam books reviewed by Joseph Alsop (who approves of the Johnson policy)."

It is natural for a President to care deeply about his coverage in the press. Personally and politically, every Chief Executive wants to project the most positive image possible and to have his administration's policies and actions cast in the most favorable light. With only one recent exception—Dwight D. Eisenhower—each President has devoted much of his precious time to scrutinizing his press notices and to cultivating or chastising the men who write them. A President's relations with the press reflect his personal style, as well as the issues and circumstances of his time. Franklin D. Roosevelt's generally cordial relations with the Washington correspondents were marred by petulance and even vindictiveness when he disapproved of what they wrote (though Roosevelt was utterly delighted when a typographical error in the Washington *Post* produced the headline FDR IN BED WITH COED; he ordered extra copies for his friends). Harry S. Truman, who fulminated against the "One-Party (Republican) Press," nonetheless enjoyed shirt-sleeved poker sessions with his press corps cronies, but when a music critic panned his daughter's singing, he dashed off a handwritten note that still stands as the unmatched classic of Presidential invective.

Most politicians develop a keen interest in the press early in their careers. Eisenhower, who came late to politics, never acquired the habit. He knew that the Washington *Post* was likely to be criticizing his administration, and so he generally confined his reading to the sports section. His acquaintance with what was printed in the press came principally from a daily digest prepared for him by the White House staff, and he left the fine art of Presidential news management to his press secretary, James Hagerty. In the view of most correspondents, Hagerty performed in the job with considerable skill. One of his major accomplishments was the creation of Presidential pseudoactivity; when Eisenhower went on vacation, the press secretary could be counted on to produce a flurry of announcements and news releases that gave the appearance of a furiously busy President. Hagerty also carefully restricted access to the White House staff, insisting that all press contacts be cleared through him— and reporters who had written critically about the President found that such clearance was difficult to obtain.

Reporters soon learn that public officials—even Presidents— are only human and have human frailties. Not surprisingly, Presidents make the same discovery about the press. Even the most cynical journalist can be flattered by a show of attention from the nation's Chief Executive. Even the most fiercely independent can be cowed by the prospect that his news sources will cut him off. A system of rewards and punishments—a carrot-and-stick approach to the press—has long been in force at the White House, but it has been elaborated and expanded—almost institutionalized—in recent years. Blandishments, as well as rebukes, have become burdens to the correspondents. Hugh Sidey, *Time* magazine's White House correspondent, was a personal friend of President Kennedy's, but he received frequent scoldings from the President about the contents of the magazine. On a day when Kennedy was offended by a critical piece in *Time*, Sidey would arrive at the White House and be told by Ted Sorensen, "The boss wants to see you." On occasion Kennedy would ask in exasperation, "What can I propose that Luce [the late Henry Luce, publisher of *Time*] will support?" Quite a few Washington correspondents have unpleasant recollections of complaining telephone calls from Kennedy to their editors or publishers.

That practice has continued and grown in the Johnson White House. The stick is bigger, but so is the carrot. Jack Bell, the veteran political writer who heads the Associated Press staff in the U.S. Senate, recalls a massive show of Presidential interest that was mounted in his behalf. One spring day in 1965, Bell received a call from the White House. "I have a friend of yours sitting here in my office, and he says you've written a book about me that's the best thing anyone has done," Johnson informed Bell. The friend in question, he learned upon inquiry, was Roy Roberts of the Kansas City *Star*. "I didn't know until Roy told me that you had written a book about me," the President continued. The fact was that Bell had tried to interview the President when he was writing *The Johnson Treatment*.[16] Johnson, however, declined to see him after suggesting that Bell submit written questions. Instead, he had George Reedy, then his press secretary, and McGeorge Bundy, then a special assistant, handle the questions for him. Without bothering to remind Johnson that he could hardly have been unaware of the book project, Bell told the President he would arrange to have a copy sent him. "Don't send it, bring it," Johnson commanded. "O.K., but you'll have to tell somebody to let me in," Bell said, and was told to arrange it through Marvin Watson, the appointments secretary. A few days later Bell was instructed to come to the White House, using the back entrance. When he was ushered into the Oval Office, Johnson greeted him effusively. He had received the book and stayed up until three o'clock that morning to finish it, "and I liked it," the President said. The

16 Jack Bell, *The Johnson Treatment* (New York, Harper & Row, 1965), p. 139.

book, which included an account of Johnson's years in the Senate, was not entirely complimentary. Bell wrote that Johnson had a reputation as a "whiner" among the newsmen who covered his activities and that a critical report "could set him off for days." He would "call the reporter to his office and tell him how disappointed he was that an old and trusted friend had written about him in such a manner. Moreover, he would often harangue one newsman about what another newsman had written. At times such discussions would last an hour, even though the newsman would explain over and over again that he had had nothing to do with the article at issue."

Bell's book, however, also contained favorable comment about Johnson, and at the White House the President praised it as "a great job." As Bell later sized up Johnson's behavior on this occasion, "he figured here was a reporter he might be able to win over with a little Presidential attention. So he began to turn on the circus. He ordered Reedy to bring the White House regulars into the office. Then he said, 'Let's take a walk.'" The President, Bell, and the rest of the correspondents trooped out into the garden and began one of the marathon walking news conferences that Johnson favored that year. When Bell dropped back three or four rows, Johnson turned and said, "Where's Jack Bell? You come on up here with me, Jack." At one point he told Bell that people were not supposed to walk on the right side of the President, but he wanted Bell to walk there. Finally, he led the reporters back to the White House and told them to join him on the south balcony overlooking the garden. When Bell started to climb the stairs to the balcony with the other reporters, Johnson pulled him back and said, "I want you to take the elevator with me." The group sat on the balcony for an hour and a half while the President talked off the record, and, Bell said, "he did not say a damned thing that he had not already said in public." A French correspondent with a Paris deadline coming up whispered to an American colleague that he was going to have to leave while the President was still talking. "You can't possibly do that," the American whispered back. "But we have been here for an hour and a half and he is saying nothing and I have a deadline," said the French reporter. "Would you leave if Charles de Gaulle were doing this?" the American inquired sternly. "Charles de Gaulle would not spend fifteen minutes talking about the rust on his balcony," the French correspondent snapped.

Johnson's relations with the press still follow patterns established when he was in the Senate. "If you could face him down with something you knew he was doing, you would generally get an answer out of him," Bell says. "Otherwise, you would spend an hour in his office and come away with nothing but a pile of manure, all designed to demonstrate what a great man he was." Robert G. "Bobby" Baker was the key to covering Johnson in those days. As secretary to the Senate Majority—he was not yet caught up in the investigation that brought his conviction on charges of theft and tax evasion—Baker knew everything that his boss was doing and shared much of his information with the Senate reporters. "We would find out from Bobby what Johnson was doing, then go ask him about it," Bell relates.

When Johnson, as the Senate Majority Leader, called the press in, it was usually to conduct a monologue about what he was doing or was going to do. He had little patience for the normal press conference give-and-take, in which correspondents try to elicit information of legitimate public interest. One such session, on July 2, 1955, sheds some light on the attitude toward the press that was to be reflected during Johnson's tenure in the White House. AP reporter John Chadwick recalls that the Majority Leader was talking that Saturday morning about how he was going to get "a whole string of bills out of committee and have them passed." Chadwick asked about the pending immigration bill, and Johnson replied that he could not comment on this as it was in committee. The Senator turned to other matters, but Chadwick felt the immigration bill deserved a more specific answer; it was controversial legislation and had aroused much public discussion, since it would have liberalized the McCarren-Walter Act and ended the nationalities quota system. Once he became President, Johnson did an about-face, pushed a similar bill through Congress, and signed it with a spectacular flourish at the Statue of Liberty. But at this point in his Senate career he clearly wanted no part of immigration reform. He had not said so on the record, however, and when an opportunity arose, Chadwick cut in again with a question.

"Senator, you have agreed to talk about other bills which are in committee. Why can't you talk about the immigration bill which is in committee? What is so different about it?" The Majority Leader exploded. "Don't tell me how to answer questions," he stormed. "You can get the hell out of here." A couple of other reporters rose to Chadwick's defense, but the press conference came to an abrupt end in an atmosphere charged with anger and embarrassment. That afternoon, Johnson, suffering from nausea, set out for a weekend at the Middleburg, Virginia, estate of George Brown, a wealthy Texas contractor and longtime Johnson supporter. There he suffered his major heart attack. Johnson was a heavy cigarette smoker at that time, and he was exhausted from six hard months of eighteen-hour days. But when he searched around for a reason for his heart attack, he decided that Chadwick had provoked it with his press conference question. Chadwick confirms that he heard indirectly from Senator Clinton Anderson of New Mexico and some others that Johnson had told them, "Chadwick caused my heart attack."

Johnson set no records in winning friends among the press during his Senate tenure. But the Presidency offered him vast new opportunities, which he quickly seized. He began to exploit the possibilities of the White House social side, as he had seen John F. Kennedy do. It was not a new idea, but no Presidents until Kennedy and Johnson were so generous in dispensing White House hospitality to large numbers of correspondents and their wives. In the words of Nat S. Finney, the Washington bureau chief of the Buffalo *Evening News*, Kennedy made a "royal court" out of the White House and created a problem: "A reporter himself might not care much about an invitation to the White House, but his wife would like it very much." Finney is convinced that a reporter exposes himself to subtle pressure if he accepts a White House social invitation. Peter Lisagor, who agrees with Finney, points out this is one way a President can create a "psychological undertow" against reporters. Lisagor has observed during his long tenure as Washington bureau chief of the Chicago *Daily News* how reporters can be tempted to soften the edges of criticism and to "obscure and minimize things that the public generally ought to be hearing about." Finney feels so strongly about this that he informed his editors if he ever were invited to the White House, he would decline. The seductive lure of the White House invitation applies not only to those who are on the list but also to those who aspire to it. "A lot of reporters pull their punches," in the opinion of Edwin A. Lahey, "either because they hope this will help them get invited to the White House or, if they have been once, because they hope to be invited again." For his part, adds Lahey, a veteran Knight newspapers columnist, "I always considered that the press should expect to use the servants' entrance."

Whether or not they are deliberately sought after, there are professional rewards for the reporter who enjoys a personal relationship with the President. William Lawrence, the ABC commentator who covered the White House for the New York *Times* when Kennedy became President, was a golf companion of Kennedy, and was first with the news on some of his key cabinet appointments. Arthur Sylvester, who was then Washington bureau chief of the Newark *News*, was another friend who came up regularly with news beats—until he accepted a full-time job in the administration. Two of Kennedy's close friends, Charles Bartlett and Ben Bradlee, were more circumspect with the information that came to them as a result of their personal relationship with the President, but their careers advanced notably during Kennedy's tenure in office. Bartlett, who had introduced Jack to Jacqueline and served as an usher at their wedding, moved up from covering Washington for the Chattanooga *Times* to being the Chicago *Sun-Times'* nationally syndicated columnist. Bradlee, a member of the *Newsweek* Washington bureau, was promoted to bureau chief and later moved on to become managing editor of the Washington *Post*. Another Kennedy favorite, who has managed to become a Johnson favorite, is Marianne Means, the Hearst columnist. She was a young, pretty blonde working on a Nebraska newspaper when Kennedy, then a Senator, first met her during a visit to the state in his quest for the Presidential nomination. Kennedy helped her land a job with the *Northern Virginia Sun*, a small daily published in a Washington suburb. This was a springboard to a job in the Washington bureau of the Hearst newspapers, and when Kennedy became President, her bureau chief, acting on a Kennedy suggestion, assigned her to cover the White House.

Kennedy made free and frequent use of prominent correspondents to put his foreign policy failures and successes in the best possible light. He was partial to James B. Reston of the New York *Times* despite Reston's fierce independence. In April, 1961, Reston was called in, along with Murrey Marder and Chalmers Roberts of the Washington *Post*, and the late Marguerite Higgins, then with the New York *Herald Tribune*. They were summoned to hear Kennedy's self-serving explanation of the Bay of Pigs fiasco on the same day that he had cut off all questions about it in a press conference. "I think that the facts of the matter will come out in due time," he said at the news conference. "I am sure that an effort will be made to determine the facts accurately." Then, implying that the matter was still too sensitive for him to discuss any further, he said that he was confining himself "for good reason" to a general statement about the Cuban affair which he had issued the previous day.

A correspondent who agrees to confer with the President risks involvement in an "unequal proposition." No one is more aware of this than Reston, who has described the danger in those words, noting that it is difficult to enter the White House without being impressed with it and the "terrible burdens" that the President must bear. "How could you help but be sympathetic?" Reston asked. And once you became sympathetic, it would become "increasingly difficult to employ the critical facilities," he added. Reston, however, did not hesitate to ask Kennedy for a private briefing in Vienna after the summit conference with Soviet Premier Nikita Khrushchev in June, 1961. Kennedy granted the request, making it possible for Reston to scoop several hundred of his colleagues who received only routine accounts of the conference through the usual channels.

Late in 1962, Kennedy opened doors for two correspondents, his friend Bartlett and Stewart Alsop, to help them write an inside account of his triumphant handling of the October Cuban missile crisis. The effort backfired, at least temporarily, because of something Kennedy had not intended. The article, which appeared in the *Saturday Evening Post*, contained material which derogated the role that UN Ambassador Adlai Stevenson had played in the crisis. In the ensuing uproar the White House issued a formal denial that a hatchet job had been undertaken in behalf of the President.

Still another way that Kennedy cultivated correspondents, as did Presidents before him, was by cooperating with those who wanted to write books. Franklin D. Roosevelt was largely responsible for the books on the New Deal that were written by Ernest K. Lindley, former Washington bureau chief of *Newsweek*, who is now a State Department executive. Dwight D. Eisenhower made it possible for Robert J. Donovan of the New York *Herald Tribune* to write *Eisenhower: The Inside Story*.[17] Donovan, now Washington bureau chief of the Los Angeles *Times*, scored again under Kennedy. *PT 109, John F. Kennedy in World War II*,[18] the book he wrote about Kennedy's harrowing adventures as a young naval officer in the Pacific in World War II, was authorized by the President. The book, which Kennedy helped materialize with a series of exclusive interviews, was a best seller. The President's father, Joseph Kennedy, drew on his old contacts in Hollywood, at his son's request, to arrange for a film to be made from the book. Another Kennedy friend who wrote a book was Hugh Sidey, the White House correspondent for *Time* and the author of *John F. Kennedy, President*.[19]

Very early in his Presidency, as he was returning to Washington from spending Christmas in Texas, Lyndon Johnson passed the word through the press pool riding with him on Air Force One that he would make great men out of those correspondents who played ball with him. Johnson was confident that he and the correspondents were going to get along famously. Johnson's two closest reporter friends when he moved into the White House were a fellow Texan, William S. White, and Philip Potter. White, who at one time covered the Senate for the New York *Times*, writes a syndicated column that rarely causes Johnson any anxiety. Only Max Freedman, in the days when he, too, was writing a column, exhibited such undeviating admiration.

On the strength of his friendship, White was chosen by a publisher to write a book about the President in 1964. *The*

17 Robert J. Donovan, *Eisenhower: The Inside Story* (New York, Harper, 1956).
18 Robert J. Donovan, *PT 109, John F. Kennedy in World War II* (New York, McGraw-Hill, 1961).
19 Hugh Sidey, *John F. Kennedy, President* (New York, Atheneum, 1963).

Professional: Lyndon B. Johnson [20] was a typical campaign biography, but it was selected by the United States Information Agency as a suitable work to ship to USIA libraries around the world. Two other books about the President by Washington newspapermen, *Lyndon B. Johnson: The Exercise of Power* [21] by Rowland Evans and Robert Novak and *Lyndon B. Johnson and the World* [22] by Philip L. Geyelin, were deemed less suited to USIA's purposes. Both were acclaimed as balanced and objective studies of the President, and both were recommended by the USIA selection board, but both were vetoed by the agency's director. When called on later to explain the veto, USIA Director Leonard Marks said there just wasn't enough money to buy *every* book.

Freedman, who wrote speeches on the side for Johnson, was launched as a syndicated columnist by the Chicago *Daily News* after he had been Washington correspondent for the Manchester *Guardian*. Johnson gave Freedman the same White House visiting privileges he had extended to White and, in addition, lent his prestige to an occasion when Freedman was eager to increase his status with editors of his client newspapers. The columnist invited newspaper editors around the country to fly to Washington for a private dinner at his home. When they arrived, they were impressed, as Freedman meant them to be, to find the President there, too.

In 1966, Jack Valenti, the former White House special assistant who still undertakes an occasional chore for the President, visited newspaper offices far from Washington to urge editors to subscribe to two of Johnson's favorite columns. Such efforts can cut both ways. Eliot Janeway, who writes a business column that has criticized the administration's policies, says one Texas daily dropped his column after Valenti called on the editor. In another instance Valenti told a West Coast publisher that a Washington political column was "notoriously inaccurate." The publisher made an investigation and decided to keep the column. Johnson himself told William Randolph

---

[20] William S. White, *The Professional: Lyndon B. Johnson* (Boston, Houghton Mifflin, 1964).

[21] Rowland Evans and Robert Novak, *Lyndon B. Johnson: The Exercise of Power* (New York, New American Library, 1966).

[22] Philip Geyelin, *Lyndon B. Johnson and the World* (New York, Praeger, 1966).

Hearst, Jr., that the short-lived New York *World Journal Tribune* was giving too much play to the same column.

Valenti has also acted as Johnson's "agent" in contacts with publishers of books the administration fears will be harmful or unfriendly. In one such case the White House dispatched an aide to the vice-president of a publishing firm to ask, "Do you *have* to publish this book?" The aide implied that the firm, which hoped to obtain publication rights to the Johnson memoirs, might lose out if it went ahead with the critical book. The book was published, and the firm lost the Johnson business. In this instance the White House also tried, unsuccessfully, to obtain a copy of the book's prepublication manuscript; Valenti made the attempt by calling the book's editor from the office of one of the publishing firm's corporate officers.

When Phil Potter of the Baltimore *Sun*, for many years a close friend of the President, upset Johnson in January, 1966, with an exclusive story on the new Food for Peace program, it was Valenti who took him to dinner and questioned him about his sources. Potter told Valenti that he could tell the President he would disclose his sources neither to Valenti nor to the President himself. Potter later learned that an official of Cabinet rank who had nothing to do with the story was blamed for the leak and given "unshirted hell." Johnson would have been even angrier had he known that Bill Moyers, then the White House press secretary, was one of Potter's actual sources. The inside story of how Potter broke his exclusive is an example of what a resourceful reporter can occasionally accomplish in Washington with a little high-level help—and of what the consequences can be if the story fails to meet with the President's approval. Potter obtained much of his information from Richard W. Reuter, director of the Food for Peace agency. Then he went to Moyers and told him what he knew. The press secretary told Potter he was on the right track but urged him to hold up publication, and Potter agreed. One day, after a routine White House press briefing, Moyers slipped a piece of paper to Potter. On it was scribbled just one word: "Tomorrow." Moyers had announced in the briefing that Johnson had called a Cabinet meeting for the next day. Potter put two and two together and wrote in the Baltimore *Sun* that the President would announce the new food program at the Cabinet meeting. When the story appeared, Johnson flew into a rage, canceled the Cabinet meeting, ordered the news releases on the food program destroyed, and launched a full-scale investigation of the "leak." It was one of the most vivid demonstrations of how far the President would go to suppress a story he had not announced.

Potter's relations with the President are not as close as they once were, and the White House has made it known that the Baltimore *Sun* has been replaced by the *Christian Science Monitor* as the President's favorite newspaper because the *Monitor* is "more fair." (This news prompted one of the *Monitor*'s senior correspondents to comment, "We must be doing something wrong.")

The Washington press corps has had ample warning of the dangers of becoming too friendly with a President. Two correspondents whose experience spans many administrations, Arthur Krock and Walter Lippmann, have eloquently described the hazards. In a farewell address at the National Press Club on his retirement from the *Times* in January, 1967, Krock sounded a cautionary note about the perils of White House hospitality. No reporter should "become bemused by the heady wine" of White House invitations, he said, speaking from his experience of sixty years as a newspaperman. "The objectivity of news reporting in the capital depends upon the conscience of the king and the susceptibility of the press corps," he continued. "I am a walking allergy to Presidents. Too much hospitality is usually an effort by an administration to shape official news the way it would like to see it."

Lippmann told the International Press Institute at its London meeting in May, 1965, that there was a growing conflict between the reporters' pursuit of the truth and their need and desire to be on good terms with the powerful. "The powerful are perhaps the chief source of the news but they are also the dispensers of many kinds of favor, privilege, honor and self-esteem," he said. "The most important forms of corruption in the modern journalist's world are the many guises and disguises of social climbing on the pyramids of power. The temptations are many; some are simple, some are refined, and often they are yielded to without the consciousness of yielding. Only a constant awareness of them offers protection." Lippmann has experienced the heady wine of having Presidents honor him by visits to his home. Both Kennedy and Johnson made pilgrimages early in their Presidencies to the stucco home at 3525 Woodley Road, in a fashionable section of northwest Washington, where he formerly lived. Both sought his advice. He and Kennedy hit it off well together, and he continued to be a regular visitor at the White House during the first year or so of the Johnson administration.

It was not unusual for Lippmann to spend hours at a stretch at the White House. On one occasion he arrived before lunch and stayed for seven hours. But he broke with Johnson over the President's decision to expand the war in Vietnam, and by December, 1966, he had reached the point where he was willing to speak candidly for publication. He did not go to see Johnson anymore, he told Andrew J. Glass of the Washington *Post*, because he felt that Johnson had misled him. "He was saying different things to me than to other people." Then seventy-seven and getting ready to move to New York after nearly three decades in Washington, Lippmann was also moved to comment about the professional hazards involved in becoming a President's crony. "Cronyism is the curse of journalism," he declared. "After many years, I have reached the firm conclusion that it is impossible for an objective newspaperman to be a friend of a President. Cronyism is a sure sign that something is wrong and that the public is not getting the whole journalistic truth." Johnson, he asserted, should not be calling him and other columnists and asking their advice. "That sort of relationship is very corrupting."

Asking a correspondent for advice is one way of attempting to influence him. Another, practiced by both Kennedy and Johnson, is to call a correspondent and praise him for a story he has written—or, conversely, to complain about a story that displeased. Each President developed his own style for such approaches, as did the various press secretaries and other officials who made them. Pierre Salinger, who served both Kennedy and Johnson, adopted a belligerent tone toward authors of unfriendly articles. "Now who the hell gave you that bum dope?" he would ask. Moyers would diplomatically reproach reporters, more in sorrow than in anger, with the words, "I just hate to see you go off the beam that way." As the 1968 political campaign approached, the embattled Johnson White House stepped up the volume and tone of its complaints. Stuart H. Loory, the White House correspondent of the Los Angeles *Times*, reported that he had been denounced by the associate press secretary, Loyd Hackler, for a foreign policy story he had written for his paper. "This is the most biased story I have ever seen," Hackler protested. "You are so biased you don't even recognize the facts." "His voice grew louder and louder," Loory said, "and as I walked away Hackler was shouting obscenities."

One morning late in 1967, Martin Nolan of the *Reporter* appeared as a guest on a Washington television program and talked about the Credibility Gap. "I think what the press—that is, the working reporters—most resent is not that they are not always being told the truth, but that the President and his staff kind of brag about the fact that he hoodwinks them. And I think that is a dangerous business—not if you deceive them and then you don't let them know about it, but if one is deceived and then your deceiver brags about it, you feel a little upset," Nolan said. Minutes after he was off the air, the White House was checking on Nolan's background. A little later one of the President's special assistants called. Johnson, it turned out, had been watching the program, and the aide wanted to know what proof Nolan had for his "very serious charge." Nolan offered a few examples, and his interrogator replied that they weren't very recent. The interview, Nolan said, had "a faintly accusatory tone."

There are many ways of harassing correspondents who seem immune to the techniques of White House seduction. Harassment can take the form of a mild rebuke—the President's refusal, for instance, to attend a dinner of the White House Correspondents' Association or the Gridiron Club. Johnson showed his displeasure with the press corps in 1967 by declining to go to the Gridiron dinner. The previous year he had sent his regrets when invited to attend it, and arrangements had accordingly been made for Vice-President Humphrey to be the guest of honor. But 1966 was an election year, and Johnson put in an appearance at the eleventh hour, arriving just in time to oust Humphrey from his role as guest speaker, and gave the principal speech himself. It had been put together at the last minute by Bill Moyers, with the help of Art Buchwald, who was called away from the dinner to supply Moyers with humorous material.

Harassment can also take the ugly form of an FBI investigation of a correspondent to ascertain the source of a leaked story which the President did not want printed. Lloyd Norman, the military correspondent of *Newsweek,* suffered this experience under the Kennedy administration; Philip L. Geyelin (who moved in 1967 from the Wall Street *Journal* to the Washington *Post*) was given the FBI treatment on Johnson's orders.

Harassment does not have to take so blatant a form to achieve the desired effect. James McCartney, now city editor of the Chicago *Daily News,* has pointed up an inhibiting factor which he learned about during his days as a Washington correspondent. "A reporter may hesitate to take a critical view of regularly tapped sources," he wrote in *Nieman Reports,* "for the very human reason that he prefers to be greeted pleasantly when he walks into an office, rather than to be treated as though he were poison." McCartney illustrated his point by recalling how little publicity there had been on the antics of Brumas, Robert F. Kennedy's giant black Labrador, which accompanied Kennedy to the Justice Department every day when he was Attorney General. One Justice Department correspondent, William J. Eaton of United Press International (now with the Chicago *Daily News* in Washington), broke the story of Brumas in a dispatch that called attention to a regulation, plainly posted on the walls, forbidding dogs in government buildings. It was a legitimate, if trivial, story, but Kennedy was not amused. He and his press aide, Edwin O. Guthman, were furious and gave Eaton the cold shoulder after the story appeared. Brumas led an adventurous life at the department. Once he jumped up on Associate Justice John M. Harlan during a solemn swearing-in ceremony. Another time he escaped from the building, and FBI agents had to rush out to retrieve him in the midst of traffic on Pennsylvania Avenue. These and other escapades were well known to the reporters who covered Justice. But rather than land in Kennedy's doghouse because of a dog, they prudently decided to let the Brumas story go unchronicled.

Harassment, however, is one of the lesser problems of the Washington correspondent. One of the most serious obstacles to more competent reporting of Lyndon Johnson's Presidency has been, as columnist Joseph Kraft has observed in *Harper's*, "the inability of the press to see the President as just another flack." Johnson, Ben Bagdikian notes in the *Columbia Journalism Review*, is essentially a public relations man in his obsession with image, his unrestrained attempts to create illusion for tactical reasons, and his concern with appearances no matter how implausible. "The problem," Bagdikian comments, "is that Lyndon Johnson appeals to reporters with all the dignity and power of his position as President and when this does not produce the results he wants, begins manipulating them and the news in ways that are not highly regarded even at the Press Club bar. He is trying to have it both ways. The weakness of many correspondents is that the President is too valuable a source in the competition for news to be ignored as a lesser PR man would be. But deeper than that is the conflict the President creates in many serious correspondents who respect the office of President and the man in it, but whose professional standards tell them that what is going on is common, ordinary press agentry. . . . Too often correspondents are asked to choose between disrespect for the reader and disrespect for the President."

8. The Great Snow Job

When the Eighty-ninth Congress passed the Truth in Packaging Act in 1966, it made no provision for policing the packaging of government information. The omission was regrettable, for the gaudy wrappings in which the government purveys its policies and programs are often at least as deceptive as the misleading labels placed on consumer products by unscrupulous manufacturers. Such commercial absurdities as the "giant quart" and the "king-sized gallon" become mere modest marketing claims compared to the hyperbolic excesses that have marked the merchandising of the Great Society. Some years ago an enterprising mouthwash manufacturer enjoyed a brief, but spectacular, success with a product that had been carefully engineered to please the public's preferences in color, taste, and smell; unfortunately, it caused tooth decay. With similar ingenuity, the Johnson administration advised Congress early in 1966 that it would seek to amend the federal school lunch and school milk programs to "focus more on needy children, helping to provide them with adequate and well-balanced meals." The measure went to Capitol Hill as the Child Nutrition Act of 1966—and astonished Congressmen discovered that it provided for an $82,000,000 *reduction* in the federal milk subsidy for schoolchildren.

Nineteen sixty-six was the year in which President Johnson made every effort to convince the American people that they could afford both guns and butter—that the rising costs of the war in Vietnam would necessitate no sacrifice of domestic welfare programs. "This nation is mighty enough," the President

161

declared in his State of the Union address, "its society is healthy enough, its people are strong enough to pursue our goals in the rest of the world while still building a Great Society here at home." In fact, the building of the Great Society had already been drastically curtailed and was to be cut back still further. But what was lacking in money was more than made up in rich Presidential rhetoric.

The nation's first eighty-eight Congresses, Johnson told a Washington audience, "invested $5 billion 800 million for education, or an average of $33 million per year in educating our children. The 89th Congress invested not $5 billion 800 million, but $9 billion 600 million, almost twice as much as all those other Congresses put together." As happens all too often with the President's facile statistics, these wilted under close analysis. The impressive total for "educating our children" included, as it turned out, $2 billion spent by the Pentagon for training of military personnel, most of the budget of the Office of Economic Opportunity, the Agriculture Department's Extension Service, the operations of the Library of Congress and the Smithsonian Institution, and a wondrously varied list of other foreign and domestic efforts which the federal budget classifies as "education, training and allied programs broadly defined."

The baroque complexity of federal bookkeeping is strikingly suited to such manipulative calculations, and the administration has made the most of its opportunities. The President's budget for fiscal 1968, still striving to demonstrate that the Great Society was a going concern, noted a total expenditure of $25.6 billion for "poor people under all government programs." The figure, often cited by administration spokesmen as evidence of a massive and extraordinary federal effort, included not only funds for education and training, health, economic development, and public assistance, but also such earned benefits as Social Security payments and veterans' pensions, as well as highway construction and urban renewal efforts that were of marginal usefulness—if not actually detrimental—to "poor people."

As the promises of the Great Society faded from view, administration spokesmen attained new heights of creativity in their efforts to demonstrate that domestic programs were making progress. A typical example was the news conference conducted at the White House on September 12, 1967, by Robert C.

Weaver, the Secretary of Housing and Urban Development. Weaver said he had good news for low-income families—news for which Johnson should receive the credit. At the President's urging, the Secretary reported, his agency had found ways to double the number of new low-rent housing units that would become available for occupancy within the next twelve months. Where 35,000 units had originally been planned, Weaver said, 70,000 would actually be built.

Vincent J. Burke, who writes about urban affairs for the Los Angeles *Times*, felt that "there seemed to be something wrong with Weaver's arithmetic or with his memory." He checked the records and found that the administration had told Congress early in the year that it would build 60,000 new low-income units—not 35,000—by June 30, 1968. Burke failed to see how 70,000 could be twice as many as 60,000. He put the question to a spokesman for Weaver's agency, who checked with the Secretary and then replied that Weaver's claim had been correct; the 60,000 units promised to Congress were the number newly authorized, and not the number that would be "ready for occupancy," the spokesman explained. Again Burke checked the record—and the Credibility Gap widened another notch. The administration testimony on Capitol Hill had described the 60,000 units as those that would be "completed for occupancy" in the current fiscal year. WEAVER'S HOUSING NEWS RAISES SOME QUERIES, said the headline in the Los Angeles *Times*, but the more typical headline in other papers was, HUD TO DOUBLE LOW-COST HOUSING.

Second only to the Vietnam war, the War on Poverty provides the egregious example of government management of the news in the 1960's. Conceived in haste in the early days of the Johnson administration and launched as its major domestic effort—the keystone of the Great Society—the antipoverty program was the subject of a hard-sell campaign unprecedented in Washington. From the beginning, deception was an important weapon in the arsenal of the antipoverty publicists. "Anyone who was involved with the establishment of the War on Poverty knows that it was put together by fiscal mirrors," says Daniel Patrick Moynihan, who *was* involved. Despite the "orgy of tub-thumping" that announced its birth, Moynihan wrote in *Newsday* in 1967, the antipoverty program committed "scarcely a driblet of new money." Furthermore, "even an element of fraud entered the picture: the Bureau of the Budget began calculating interstate highway funds as part of the financial aid going to the cities."

Such realities were, of course, never mentioned in the barrage of publicity that accompanied Johnson's declaration of "unconditional war on poverty" in his first State of the Union message in 1964. Even before the President submitted his initial fund request to Congress—a $962,500,000 proposal that fell considerably short of being unconditional—newspaper and magazine stories were inspired to condition the public to the need for a new federal approach to the plight of the poor. Poverty was escalated. From the invisible national disgrace of Michael Harrington's *Other America* [23] in 1962, it had at last reached the status of a headlined national preoccupation.

The dashing commanding officer of the Peace Corps, Sargent Shriver, who offered the added publicity advantage of being a Kennedy by marriage, was placed in charge of the new federal antipoverty agency, the Office of Economic Opportunity (OEO). From the outset, the imagery was compelling and self-perpetuating. Shriver became the "field general of the War on Poverty," and his subordinates were, of course, "poverty warriors." Before long the military lexicon was running rampant through the speeches, Congressional testimony, press releases, and even intraoffice memos of OEO. An "inspector general's office" was established, similar to those in the armed services. "War maps," replete with multicolored pins, flourished on the walls of OEO offices and were eagerly displayed to reporters. The Pentagon's patented cost-analysis approach to administrative efficiency was adopted, complete with computerization. Whatever the intent of all this gimmickry, its effect was to deceive Americans by creating the widespread impression that total war had been declared on poverty.

When OEO revised its income standard for defining poverty, the new figure was dubbed the second generation definition—a term borrowed from missile technology. Slipping into scientific jargon, Shriver told a House committee in 1966 that the Job Corps had not yet reached "what we call a steady state operation." A year later he was explaining that OEO had only

[23] Michael Harrington, *The Other America* (Baltimore, Penguin, 1962).

achieved some of its goals because "until we reach the critical mass, you might say, we won't get the mass reaction which is necessary." Joseph Kershaw, OEO's former assistant director for research, told Congress that "our programs in OEO have a given throughput." Congressmen found such terminology confusing, but dazzling.

Within the antipoverty agency, there was much talk of "weapons" and "target areas," "delivery systems," and "alternate strategies." Pentagon maps showing the potential destructive impact of a nuclear explosion in a given urban area were redrawn to show the constructive impact of an antipoverty grant. The constant use of the war analogy, OEO officials were convinced, was an effective public relations device. "In the kind of world we live in, in which the greatest part of our budget is going into a war, this war we're fighting almost has to be phrased in dramatic terms to get the public's attention. We can measure this war in terms of our victories, our defeats, our enemies," said Herbert J. Kramer, OEO's director of public affairs. Kramer's former deputy, James F. Kelleher, once told reporters, "While I don't cotton to the war analogy, it's now become a part of the American folklore."

But folklore building needs professional assistance in modern America, and OEO provided it through a public affairs office surpassed in government only by the Pentagon's elaborate press relations apparatus. Kramer, former vice-president in charge of public relations and advertising for the Travelers Insurance Company, brought some fascinating innovations to the long practiced art of Washington press agentry. Operating in fiscal 1967 with what Representative Charles E. Goodell, New York Republican, called a "ballyhoo budget of $2.4 million" and a staff of forty-seven, the public affairs office trumpeted the victories in the poverty trenches, issued rebuttals to critics, conducted seminars for the press, and generally worked long and hard to accentuate the positive about Shriver and all phases of his war. Its most formidable weapon was a massive Xerox copying machine with a firepower of 2,400 news releases an hour, which one staff member proudly described as "the nerve center of our whole operation."

"We're organized in a sense like an in-house advertising agency," Kramer once explained. "It's patterned after my own experience in a seventy-two-man operation in a multiproduct organization." The public affairs office, he elaborated, was organized along vertical, as well as horizontal, lines. Vertically, staff members specialized in information about major OEO programs—the Job Corps, VISTA, Project Head Start, Upward Bound—whose very names were a tribute to the publicists' inventiveness. Much time and effort went into the creation of catchy acronyms—such coinages as Project FIND, for "Friendless, Isolated, Needy, Disabled," described, in typical OEO fashion, as "a new and innovative assault against the problems of the nation's 5,400,000 elderly poor. . . ." Horizontally, the public affairs office assigned specialists in the media—radio-television, graphics, display and publication, public speakers, magazines and supplements, and the daily press. A host of OEO publications, ranging from austere newsletters to slick and elaborate magazines and reports as bulky as telephone directories, were produced primarily for local antipoverty agencies but were also widely disseminated to the press.

The agency's information program was specifically authorized by Congress in the Economic Opportunity Act of 1964, which empowered the director of OEO to distribute "data and information, in such form as he shall deem appropriate, to public agencies, private organizations and the general public." The agency construed this mandate in various ways and with varying degrees of success. A comic book, commissioned from Al Capp, the creator of *Li'l Abner*, was printed in an edition of 501,000 to publicize the Job Corps; more than 435,000 undistributed copies were consigned to gather dust in Washington warehouses. A network rock-'n'-roll television show, featuring a disc jockey who calls himself Murray the K, brought down a storm of Congressional and editorial criticism. In the beginning, Kramer explained, "a tremendous promotion program had to be launched. The techniques of mass communications had to be used almost with a bludgeon effect. . . . We had to create a market. We had to oversell."

The grave question raised by OEO's extravagant merchandising effort is to what extent it has, by raising false hopes, contributed to the fury and frustration to be found in the nation's urban ghettos—and to the Credibility Gap. In the search for causes of the ugly violence that has flared across the country in recent summers, serious students have not over-looked the implications of the antipoverty agency's hard sell. "We raised hopes out of all proportion to our capacity to deliver on our promises," says Moynihan. And Bayard Rustin, chief organizer of the 1963 Civil Rights march on Washington, has written that "if a society is interested in stability, it should either not make promises or it should keep them." The record leaves no doubt that the War on Poverty has failed to keep its promises. Testifying before Congress in 1966, Shriver set 1976 as "the target date for ending poverty in this land." A year later he conceded that "it will take a lot longer than ten years," but almost in the same breath he assured Congress that "we have never exaggerated what we are doing."

Many of OEO's highly publicized early projections came to be dismissed by Shriver and his aides as "visionary" or "unrealistic." The Job Corps, originally planned to enroll 100,000 youths, had about 41,000 in the fall of 1967. Project Head Start, the preschool program launched in 1965 under Mrs. Johnson's personal patronage, was mired in delays and confusion because OEO lacked the funds to meet all the requests its promotion engendered. The need to follow through with educational benefits when Head Start pupils entered the first grade was acknowledged from the beginning of the program, but it was not until July, 1967, that the government announced "launching of the pilot phase of a nationwide follow through program to carry the benefits of Head Start into the regular school system. . . ." Only thirty school districts in the entire nation were designated to take part in the pilot phase. Since costs of the Vietnam war began to rise rapidly in 1966, big cities have been curtailing antipoverty community action programs because available funds have to be spread thinner.

Such setbacks spurred the antipoverty agency to ever more strenuous publicity efforts. OEO conducted seminars on its programs for Washington correspondents and hometown reporters. Correspondents who attended one such session learned later that their publisher had received a personal note from Shriver thanking him for their participation. Articles that met with OEO approval were regularly reproduced and distributed to the media, with form letters signed by Kramer. "This enclosed article was on page one of the Hartford *Times* last week," one such letter said. "In a fairly short piece, I thought, the writer summarized significant local results of the anti-poverty campaign. Perhaps a similar story exists in your community. In any case, I thought this treatment might be of special interest to you. Please feel free to call us at any time." Another letter from Kramer, accompanying a pamphlet in which four "excellent series" were reprinted, concluded, "If you have written or are planning a series of articles, please send us tear sheets for possible inclusion in future reprints." Late in 1966 the Washington bureau of the Newhouse newspapers assigned six reporters to look into various aspects of the War on Poverty. They found successes, as well as failures, and wrote about both. The most favorable article dealt with OEO's efforts in the health field, and inevitably this was the one—and the only one out of seven—that the agency chose to reprint and disseminate.

Much of OEO's manipulation of the news was conceived and executed as much to impress the Congress of the United States as to mislead the public. In the fall of 1966, for example, when Shriver's administrative talents came under Congressional fire, the agency dispatched to its seven regional offices around the country a series of statements by business leaders supporting Shriver. "Suggest these telegrams, together with story guidance, be given immediately to local newspapers and editorial writers as good weekend story indicating that among people who really know administration, Shriver is tops," the regional offices were advised by Washington headquarters. "Important that we try to get this story across."

At least one regional office, in Kansas City, was carried away by the suggestion and dispatched three-and-a-half-page telegrams in praise of Shriver to forty newspapers—including five within Kansas City itself—at a total cost of about $2,900. One recipient, Al Schmahl, managing editor of the Grand Island *Daily Independent* in Nebraska, was sufficiently annoyed to protest to his Congressman, who in turn demanded an investigation by the General Accounting Office. The GAO later reported: "We have been informally advised by Office of Economic Opportunity officials that Mr. Shriver is of the view, apart from any question of legality, that it would be inappropriate to charge public funds with the cost of these telegrams and that the administrative determination in Kansas City to utilize telegraphic means of communication was most injudicious. He has, therefore, determined that appropriated funds will not be utilized to pay for the costs of the telegrams, despite advice from his General Counsel that the use of such funds for this purpose would be legal." Who wound up paying for the telegrams was never made clear by OEO, and no one in government bothered to address himself to the propriety of using a federal agency's publicity apparatus to promote the managerial skills of its director.

The aim of OEO's public affairs office, Kramer has said, was to "maintain a frank and candid relationship with the responsible press," but Washington correspondents who have covered the antipoverty program over the years have had no difficulty recalling occasions when frankness and candor were notably absent. They noted, indeed, striking parallels between the Credibility Gap afflicting the War on Poverty and that involving the Vietnam war. Just as the White House, for example, refused to acknowledge each successive stage of escalation of the Vietnam war, so OEO denied or soft-pedaled its successive retreats. The practice prompted some reporters to suggest a few years ago that the motto of the public affairs office ought to be: "We've Said Right Along That. . . ." Similarly, OEO appointments, even on relatively low staff levels, were announced with fanfare, while significant resignations were passed over in silence.

On occasion, OEO "information" ran directly counter to the facts. When Joseph Loftus of the New York *Times* and Tom Joyce of the Detroit *News* tried to verify reports that VISTA volunteers in Alabama were carrying arms for self-protection, they received a flat denial from OEO's public affairs office. They later verified the story. Similarly denied were reports that Rutgers University consultants to the Job Corps center at Camp Kilmer, New Jersey, were highly dissatisfied with the center's operations. When the consultants issued a scathing report, OEO explained its earlier denials by saying that its contract with the corporation operating the center gave the firm full control over the release of information. Figures released by OEO on Job Corps costs per enrollee were revised substantially upward after they had been challenged in Congress. "I get a little weary of this snow job," Congresswoman Edith Green, the Oregon Democrat, told Shriver when he appeared to testify on his agency's fiscal 1968 authorization bill. And Representative Goodell chimed in, "You people pile propaganda to the skies, but you don't answer our questions."

Though Kramer urged reporters to "go out and look at the program," their access to information was not invariably free and unfettered. When Loftus of the *Times* visited the Kilmer Job Corps center in 1965, he was led around on a guided tour. The camp's public information officer, a former Air Force man, discharged his duties in the best military tradition. John Carmody, who reported extensively on the Job Corps camps for the Washington *Post*, found himself followed by staff members assiduously taking notes. In Washington, reporters who wrote "unauthorized" stories about OEO were questioned about their sources within the agency—and discovered that staff members were interrogated by the Inspector General's office to determine whether they were responsible for leaks. OEO officials challenged the accuracy, integrity—even the sobriety—of reporters who wrote critical articles. In some instances, public denials of stories were followed by private confirmation—from the same officials who issued the denials.

Early in 1966 some OEO staff members believed—and told reporters—that they were under orders to clear with the public affairs office any conversation with a newspaperman. This was the rule then in effect at the Pentagon, but Kramer categorically denied that it applied to the antipoverty agency. "It's not my intention to serve as a thinking man's filter," he said. "I think we have a more open shop here than any other agency in the government." An "absolute misunderstanding" arose, Kramer explained, from a senior staff meeting at which he discussed "the philosophy of communication and maintenance of a full and free flow of information." In the course of the discussion he mentioned leaks "and the detriment they can cause to a program" and suggested that "it would be helpful if someone would let us know when a reporter spoke to him." It was, Kramer added, "a rather innocent request blown out of proportion" and involved "no report, no debriefing, or anything like that. I thought it was little enough to ask." But reporters thought it was too much and lodged protests. The result was a memorandum to OEO's senior staff from Shriver, issued, Kramer said, "at my request." The memo stated: "I would like to reaffirm the press policy of this agency. OEO recognizes that its programs cannot succeed unless they are communicated fully and openly to the American public. The press has demonstrated overwhelming interest in the War on Poverty. It is our desire and policy to support the interest with the most comprehensive possible dissemination of facts and interpretive information. OEO officials responsible for programs and in possession of these facts are available to the press at any time. It is my hope that such officials will continue to regard representatives of the communications media as an indispensable aid to the success of our programs and will make certain that they are furnished with the information they need in reporting the War on Poverty."

The Shriver memorandum, Kramer insisted, was merely a "clarification": "The fact of the matter is that we have always operated on that basis." Nonetheless, it apparently had some effect on relations with the press. "I think the credibility of this agency has increased greatly," Kramer said a few months later.

Shriver, obviously, was under no obligation to clear his press contacts with OEO's public affairs office, but reporters complained that he was often unavailable for comment when they were working on unfavorable stories, though he was generally accessible when the news was good. Shriver, Kramer said, "is his own best PR man." He often presided at news conferences held in OEO's eighth-floor conference room to announce new grants or programs. As a rule, his facile charm on these occasions carried the day, though unpleasant revelations were glossed over in the process. When the Johnson administration's proposed budget for fiscal 1967 was released, Shriver conducted a briefing for the press on OEO's share. The chore could not have been a pleasant one: Only a few months earlier he had been talking about doubling the $1.5 billion budget for the War on Poverty to $3 billion; now the demands of Vietnam had held the amount to only $1.75 billion. Nonetheless, Shriver made the best of it. He called the allocation "a substantial vote of confidence in the work of this agency" and cheerfully announced that "the percentage of increase in expenditure for the Office of Economic Opportunity is, as a matter of fact, larger than that of the Defense Department."

Some of Shriver's news conferences took on the appearance of television variety extravaganzas. Folk singers, star quarterbacks, twenty-game winners, cowboy actors, and full-blooded Indians were persuaded to make guest appearances to say a few kind words about the War on Poverty. At appropriations time, similar productions were mounted for the benefit of wavering Congressmen. A star attraction in 1967 was the Reverend Billy Graham, who went to the Capitol to give Shriver his endorsement. "If you criticize the War on Poverty, you're sacrilegious," grumbled Congresswoman Green.

Only one major misfortune marred Shriver's image as his own—and OEO's—best PR man—the Washington convention in the spring of 1966 of the Citizens Crusade Against Poverty, at which he was booed off the stage and out of the hall by delegates who were angry, disillusioned, and poor. The incident raised significant questions about OEO's publicity effort—indeed, about the whole Great Society merchandising program. Newspaper accounts of the incident jarred the office of public affairs. Particularly resented was the front-page story in the New York *Times* by Nan Robertson, though her account of what had happened differed in no significant respect from other newspaper and wire service reports. In New York, Turner Catledge, the executive editor of the *Times,* received protests against the story. In a long telegram one prominent citizen informed the newspaper that "I resent and object to today's news story" and went on to praise Shriver as a man who "to the best of my knowledge has never ducked out of any meeting in his life including yesterday's." Another, shorter telegram advised the *Times* that Shriver had "conducted himself with calm, dignity and decorum." Neither sender mentioned the fact that his message to the *Times* had been encouraged—in fact, solicited—by OEO or that others had been importuned to send similar protests but had refused.

Shriver blamed "professional demonstrators" for the incident, but there were other appraisals that laid the blame closer to the door of OEO's in-house advertising agency. Walter Reuther, the chairman of the Citizens Crusade Against Poverty, was quoted as pointing out that the demonstrators started booing as "Shriver was trying to overwhelm them with success statistics. They released their anger and their deepest frustrations at not seeing results." The shouts of the protesters lent weight to Reuther's assessment. "Tell us where the poor are being helped," one woman screamed. "It's just a big publicity deal." "Shriver tells us what has been done, but what about what hasn't been done?" another shouted. The Washington *Post* commented in an editorial that Shriver "was hearing from the people who have taken literally every word of every official pronouncement. These true believers now consider themselves betrayed, for the performance turns out to be less splendid than the promise."

Haynes Johnson, writing in the Washington *Evening Star*, had a similar thought. In its early planning stages, he recalled, the War on Poverty "was viewed only as a beginning, and an experimental one at that. Yet from the beginning the program was sold as if it were the remedy. The program has suffered from too much, and too effective, salesmanship. As a consequence it is, in part, a captive of its own promises."

And the nation is a captive of its promises, too. There are Americans who believe that their government has, indeed, waged "unconditional war on poverty" and is winning that war. It isn't true, but those who believe it are understandably baffled by the riots in the streets. Other Americans believe the War on Poverty has been fought and lost. That isn't true either, but those who believe it wonder why still more money is to be "squandered on the poor." And then there are those who no longer believe their government. Many of them are poor, and some riot in the streets. "When the electorate no longer trusts the government," Arthur Krock observed, "the deterioration of public order begins."

9. To Close the Gap

How to get at the truth in Washington? One way is to search through the reams of official rhetoric for the internal conflicts and contradictions that occasionally offer glimpses of reality. The government is fallible, even in its efforts to suppress or manipulate the news, and sooner or later—though often later than the best interests of the nation dictate—the facts the public needs to know are brought to light. Conscientious correspondents have become, in the words of Peter Lisagor, Washington bureau chief of the Chicago *Daily News,* "nuance detectors" attuned to the subtle shades of meaning that may disclose a shift in policy or a new decision the administration is not yet ready to divulge. The process is an arduous and risky one, but it has its rewards. Take, for example, the case of the missing "whatever."

On the afternoon of Wednesday, May 18, 1967, President Johnson summoned White House reporters into his Oval Office for an impromptu news conference. Newspaper stories in the preceding day or two had reported that rising costs of the Vietnam war were likely to add $4 billion or $5 billion to the administration's budget estimates. Johnson was asked for his current budget estimate, and he replied: "We don't have any. We will just say without being critical of anyone—I want to tread very lightly now because I don't want to touch any sensitive toes—that the stories I have read are without any basis whatever in fact." That, at least, was the way the President's answer was recorded in the reporters' notebooks. But when the official transcript—supposedly a verbatim record of the President's remarks—was distributed to correspondents an hour later, the word "whatever" had been deleted. Those who noticed the omission concluded that the stories did, indeed, have a basis in fact and that Johnson had, on reflection, softened his denial. Three months later, speculation turned into fact when the President announced that additional troop commitments to Vietnam would cost an estimated $4.5 billion.

In the topsy-turvy world of Washington news coverage, an absolutely firm denial is often the best confirmation that can be obtained; a graciously regretful acceptance of a resignation may denote that an official has been fired; an effusive display of harmony possibly—indeed, probably—points to the existence of deep, but hidden, disagreements. If that sounds cynical—well, Washington reporters have much to be cynical about. Seldom, for instance, have they witnessed such a show of total accord as the one staged by the President in the White House sitting room on July 12, 1967. Seated on a green sofa were Defense Secretary McNamara; General Westmoreland, the American military commander in Vietnam; and General Earle G. Wheeler, Chairman of the Joint Chiefs of Staff. The President, sitting in an armchair to their left, assured the assembled correspondents that published reports to the contrary notwithstanding, there was absolute unanimity within the administration on the number of new troops to be sent to Vietnam. "The troops that General Westmoreland needs and requests, as we feel it necessary, will be supplied," Johnson said. "Is that not true, General Westmoreland?"

"I agree, Mr. President."

"General Wheeler?"

"That is correct, Mr. President."

"Secretary McNamara?"

"Yes, sir."

The chorus of unity barely concealed the discord, for, as William Beecher subsequently reported in the New York *Times*, Westmoreland had asked for an increase of at least 70,000 men, while McNamara had recommended a top figure of 30,000. The President, characteristically, split the difference at 45,000. A few weeks later, when the generals rose in almost open insurrection against the administration's bombing policies toward North Vietnam, Johnson again erected a façade of harmony in the face of manifest evidence to the contrary.

"I don't think we're going to have a healthy relationship between press and President—with mutual respect and lessened hostility—until Mr. Johnson is convinced that Presidents of the United States must tell the truth, and nothing but the whole, unvarnished truth," says Charles Roberts, *Newsweek*'s White House correspondent. "We do not want fraternization—only full disclosure within the bounds of national security. We do not want to be captivated by the President's charm any more than we want to be intimidated by his anger." Johnson's press relations, Roberts observes, "are important, not just for the newsmen or the President but for our national security." The Presidency is "too important an office to be covered by an habitually disgruntled press," he says. "And the role of the press in covering the President is too important for the President continually to deride and derogate it."

The duty of a free press in a free society has never been more eloquently stated than it was in the *Times* of London more than a century ago. It declared: "The purposes and duties of the [Ministers of the Crown and of the Press] are constantly separate, generally independent, sometimes diametrically opposite. . . . The Press can enter into no close or binding alliances with the statesmen of the day, nor can it surrender its permanent interests to the convenience of the ephemeral power of any Government. The first duty of the Press is to obtain the earliest and most correct intelligence of the events of the time, and instantly, by disclosing them, to make them the common property of the nation. The statesman collects his information secretly and by secret means; he keeps back even the current intelligence of the day with ludicrous precautions. . . . The Press lives by disclosures."

The press enjoys a unique and privileged status in American life; it is the only private, profit-making institution whose freedom from government restraint is guaranteed by the Bill of Rights. The Founding Fathers recognized, as enlightened men everywhere have long recognized, that the press has an indispensable function as the public's monitor on government. It is a responsibility that has always been imperfectly discharged. In recent years, as the pressures of official secrecy and deception have mounted, as the "ludicrous precautions" have multiplied, and as the nation's highest elected and appointed officials have resorted to outright falsehood, the news media have performed with all too little distinction as the guardians of the public's right to know. With only a few notable exceptions, the press has been acquiescent rather than enterprising, docile rather than intransigent, in the face of unprecedented efforts to suppress the news. Editors and publishers—the men who run the media—have, by and large, been content to produce sonorous freedom-of-information resolutions at their annual conventions. And altogether too many of the reporters, the men in the front lines, have turned aside from the battle.

To cope with the enormous flow of news in Washington today is a formidable assignment. To look beyond the handouts and to dig below the obvious are challenges to any correspondent's enterprise and ingenuity. But the fact that some reporters rise to the challenge proves that it can be done—and the fact that many do not demonstrates that more than physical limitations of time and energy impede the news-gathering process. Clark R. Mollenhoff, an investigative reporter for the Cowles publications, has pointed out that the Washington correspondent has the choice of becoming either a watchdog or a lapdog. "I am not being critical of all political figures when I say that all political figures will, to some degree, use public relations gimmicks to make themselves look better than they are," Mollenhoff said in a lecture at the University of Iowa. "I am being critical of the newsmen who take part in presenting one-sided hero images of high public officials, and end up as little more than high-level handout collectors. This may be a most convenient way to become the favorite columnist or the favorite reporter of public figures from the county courthouse to the White House. However, it is not filling the role that the press must fill if it is to be a true watchdog on government."

There is, Mollenhoff added, "an overabundance of Washington newsmen who are afraid of the frown from the President, and who wince at an unkind word from other high government figures. There are too few men who are willing to be identified as an 'unfriendly questioner.' There are too few who are willing to be singled out as fighting for any principles. 'Crusader' has even become a derogatory term in some newspaper circles.

When a White House invitation becomes more important than aggressive reporting, the watchdog has become a lapdog. When general popularity with political figures is more important than principle, the watchdog is dead."

Some practices have grown up in Washington that tend to destroy the semblance, if not the substance, of reportorial independence and objectivity. Correspondents who cover the State Department can pick up pin money by making occasional broadcasts for the Voice of America. Pentagon correspondents have been offered tempting trips to London, Paris, Berlin, Istanbul, Athens, Oslo, San Juan, and Saigon at government expense, and though some news organizations flatly bar participation of their staff members in such junkets, many do not. It would be unfair and inaccurate to suggest that every newsman who has been paid for a Voice broadcast or who has accepted a Pentagon tour has sold out his right to take an independent stance. There is no question, however, that he has cast doubt on his credentials.

A hoary British jingle aptly sums up one aspect of the problem. It goes:

> No power on earth can bribe or twist,
> Thank God, the British journalist.
> But seeing what the man will do
> Unbribed, there's no occasion to.

All too many correspondents assume, after a while, the protective coloration of the beats they cover. After years of reporting from the Senate press gallery, for example, a correspondent is likely to think of himself more as part of the Senate than as part of the press. Jim McCartney of the Chicago *Daily News* called this the "vested interest" problem when he discussed it a few years ago in *Nieman Reports*: "In the Pentagon," he states, "it is commonplace for reporters to make alliances with one or another of the armed services, presenting by and large that particular service's views on highly controversial problems of national defense." In McCartney's terms, the counterparts of Mollenhoff's lapdogs and watchdogs are called ins and outs. Each type of reporter, he notes, is likely to be found on almost any beat in Washington. "The ins," he says, "are those who play along with the news sources, handle it their way, tend to overlook minor indiscretions and in general protect their sources. The outs fight their sources, or at least needle them. They get their news by insisting on their right to it by sheer perseverence. . . ."

Writing on the basis of his experiences in the Eisenhower and Kennedy administrations, McCartney observes: "Just plain fear may play a role in White House reporting. The awesome power of the presidency is, indeed, something to contemplate and few reporters relish the thought of arousing presidential anger. The tendency even in presidential press conferences is to throw the President home run balls rather than curve balls. It takes a man of some moral courage to brave the possibility of presidential ire or of presidential sarcasm before a national television audience. But the fact is that controversial questions often are simply not asked at presidential press conferences. If they are, one may be sure that White House staff members will not fail to make a mental note of the questioner. The next time the questioner makes an inquiry for his paper at the White House on a routine matter he may find staff members unavailable—for days. . . ."

Since the beginning of the cold war, substantial and significant areas of government have become virtually off limits to the press. When the U-2 spy plane erupted into headlines in 1960, an editor of a major daily newspaper confided that he had known about the overflights of Soviet territory for several years but had withheld the news "in the national interest." Would the national interest have been better served by disclosure? Would publication of the Bay of Pigs invasion plans have averted a disaster? Would the official concealment and deception practiced in these instances have been susceptible to challenge if Francis Gary Powers had completed his flight or if the Cuban invasion had succeeded? There is no broad consensus in the press corps on the answers to these questions. In the fall, 1967, issue of the *Columbia University Forum*, Victor Bernstein and Jesse Gordon told how the editors of the *Nation* tried, in November, 1960, to interest all major news media in an article suggesting that plans for a U.S.-backed invasion of Cuba were well advanced; they found no takers for the story. In the wake

of the Bay of Pigs fiasco the New York *Times* editorialized:
"The Cuban tragedy has raised a domestic question that is
likely to come up again and again until it is solved. The cause
may be something that is happening in Laos, in Central Africa
or in Latin America, but the question remains the same: is a
democratic government in an open society such as ours ever
justified in deceiving its own people? . . . A democracy—our
democracy—cannot be lied to. . . . The basic principle is that of
confidence."

Yet there is reason to doubt that this lesson has been learned.
In the spring of 1967 it fell to *Ramparts,* a rambunctious but—
up to that point—obscure West Coast monthly, to reveal that
the Central Intelligence Agency had secretly been subsidizing
the National Student Association. Once the news was out,
Washington correspondents did a creditable job of running
down other covert CIA subsidies to American institutions and
organizations. But it reflected little credit on them that this
sensational and significant story had been under their very
noses for fifteen years. At least one Washington bureau had
advance knowledge of the *Ramparts* exposé—and timidly decided to let the magazine have the scoop.

What can be done to close the Credibility Gap? There has
been no shortage of proposals from various quarters in government, the press, and the public. Many of them center on that
great bureaucratic panacea, the committee or commission.
Pierre Salinger, who believes most problems of news management grow out of the "subtle area" of national security, has
revived the idea first advanced by Kennedy after the Bay of
Pigs for a joint press-government conference to study the issue
and perhaps establish a voluntary censorship operation. "There
has been no march on Washington to get it accomplished,"
Salinger concedes—and there should be none. The editors and
publishers to whom Kennedy submitted his plan, CBS news
correspondent Walter Cronkite has observed, were "correctly
suspicious of such overtures." To involve the media in the news
management process—or even to cast them in the role of advisers
to the government on information matters—"is an involvement
that strips them of the impartiality required to serve properly
their charge in our democracy," Cronkite told members of the
Inland Daily Press Association in 1966.

Cronkite offered a proposal of his own: He suggested that the House Foreign Operations and Government Information Subcommittee, better known as the Moss Committee for its chairman, California Democratic Representative John Moss, should be constituted as a "people's court" to which the media could carry cases of news management or suppression. But the history of the Moss Committee offers little encouragement to those who would look to Congress as the guarantor of the people's right to know. It performed with telling effectiveness in the Eisenhower administration but lost its zeal when the Presidency passed into Democratic hands. Robert O. Blanchard, acting chairman of the journalism department at American University in Washington, has called the committee "a watchdog in decline" and documented the case in a doctoral dissertation condensed in the summer, 1966, issue of the *Columbia Journalism Review*. "To measure the Moss Committee's decline as a watchdog," Blanchard wrote, "one may point to the quality and quantity of hearings—the major source of all other subcommittee publications. From November 7, 1955, to April 23, 1959, the subcommittee held seventeen hearings, many of them vigorously critical of the Eisenhower administration's security and information policies." After Kennedy's inauguration, Blanchard noted, no further hearings were held until 1963. "After breaking this four-year silence, the Moss Committee conducted seven hearings connected with information issues. Significantly, however, these hearings were not part of the 'availability of information' series started during the Eisenhower administration. The first five Kennedy administration hearings were labeled 'Government Information Plans and Policies.' Moss was no longer attacking barriers but seeking 'guidelines which can and should be imposed on information during periods of crisis.' " Moss, Blanchard pointed out, had risen rapidly in the House leadership during this period and "is now within eventual striking distance of the House Speakership. One does not, as a party leader, unduly, unnecessarily, or willingly embarrass or challenge party leadership when it is in the White House."

Moss called Blanchard's research "extraordinarily faulty," his facts "a fantasy," and his conclusions "erroneous." The Johnson administration, the California Congressman told Saul Pett of the Associated Press, "has a reputation for an almost perfect score in not abusing the handling or withholding of information." So much for the "people's court."

The chief product of the Moss Committee's recent labors was the Federal Public Records Law enacted, after many delays, in 1966. The measure, substantially diluted at the administration's insistence, went into effect on July 4, 1967. It requires that disclosure of information be the general rule, not the exception, among federal agencies and puts the burden of proof on the government to justify the withholding of news. However, the law also provides nine major categories of exceptions, including provisions designed to ensure the right of privacy, safeguard the public interest, and protect trade secrets of firms whose products are subject to government review. "Some agencies appeared to be making a maximum effort to push such exemptions to the limit," the Washington *Post* reported as the law went into effect. The Department of Health, Education, and Welfare, for example, declared exempt "records of correspondence between federal and state or local officials, privileged through custom or usage or where disclosure might prejudice negotiations in progress." "Privileged through custom or usage" could mean, of course, anything that was kept secret before the law was put in force.

In August, 1967, columnists Rowland Evans and Robert Novak reported that the Defense Department was trying to suppress a report by Assistant Secretary of the Air Force Robert H. Charles casting doubts on the government's generous financing arrangements for the supersonic transport plane. They wrote: "Although the Charles report is well known inside the administration, Pentagon bureaucrats flirt with violation of the new freedom-of-information law and refuse to make it public. They contend this was Charles's personal effort (although they acknowledge that the Charles report became an Air Force working paper) and therefore doesn't rank as an official document."

The information law was credited with prompting Secretary McNamara to abolish the Pentagon's five-year-old rule requiring Defense officials to report the substance of all press contacts to the public information office "before the close of business that day." But in the memorandum rescinding the rule, McNamara offered an intriguing explanation for his action. "While there will always be some degree of parochialism," he wrote, "special pleading by special interests has largely been ended within the department." The rule "has served its purpose and it is rescinded immediately," McNamara continued. "In other words," Neil Sheehan observed in the New York *Times* for October 22, 1967, "officials were now so well indoctrinated that McNamara did not have to worry about subordinates expressing disturbing and possibly independent opinions to journalists. The rule has, in fact, 'served its purpose' and reporters have noticed no perceptible change since its abolition. Pentagon officials are as cautious as ever and most still have a public information officer present to protect themselves."

The Associated Press, in a survey of the reaction of government information men to the new law, found that "few of them expect important changes in the way they disclose public records." One official told the AP, "I don't see three cents' worth of difference." With respect to those files not specifically exempted from disclosure by the law, the AP reported, "many agencies said in the survey that they had been making them available to the public all along. A typical comment in this regard came from George Christian, the White House press secretary, who said, 'We give you everything that isn't classified.' Christian noted that routine working papers were stamped 'for administrative use only,' which in effect makes them secret. It came to light recently that one White House aide was stamping newspaper clippings 'confidential.' "

No citizens' committee and no act of Congress can cope effectively with today's crisis in credibility. No ready gimmick is at hand to induce candor in a government deeply, increasingly committed to conducting its affairs behind a curtain of secrecy or in the disguise of deception. Perhaps a first, modest step back to credibility would be the return of the regular, scheduled, no-holds-barred news conference that served in earlier administrations as the principal vehicle of communication between the President and the public. It is an imperfect device, to be sure, but it is the best yet devised in the United States to elicit information from the executive branch. "If the President would hold one pre-announced, live TV news conference every fortnight instead of three unannounced quickies a week (and not consume most of them reading prepared announcements), then the reporters would ask more intelligent questions," says Charles Roberts. That would be a start.

But the basic problem will not be solved until there is full and frank acknowledgment that it exists. The easy answer when the question of credibility is raised is the cynical one: Governments always lie. Washington abounds today in supporters of President Johnson whose defense of the Credibility Gap is that John F. Kennedy practiced news management; in Democrats who point out that Republican Presidents have also lied; in patriots who righteously cite the falsehoods of foreign governments. All this may well be true, but it all is irrelevant. The crisis is now, it is here in the United States, and there is growing evidence that it is grave. "Everything secret degenerates," Lord Acton observed, "even the administration of justice; nothing is safe that does not show it can bear discussion and publicity."

Nothing is safe—not even the government of the United States—when the citizens who are its sovereigns are told so little of what they need to know, and can believe so little of what they are told. Official secrecy and deception do not produce pliant, cheerful, obedient subjects—at least, not in America. They do produce suspicious, frustrated, cynical, or apathetic citizens, many of whom are losing faith in the workings of democracy.

One who has confidence in the democratic process must assume that in due time an aroused citizenry will demand candor and truthfulness from public officials—and that the demand will be met. But in the process the prime responsibility rests, as it always has, with the public's representatives, the press. The press will meet its obligation and render its greatest service to America when it makes it unmistakably clear to its government and to its public that it will not accept, it will not believe, it will not publish—as it has done too often in the past—anything but the truth.

Appendix A

Dwight D. Eisenhower Meets the Press

The Presidential press conference came into its own in the Eisenhower administration. For the first time, television cameras were admitted to the proceedings, and overnight many millions of Americans were initiated into the mysteries of the press conference. President Eisenhower was from the beginning an outstanding performer on TV.

The following are excerpts from the official transcript of a news conference Eisenhower held on Wednesday, August 1, 1956. The site was the ornate Indian Treaty Room of the Executive Office Building, next door to the White House. The President had just recovered from his ileitis operation, the Republican nominating convention was in the offing, and correspondents pressed Eisenhower on the state of his health, his plans to seek election to a second term, and his desire to retain Vice-President Richard M. Nixon as his running mate. The questions and the President's answers produced what *Life* magazine later called "perhaps the frankest, most searching interview since Wilson inaugurated regular conferences in 1913."

PRESIDENT EISENHOWER: Please sit down. It's been quite a while since I visited with you. And one of the latest incidents in my own activities was my visit to Panama, which I would like to mention briefly.

It was a unique sort of visit, as you know, and one from which I personally felt I derived a tremendous profit of knowledge and understanding, and I am certain that the other heads of state there did the same. It is the kind of meeting which I am convinced could, with benefit to all, be held—not often—but at reasonable periods. Of course, it's always awkward to arrange a meeting like that to which heads of states can go.

I understand that now, guests of the State Department here this morning, are a number of reporters from the Latin American countries. And I want to assure them of my personal and official welcome to them, and I hope they have a fine time in our country, and learn something of us, as I know I did of Panama.

I think we shall go to questions.

MARVIN L. ARROWSMITH OF THE ASSOCIATED PRESS: Mr. President, would you tell us how you feel about Harold Stassen's campaign to block the nomination of Vice President [Richard M.] Nixon, and to put Gov. [Christian A.] Herter [of Massachusetts] on the ticket in his place? And can you tell us what you said to Stassen when he first informed you of his plan?

THE PRESIDENT: Well, to answer your last part first, I said very little, because Mr. Stassen didn't come to me for advice. He came to tell me what he expected to do.

And, as you know, I firmly believe in the right of any American citizen to express his own political beliefs and political preferences as he chooses. This applies to me as well as to the Vice President; and the Vice President has assured me of the same kind of thinking himself.

Now, Mr. Stassen said that. I assured him that that was his right as far as I was concerned, but he had to do it as an individual not as any member of my official family; that he had to make that distinction very clear.

A little later I think he found he probably—and I am speculating a little—but apparently he found that he had stirred up more of a storm than he had anticipated. And he came to me and said in order to carry out his purpose of separating his efforts from the Administration and from the White House, he wanted to ask for a leave, which I personally thought was a wise act on his part, and I promptly approved. And he is on leave and will remain on leave as long as he is working for this.

Now, as to my feelings about it, I say my feeling is he has got a right to do, to express himself, as any other American has.

EDWARD T. FOLLIARD OF THE WASHINGTON *Post*: Mr. President, do you feel that you have committed yourself to Vice President Nixon as your running mate this year?

THE PRESIDENT: Well, Mr. Folliard, I am not exactly sure what you mean by "committed yourself."

I have expressed my opinion in front of this body of Dick Nixon so often that I think there should be no doubt about my satisfaction with him as a running mate. But I have also said I am not even nominated yet; you must not forget that. (Laughter.)

And I do uphold the right of the delegates to the convention to nominate whom they choose.

I believe I once said here if any man were nominated as Vice President that the President felt he could not, in good conscience, run with, he would have just one recourse: to submit his own resignation.

Q: Mr. Stassen is going on the assumption that your position is now what it was on February 29, that is, that the No. 2 place on the ticket would remain open until the convention, until the No. 1 nominee had been selected.

THE PRESIDENT: I think it is open. Mr. Nixon himself said to me that the last thing that he hoped anyone would consider was that this was a cut and dried affair, and that we were trying to foreclose the delegates their right to choose whom they please. He said that within my own office within the last few days.

So I have said, I think I made myself so clear on this subject time and again, that there is really nothing more to be said about it that I can add to it.

ANDREW F. TULLY, JR., OF THE SCRIPPS-HOWARD NEWSPAPERS: Mr. President, in 1952 you had a list of names of men who would be acceptable to you as a Vice-Presidential candidate.

THE PRESIDENT: Yes.

Q: Do you have such a list today?

THE PRESIDENT: I haven't made any up yet.

But I might say a little further to that question, if I did I would not by any manner of means ever give it to anyone except on the most confidential basis, because I certainly would not be drawn into the great error of saying I would run with this man, with this man, with this man, and finally get to someone and I said, "No, I would not do it."

Q: Sir, can I ask if you are planning to make up such a list before the convention?

THE PRESIDENT: I haven't any idea.

MERRIMAN SMITH OF THE UNITED PRESS: Mr. President, some

weeks ago you said that if anyone ever proposed a dump Nixon movement, that you would create quite a commotion in your office.

Have you created such a commotion in the wake of Mr. Stassen's recommendation?

THE PRESIDENT: No, no one ever proposed to me that I ever dump Mr. Nixon. No one, I think, would have the effrontery.

MRS. MAY CRAIG OF THE PORTLAND (MAINE) *Press Herald*: Mr. Stassen said, in announcing his preference for Herter on the ticket, that large portions of our populace overseas, and uncommitted nations would prefer an Eisenhower-Herter ticket. Aside from commenting on Stassen, do you believe an Eisenhower-Nixon ticket would not have the support of people overseas, and would be detrimental to you in relation to uncommitted nations?

THE PRESIDENT: Well, I haven't any source of information, Mrs. Craig, that would allow me to make a positive answer to such a thing. But this is what I do have: As you know, I have sent the Vice President on innumerable trips, and from every country, both from the people, the citizens of that country, and from Americans in the country, I have received only the most glowing reports of his acceptability while there. Now, that's all I have on it.

CHARLES S. VON FREMD OF THE COLUMBIA BROADCASTING SYSTEM: Mr. President, would you be equally pleased, sir, to have some other well-qualified Republican, other than the Vice President, as your running mate this year?

THE PRESIDENT: I am not going into comparisons at all.

THOMAS N. SCHROTH OF THE *Congressional Quarterly*: Mr. President, in its annual analysis of your legislative program, *Congressional Quarterly* found this session of Congress acted favorably on 103 of your 224 specific requests.

The Republican-controlled Eighty-third Congress did considerably better than that.

Considering the substance of the legislation passed as well as the amount, what is your—were you satisfied with the performance of Congress this year on your legislative program?

THE PRESIDENT: Well, with respect to this Congress I have more than one emotion. In certain respects I was highly pleased. In some I was most regretful; and in some I was frankly disappointed.

There were essential parts of the program that I had laid out in my State of the Union speech that were enacted into law. For that I was highly pleased, I was grateful.

There were other parts that seemed to me were handled in such a way as to delay their enactment for a long time: the farm program, the road program which I wanted to get busy on; and I regretted that delay.

And there were other parts that we didn't get at all, particularly some of them that applied to human welfare. For example, we didn't get the school program. We didn't get reinsurance for sickness, that sort of thing. There is a whole list of the things we didn't get, which I could have the press section give you in detail. But it is one of those human things you can't be—you are never completely satisfied, I am sure.

ROSCOE DRUMMOND OF THE NEW YORK *Herald Tribune*: Mr. President, would you give just your own report on how you feel, and on your decision to remain in the race after the operation?

THE PRESIDENT: Well, I don't mind telling you this much and, of course, I mean as far as I know I can tell you everything on it, but I don't know everything.

Like anybody else, my condition has to be determined for me somewhat by the doctors. As far as I—my feelings—are concerned, from the day I was operated on—and you must remember I was in— I was having a pretty rough ride there for two or three days—from that day on I have improved every day.

Now, the doctors warned me at that time it would be certainly four months before I would feel myself, would really want to do the things I have been accustomed to doing. But as far as I know, I have improved every day, and I have nothing that keeps me from going ahead and doing my work.

When I get home they come in—one of them, my personal physician—come in, look me over, and say I am in good shape.

Now I feel good, but I don't feel as well as I did a year ago at this time.

*   *   *

EDWARD P. MORGAN OF THE AMERICAN BROADCASTING COMPANY: Mr. President, there must be times, sir, when you recoil against the constant probing into your personal affairs, and I ask this question in that light.

There have been repeated reports, sir, that you have been suffering since the operation from some kind of dysentery-like disturbance. Is that true?

THE PRESIDENT: No. As a matter of fact, they warned me that I should have a little of that and I never did. They remarked on it several times and I never did.

RICHARD L. WILSON OF COWLES PUBLICATIONS: Mr. President, do you think that Mr. Nixon would detract from the strength of the Republican ticket this fall?

THE PRESIDENT: Well, I don't know, Mr. Wilson, because people go by many different guides with which I am not familiar.

But I can say this: He certainly didn't seem to in 1952, and I can't believe that the United States does not consider that Mr. Nixon has made a splendid record as Vice President in these past four years. Now that's—

Q: Would you oppose a poll to determine whether or not he has strength and will not subtract—

THE PRESIDENT: I don't oppose any poll. I see they are made all the time. I don't think it makes any difference whether I oppose them or not.

Q: Do you think it makes any sense to have one?

THE PRESIDENT: Well, again, I don't believe it makes much difference. I think they will probably have one anyway, don't you? (Laughter.)

RAYMOND P. BRANDT OF THE ST. LOUIS *Post-Dispatch*: Mr. President, Mr. Stassen was compelled to speak as an individual. Other members of the Cabinet or of Cabinet rank came out for Mr. Nixon. Was that because you regard Mr. Nixon as a member of the team?

THE PRESIDENT: Well, at that time, you remember, I mentioned Mr. Nixon myself because he was then occupying the position, and I thought it was only proper and appropriate that in front of such a body as this that I should express my complete satisfaction with him, as I would about Mr. [George M.] Humphrey [Secretary of the Treasury], of Mr. [Marion B.] Folsom [Secretary of Health, Education, and Welfare], or anybody else in my official family.

Now, when you go beyond that, we begin to get into a field which I don't care to venture because eventually I would be doing somebody an injustice.

Q: Well, the point is, you and the Cabinet seem to have given the candidacy of Mr. Nixon your tacit consent.

THE PRESIDENT: I—well, certainly given it consent.

Remember this, though, none of us is conducting a campaign for anybody.

Now, Mr. Stassen, as I understand it, says he is going out to conduct a campaign; and that is a different story.

FLETCHER KNEBEL OF COWLES PUBLICATIONS: Mr. President, do you have a preference for your running mate?

THE PRESIDENT: I think that is a question—as Mr. Morgan says, there are certain of my personal likes and dislikes I can keep to myself.

PETER LISAGOR OF THE CHICAGO *Daily News*: In the light of what you said about your health, would you have any personal objections to your doctors having a press conference?

THE PRESIDENT: Well, I don't know that I have any personal objection, but I understand they had one this morning—so I—I didn't know anything about it—but they had it. So—

MRS. CRAIG: We didn't either.

THE PRESIDENT: Well, it was some place; isn't that true? Some of you must have been there.

JOHN L. STEELE OF *Time* MAGAZINE: Mr. President, you told us in the past that you would be happy to have Vice President Nixon as your running mate, if that is the will of the convention.

Does that pertain, too, to Governor Herter if that should be the will of the convention?

THE PRESIDENT: I told you I would not go beyond Mr. Nixon in this regard because he now occupies the position, and did occupy it when I made my statement.

If I go beyond that, inevitably I am called upon to comment on someone whose name has not probably been mentioned, but where I might have reservations. So I am not going to comment beyond that.

RUSSELL BAKER OF THE NEW YORK *Times*: Could you tell us whether you underwent a long period of indecision after your operation as to whether you would stay in the race, and when you made that decision firmly?

THE PRESIDENT: Well, you must remember this: When you're hurting like I was at that moment you don't read the papers, so I didn't know how much renewed interest had been stirred up in this thing.

As far as I was concerned—and as far—and this is what the doctors told me—I was suffering from a chronic ailment that had probably begun some thirty years ago—this was after the operation.

You see, the difficulty I had was a disease of young people. There is only five—I believe I am the fifth case that is of record where anybody sixty-five years old ever had this.

So all they said was they had corrected a condition that existed with me for a long time, and I was going to be a lot better. So it never occurred to me there was ever any renewed question.

I didn't begin to have any of this period of indecision you talk about, or doubt, until I got out and read the papers. (Laughter.)

And I have told some of you people at times about the so-called Battle of the Bulge. I didn't get frightened until three weeks after it had begun when I began to read the American papers and found out (laughter) how near we were to being whipped.

Well now, this had a little bit of that same thing, because I had at that moment no question on my mind. I was merely being improved, not hurt, except that I did hurt physically.

DAVID P. SENTNER OF THE HEARST NEWSPAPERS: Mr. President, have you had any discussions with Vice President Nixon or sent him any word regarding the Stassen anti-Nixon campaign or your attitude toward it.

THE PRESIDENT: Mr. Nixon was in my office, what, about three days ago. We had a long talk and, of course, we mentioned it casually. There was no point in making it a great matter of debate.

Mr. Nixon, like myself, considers this anyone's privilege, and I believe it was, I believe it was the day—well, I don't know, I am not going to guess on what day it was—but it was a very casual and not an important conversation on the matter.

*   *   *

WILLIAM McGAFFIN OF THE CHICAGO *Daily News*: Mr. President, this again is one of those personal questions about your health, sir, but I think, perhaps, you don't realize the impact it's had on the people of the country, your having the attack of ileitis and the operation, and a major operation after your heart attack, and when we were all in Gettysburg, for instance, I went around and talked to a number of your friends and neighbors to ask them how they felt about your running again.

Well, they all love you, as you know, and they said they are going to vote for you; but really they wished that you wouldn't run because they feel you have done enough for the nation, you have made so many sacrifices and, sir, they are afraid that you won't last out, they are afraid you won't live for another four years.

THE PRESIDENT: Well, sir, I would tell you, frankly, I don't think it is too important to the individual how his end comes, and certainly he can't dictate the time.

What we are talking about here is the importance to the country, and it happens that at this moment the Republican party apparently thinks I am still important to them and to the country. And since I believe so much in the Republican party, and I believe that it needed rebuilding so badly, an effort which I have been making, as you well know, I said I would continue to try.

But this is a decision that the American people are going to have to face. I am flattered by what you tell me about my friends and neighbors at Gettysburg, but I have made up my mind this is the thing I should try, and we will see what the American people have to say about it.

*   *   *

ELIZABETH S. CARPENTER OF THE HOUSTON *Post*: Mr. President, the current primaries in the South are bringing a rather alarming outburst of violent talk on the race issue and I wonder if you feel that candidates who cater to this kind of talk do a disservice to their country?

THE PRESIDENT: Miss Carpenter, I believe that anyone that stirs up racial hatreds, other antagonisms that are based upon race or religion or differences in basic philosophy, it is always a mistake. It is a very grave error and a disservice to the United States. Extreme statements of this kind can do no one any good.

The path of human progress is not along the path of hatreds; it is not along the path of the extremes. It is along the path that represents the road where people of good will and real sensibilities can get together and say, "Here is a way we can go together."

Now, I deplore with—just as earnestly as I know how, every kind of thing that you describe. I didn't know actually it was going on at such a degree to create comment, and I am sorry.

JAMES RESTON OF THE NEW YORK *Times*: Mr. President, in the light of what you have said about Mr. Nixon this morning, and your failure to comment about other candidates for the Vice Presidency, is it not inevitable that we should conclude that Mr. Nixon is your preference?

THE PRESIDENT: Well, you have a right to conclude what you please. (Laughter.) But I have said that I would not express a preference, I have expressed—I have said—he is perfectly acceptable to me, as he was in 1952. But I am not going beyond that because in 1952 I also put down a few others that were equally acceptable to me. So I see no reason why you draw the conclusion, but you may if you so choose.

CHALMERS M. ROBERTS OF THE WASHINGTON *Post*: Mr. President, during your illness there was considerable excitement, both here and abroad, over views credited to Admiral [Arthur W.] Radford [Chairman of the United States Joint Chiefs] that the Pentagon was thinking of cutting our armed forces further by as much as 900,000 men in the next, over the next few fiscal years.

Have you discussed this with the Admiral, and could you give us your own views on this problem?

THE PRESIDENT: I have never heard of such a proposal made on any serious basis.

On the other hand, I recall the 1953 effort to produce a changed attitude toward our defense services; to stress new weapons, to stress the modern means of delivery of fire power, and to minimize, so far as we could, the use of individuals who could better be employed in building roads and schools and other things necessary.

Now, that same thought has been pursued around the world. We have only in the last few months, we have seen the Soviets announce their determination of cutting strength, but it certainly is not with any idea that they are cutting their total striking and defensive power.

So I will say only this: I would hope that we can progress in this direction of substituting power, speed, mobility, flexibility for just men, taken away from their homes and in the—and serving in the armed services.

Q: Sir, in that—

THE PRESIDENT: I think that is all I have to say.

HERMAN A. LOWE OF THE PHILADELPHIA *News*: Mr. President, assuming your renomination, could you give us some idea of your campaigning plans away from Washington?

THE PRESIDENT: As of this moment I have none.

Q: You have none.

EDWARD W. O'BRIEN OF THE ST. LOUIS *Globe-Democrat*: Do you anticipate, sir, that Mr. Stassen will return to your family as a full-fledged and permanent member after this thirty-day leave is up?

THE PRESIDENT: Well, so far as I know now, and from the knowledge I have, yes, for the simple reason that Mr. Stassen undertook one of the most difficult, sometimes frustrating, but certainly tedious tasks, and has pursued it earnestly, rigorously, and is trying to do things that very few people would have the patience, the intelligence, and really the courage to do.

He has been—I have been very delighted, and one of the reasons that this whole episode sort of disturbed the even tenor of my ways was that I thought "well now, here is a month that he won't be around."

But, as he pointed out, Ambassador [Amos] Peaslee [Mr. Stassen's assistant] did carry on his [Mr. Stassen's] job while he was over in London for six or seven weeks, and there was no reason why he could not do it for four weeks. But I think Mr. Stassen has done a very splendid job in the task that I have given him.

*   *   *

ROBERT G. SPIVAK OF THE NEW YORK *Post*: Mr. President, I understand the talk with Dr. [Howard McC.] Snyder [General Eisenhower's physician] this morning was a rather casual and informal thing.

Would you have any objections if reporters were to sit down with Doctors Heaton [Major General Leonard D. Heaton, commandant of Walter Reed Army Hospital] and [Isidor S.] Radvin [of the University of Pennsylvania] and discussed the operation and diagnosis?

THE PRESIDENT: Well, I am not going to commit them to anything until I talk to them about it. I have never discussed with them the possibility of having a press conference; and it is indeed possible that since it was an operation from which a period of convalescence is essential, they may say there is no reason for having one; but I would certainly want to talk to them before I committed them to anything.

Q: They say they are restricted from doing it.

HENRI PIERRE OF *Le Monde* (PARIS): Could you tell us something at this time about your view on the Suez crisis, and could you tell us also something about the message which was sent to you by Sir Anthony Eden [Prime Minister of Great Britain] and by M. [Guy] Mollet [Premier of France]?

THE PRESIDENT: Well, of course, I never publicly mention the substance of messages received from heads of other states and governments and/or the substance of my replies.

No, the only thing I can say is we are manifestly faced with a very grave issue, important to every country in the world that has a seacoast, and maybe even all the rest. So it is something to be handled with care, to make sure we are just and fair; but we must make certain that the rights of the world are not abused.

CHARLES LUCEY OF THE SCRIPPS-HOWARD NEWSPAPERS: Mr. President, could I ask just one more question on the health matter, sir? As nearly as you can tell now, have you any doubts or any reservations about your ability to carry on the Presidency for another four years? That relates to the health matter, sir.

THE PRESIDENT: Well, so far as I know, my answer is I have no doubts.

Now, I have got only what?—twenty more days before the convention, isn't it?—and I wouldn't expect any great change in that time.

As I said before, what I have is this: the prognosis of the doctors and the constant improvement I have experienced.

*   *   *

MR. ARROWSMITH: Mr. President, could you tell us what information your doctors have given you as to the possibility of a recurrence of your ileitis trouble?

THE PRESIDENT: Well, there is only four cases, as I told you before, in which they have a record, and they say none of those four, I believe, was there ever a recurrence—I mean four cases in a man of my age. That is about all they have told me.

MR. SMITH: Thank you, Mr. President.

Appendix B

"The Press and National Security"

On June 1, 1966, Clifton Daniel, the managing editor of the New York *Times,* delivered an unusual lecture to the World Press Institute at St. Paul. He entitled it "The Press and National Security," but it might have been more precisely called "The New York *Times* and the Bay of Pigs." The speech, whose full text is reprinted below, offered a rare glimpse of the inner workings of the national government and the nation's leading newspaper—and their interrelationship—at a moment of crisis.

This morning I am going to tell you a story—one that has never been told before—the inside story of the New York *Times* and the Bay of Pigs, something of a mystery story.

First, a little background.

*   *   *

On an occasion somewhat like this one, in October, 1960, I appeared at a journalism seminar with a distinguished public servant who was also a newspaper owner. I won't name him because I am going to disagree with him, and he is not here to defend his position.

He spoke before I did.

Alluding to the problem of official secrecy, he said:

". . . I can say with certain knowledge that there are from time to time disclosures which do adversely affect our national security. It is in this area that I have the deepest concern. . . .

197

"I don't know that I advocate something like an 'Official Secrets Act,' although this may be a fair subject for debate. . . . But perhaps my question is this: Should voluntary restraints so familiar to us in time of shooting war be more onerous and less compelling in time of rugged cold war?"

A little later it was my turn:

"Obviously," I said, "American newspapermen must not be irresponsible in the reporting of news that might affect the safety and security of our own country, our own homes. But the primary responsibility for safeguarding our national interests must rest always with our government.

"Up until the time we are actually at war or on the verge of war, it is not only permissible—but it is our duty as journalists and citizens—to be constantly questioning our leaders and our policy.

"Some people argue that newspapers should not print facts that might embarrass our government in its relations with other governments. But it may be that those very facts are the ones our people need to know in order to come to clear decisions about our policy."

*   *   *

I didn't realize how quickly my principles would be put to the test—a very severe test. A month later, in its issue of November 19, 1960, the *Nation* published an editorial under the heading, "Are We Training Cuban Guerrillas?"

I had never seen this editorial and had never heard it mentioned until a reader of the New York *Times* sent in a letter to the editor. He asked whether the allegations in the editorial were true, and, if so, why they hadn't been reported by the New York *Times*, whose resources for gathering information were much greater than those of the *Nation*.

The editorial is worth quoting because it probably was the first article published in English about the invasion plan that subsequently became the Bay of Pigs operation.

The *Nation* said:

"Fidel Castro may have a sounder basis for his expressed fears of a U.S.-financed 'Guatemala-type' invasion than most of us realize. On a recent visit to Guatemala, Dr. Ronald Hilton, Director of the Institute of Hispanic-American Studies at Stanford University, was told:

"1. The United States Central Intelligence Agency has acquired a large tract of land, at an outlay in excess of $1 million, which is stoutly fenced and heavily guarded. . . . It is 'common knowledge' in Guatemala that the tract is being used as a training ground for Cuban counter-revolutionaries who are preparing for an eventual landing in Cuba. . . . United States personnel and equipment are being used at the base . . .

"2. Substantially all of the above was reported by a well-known Guatemalan journalist . . . in *La Hora*, a Guatemalan newspaper. . . .

"3. More recently, the President of Guatemala, forced to take cognizance of the persistent reports concerning the base, went on TV and admitted its existence, but refused to discuss its purpose or any other facts about it.

"The American press . . . has apparently remained unaware of the public commotion the subject has aroused in Guatemala. . . . We ourselves, of course, pretend to no first-hand knowledge of the facts; nevertheless, we feel an obligation to bring the subject to public attention. . . . If the reports as heard by Dr. Hilton are true, then public pressure should be brought to bear upon the Administration to abandon this dangerous and hair-brained project.

"There is a second reason why we believe the reports merit publication: they can, and should, be checked immediately by all U.S. news media with correspondents in Guatemala."

*   *   *

With that last paragraph, the New York *Times* readily agreed. Paul Kennedy, our correspondent in Central America, was soon on his way to Guatemala.

He reported that intensive daily air training was taking place there on a partly-hidden airfield. In the mountains, commando-like forces were being drilled in guerrilla warfare tactics by foreign personnel, mostly from the United States. (Mr. Kennedy actually penetrated two miles into the training area.)

Guatemalan authorities insisted that the training operation was designed to meet an assault from Cuba. Opponents of the government said the preparations were for an offensive against Fidel Castro.

Mr. Kennedy's article was published in the New York *Times* on January 10, 1961.

The *Nation* also printed another article in its issue of January 7, 1961, by Don Dwiggins, aviation editor of the Los Angeles *Mirror*.

And now Arthur M. Schlesinger, Jr. takes up the story in his account of John F. Kennedy's years in the White House—"A Thousand Days."

"On March 31," Mr. Schlesinger says, "Howard Handleman of *U.S. News and World Report*, returning from ten days in Florida, said to me that the exiles were telling everyone that they would receive United States recognition as soon as they landed in Cuba, to be followed by the overt provision of arms and supplies.

"A few days later Gilbert Harrison of the *New Republic* sent over the galleys of a pseudonymous piece called 'Our Man in Miami,' asking whether there was any reason why it should not be published. It was a careful, accurate and devastating account of CIA activities among the refugees, written, I learned later, by Karl Meyer. Obviously its publication in a responsible magazine would cause trouble, but could the government properly ask an editor to suppress the truth? Defeated by the moral issue, I handed the article to the President, who instantly read it and expressed the hope that it could be stopped. Harrison accepted the suggestion and without questions—a patriotic act which left me oddly uncomfortable.

"About the same time," Mr. Schlesinger continues, "Tad Szulc filed a story to the New York *Times* from Miami describing the recruitment drive and reporting that a landing on Cuba was imminent. Turner Catledge, the managing editor, called James Reston, who was in his weekend retreat in Virginia, to ask his advice. Reston counseled against publication: either the story would alert Castro, in which case the *Times* would be responsible for casualties on the beach, or else the expedition would be canceled, in which case the *Times* would be responsible for grave interference with national policy. This was another patriotic act; but in retrospect I have wondered whether, if the press had behaved irresponsibly, it would not have spared the country a disaster."

*   *   *

As recently as last November, Mr. Schlesinger was still telling the same story. In an appearance on "Meet the Press," he was asked about an article in the New York *Times* in which he was quoted as saying that he had lied to the *Times* in April 1961 about the nature and size of the landing in the Bay of Pigs.

Mr. Schlesinger replied that, a few days before he misinformed the *Times*, the newspaper had suppressed a story by Tad Szulc from Miami, giving a fairly accurate account of the invasion plans.

"If," he said, "I was reprehensible in misleading the *Times* by repeating the official cover story, the *Times* conceivably was just as reprehensible in misleading the American people by suppressing the Tad Szulc story from Miami. I, at least, had the excuse that I was working for the Government.

"I prefer to think," he concluded, "that both the *Times* and I were actuated by the same motives; that is, a sense, mistaken or not, that [it] was in the national interest to do so."

Mr. Schlesinger was mistaken, both in his book and in his appearance on "Meet the Press." The *Times did not suppress the Tad Szulc article*. We printed it, and here it is [under a one-column headline], on Page 1 of the issue of Friday, April 7, 1961.

What actually happened is, at this date, somewhat difficult to say.

None of those who took part in the incident described in Mr. Schlesinger's book kept records of what was said and done. That is unfortunate, and it should teach us a lesson. The Bay of Pigs was not only important in the history of United States relations with Latin America, the Soviet Union and world Communism; it was also important in the history of relations between the American press and the United States government.

We owe a debt to history. We should try to reconstruct the event, and that is what I am attempting to do today.

*　　　　*　　　　*

Late in March and early in April, 1961, we were hearing rumors that the anti-Castro forces were organizing for an invasion. For example, the editor of the Miami *Herald*, Don Shoemaker, told me at lunch in New York one day, "They're drilling on the beaches all over southern Florida."

Tad Szulc, a veteran correspondent in Latin America with a well-deserved reputation for sniffing out plots and revolutions, came upon the Miami story independently and quite accidentally.

He was being transferred from Rio de Janeiro to Washington and happened to stop in Miami to visit friends on his way North. He quickly discovered that an invasion force was indeed forming and that it was very largely financed and directed by the CIA. He asked for permission to come to New York to discuss the situation and was promptly assigned to cover the story.

His first article from Miami—the one I have just shown to you—began as follows:

"For nearly nine months Cuban exile military forces dedicated to the overthrow of Premier Fidel Castro have been training in the United States as well as in Central America.

"An army of 5,000 to 6,000 men constitutes the external fighting arm of the anti-Castro Revolutionary Council, which was formed in the United States last month. Its purpose is the liberation of Cuba from what it describes as the Communist rule of the Castro regime."

This article, which was more than two columns long and very detailed, was scheduled to appear in the paper of Friday, April 7, 1961. It was dummied for Page 1 under a four-column head, leading the paper.

While the front-page dummy was being drawn up by the assistant managing editor, the news editor and the assistant news editor, Orvil Dryfoos, then the publisher of the New York *Times*, came down from the 14th floor to the office of Turner Catledge, the managing editor.

He was gravely troubled by the security implications of Szulc's story. He could envision failure for the invasion, and he could see the New York *Times* being blamed for a bloody fiasco.

He and the managing editor solicited the advice of Scotty Reston, who was then the Washington correspondent of the New York *Times* and is now an associate editor.

At this point, the record becomes unclear. Mr. Reston distinctly recalls that Mr. Catledge's telephone call came on a Sunday, and that he was spending the weekend at his retreat in the Virginia mountains, as described by Arthur Schlesinger. As there was no telephone in his cabin, Mr. Reston had to return the call from a gas station in Marshall, Va. Mr. Catledge and others recall, with equal certainty, that the incident took place on Thursday and that Mr. Reston was reached in his office in Washington.

Whichever was the case, the managing editor told Mr. Reston about the Szulc dispatch.

Mr. Reston was asked what should be done with it.

"I told them not to run it," Mr. Reston says.

He did not advise against printing information about the forces gathering in Florida; that was already well known. He merely cautioned against printing any dispatch that would pinpoint the time of the landing.

Others agree that Szulc's dispatch *did* contain some phraseology to the effect that an invasion was imminent, and those words were eliminated.

Tad Szulc's own recollection, cabled to me from Madrid the other day, is that "in several instances the stories were considerably toned down, including the elimination of statements about the 'imminence' of an invasion.

"Specifically," Mr. Szulc said, "a decision was made in New York not to mention the CIA's part in the invasion preparations, not to use the date of the invasion, and, on April 15, not to give away in detail the fact that the first air strike on Cuba was carried out from Guatemala."

After the dummy for the front page of the New York *Times* for Friday, April 7, 1961, was changed, Ted Bernstein, the assistant managing editor on night duty, and Lew Jordan, the news editor, sat in Mr. Bernstein's office fretting about it. They believed a colossal mistake was being made, and together they went into Mr. Catledge's office to appeal for reconsideration.

Mr. Catledge recalls that Mr. Jordan's face was dead white, and he was quivering with emotion. He and Mr. Bernstein told the managing editor that never before had the front-page play in the New York *Times* been changed for reasons of policy. They said they would like to hear from the publisher himself the reasons for the change.

Lew Jordan later recalled that Mr. Catledge was "flaming mad" at this intervention. However, he turned around in his big swivel chair, picked up the telephone, and asked Mr. Dryfoos to come downstairs. By the time he arrived, Mr. Bernstein had gone to dinner, but Mr. Dryfoos spent ten minutes patiently explaining to Mr. Jordan his reasons for wanting the story played down.

His reasons were those of national security, national interest and, above all, concern for the safety of the men who were preparing to offer their lives on the beaches of Cuba. He repeated the explanation in somewhat greater length to Mr. Bernstein the next day.

I describe the mood and behavior of the publisher and editors of the New York *Times* only to show how seriously and with what intensity of emotion they made their fateful decisions.

Mr. Bernstein and Mr. Jordan now say, five years later, that the change in play, not eliminating the reference to the imminence of the invasion, was the important thing done that night.

"It was important because a multi-column head in this paper means so much," Mr. Jordan told me the other day.

Mr. Reston, however, felt that the basic issue was the elimination of the statement that an invasion was imminent.

Ironically, although that fact was eliminated from our own dispatch, virtually the same information was printed in a shirttail on Tad Szulc's report. That was a broadcast from CBS. It said that plans for the invasion of Cuba were in their final stages. Ships and planes were carrying invasion units from Florida to their staging bases in preparation for the assault.

When the invasion actually took place ten day later, the American Society of Newspaper Editors happened to be in session in Washington, and President Kennedy addressed the Society. He devoted his speech entirely to the Cuban crisis. He said nothing at that time about press disclosures of invasion plans.

However, a week later in New York, appearing before the Bureau of Advertising of the American Newspaper Publishers Association, the President asked members of the newspaper profession "to re-examine their own responsibilities."

He suggested that the circumstances of the cold war required newspapermen to show some of the same restraint they would exercise in a shooting war.

He went on to say, "Every newspaper now asks itself with respect to every story, 'Is it news?' All I suggest is that you add the question: 'Is it in the interest of national security?' "

If the press should recommend voluntary measures to prevent the publication of material endangering the national security in peacetime, the President said, "the Government would cooperate wholeheartedly."

Turner Catledge, who was the retiring president of the A.S.N.E., Felix McKnight of the Dallas *Times-Herald*, the incoming president, and Lee Hills, executive editor of the Knight newspapers, took the President's statement as an invitation.

Within two weeks, a delegation of editors, publishers and news agency executives was at the White House. They told President Kennedy they saw no need at that time for machinery to help prevent the disclosure of vital security information. They agreed that there should be another meeting in a few months. However, no further meeting was ever held.

That day in the White House, President Kennedy ran down a list of what he called premature disclosures of security information. His examples were mainly drawn from the New York *Times.*

He mentioned, for example, Paul Kennedy's story about the training of anti-Castro forces in Guatemala. Mr. Catledge pointed out that this information had been published in *La Hora* in Guatemala and in the *Nation* in this country before it was ever published in the New York *Times.*

"But it was not news until it appeared in the *Times,*" the President replied.

While he scolded the New York *Times,* the President said in an aside to Mr. Catledge, "If you had printed more about the operation you would have saved us from a colossal mistake."

More than a year later, President Kennedy was still talking the same way. In a conversation with Orvil Dryfoos in the White House on September 13, 1962, he said, "I wish you had run everything on Cuba . . . I am just sorry you didn't tell it at the time."

Those words were echoed by Arthur Schlesinger when he wrote, "I have wondered whether, if the press had behaved irresponsibly, it would not have spared the country a disaster."

They are still echoing down the corridors of history. Just the other day in Washington, Senator Russell of Georgia confessed that, although he was Chairman of the Senate Armed Forces Committee, he didn't know the timing of the Bay of Pigs operation.

"I only wish I had been consulted," he said in a speech to the Senate, "because I would have strongly advised against this kind of operation if I had been."

It is not so easy, it seems, even for Presidents, their most intimate advisers and distinguished United States Senators to know always what is really in the national interest. One is tempted to say that sometimes—sometimes—even a mere newspaperman knows better.

My own view is that the Bay of Pigs operation might well have been cancelled and the country would have been saved enormous embarrassment if the New York *Times* and other newspapers had been more diligent in the performance of their duty—their duty to keep the public informed on matters vitally affecting our national honor and prestige, not to mention our national security.

Perhaps, as Mr. Reston believes, it was too late to stop the operation by the time we printed Tad Szulc's story on April 7.

"If I had it to do over, I would do exactly what we did at the time," Mr. Reston says. "It is ridiculous to think that publishing the fact that the invasion was imminent would have avoided this disaster. I am quite sure the operation would have gone forward.

"The thing had been cranked up too far. The CIA would have had to disarm the anti-Castro forces physically. Jack Kennedy was in no mood to do anything like that."

*   *   *

The Bay of Pigs, as it turned out, was the prelude to an even graver crisis—the Cuban missile crisis of 1962.

In Arthur Schlesinger's opinion, failure in 1961 contributed to success in 1962. President Kennedy had learned from experience, and once again the New York *Times* was involved.

On May 28, 1963, the President sat at his desk in the White House and with his own hand wrote a letter to Mrs. Orvil Dryfoos, whose husband had just died at the age of 50. The letter was on White House stationery, and the President used both sides of the paper.

The existence of this letter has never been mentioned publicly before. I have the permission of Mr. Dryfoos's widow, now Mrs. Andrew Heiskell, to read it to you today:

"Dear Marian:

"I want you to know how sorry I was to hear the sad news of Orvil's untimely death.

"I had known him for a number of years and two experiences I had with him in the last two years gave me a clear insight into his unusual qualities of mind and heart. One involved a matter of national security—the other his decision to refrain from printing on October 21st the news, which only the man for the *Times* possessed, on the presence of Russian missiles in Cuba, upon my informing him that we needed twenty-four hours more to complete our preparations.

"This decision of his made far more effective our later actions and thereby contributed greatly to our national safety.

"All this means very little now, but I did want you to know that a good many people some distance away, had the same regard for Orvil's character as did those who knew him best.

"I know what a blow this is to you, and I hope you will accept Jackie's and my deepest sympathy.

"Sincerely, John F. Kennedy."

In the Cuban missile crisis, things were handled somewhat differently than in the previous year. The President telephoned directly to the publisher of the New York *Times*.

He had virtually been invited to do so in their conversation in the White House in September.

That conversation had been on the subject of security leaks in the press and how to prevent them, and Mr. Dryfoos had told the President that what was needed was prior information and prior consultation. He said that, when there was a danger of security information getting into print, the thing to do was to call in the publishers and explain matters to them.

In the missile crisis, President Kennedy did exactly that.

Ten minutes before I was due on this platform this morning, Mr. Reston telephoned me from Washington to give me further details of what happened that day.

"The President called me," Mr. Reston said. "He understood that I had been talking to Mac Bundy, and he knew from the line of questioning that we knew the critical fact—that Russian missiles indeed had been emplaced in Cuba. [That was on Sunday.]

"The President told me," Mr. Reston continued, "that he was going on television on Monday evening to report to the American people. He said that if we published the news about the missiles, Khrushchev could actually give him an ultimatum before he went on the air. *Those were Kennedy's exact words.*

"I told him I understood," Mr. Reston said this morning. "But I also told him I could not do anything about it. And this is an important thought that you should convey to those young reporters in your audience.

"I told the President, I would report to my office in New York, and, if my advice were asked, I would recommend that we not publish. It was not my duty to decide. My job was the same as that of an ambassador—to report to my superiors.

"I recommended to the President that he call New York. He did so."

That was the sequence of events as Mr. Reston recalled them this morning. The President telephoned the publisher of the New York *Times*.

Mr. Dryfoos in turn put the issue up to Mr. Reston and his staff.

And the news that the Soviet Union had atomic missiles in Cuba, only 90 miles from the coast of Florida, was withheld until the Government announced it.

*   *   *

What conclusion do I reach from all these facts? What moral do I draw from my story?

My conclusion is the one I started with: Information is essential to people who propose to govern themselves. It is the responsibility of serious journalists to supply that information.

When it comes to matters of national interest, American newspapermen obviously must not be irresponsible in the dissemination of information that might affect the safety and security of our country.

I have tried to give you examples from my own experience of newspapermen who, although they disagreed at times, acted with the highest sense of responsibility toward their profession, their country and their readers.

Still, the primary responsibility for safeguarding our national interests must rest always with our Government, as it did with President Kennedy in the two Cuban crises.

Up until the time we are actually at war or on the verge of war, it is not only permissible—it is our duty as journalists and citizens to be constantly questioning our leaders and our policy, and to be constantly informing the people, who are the masters of us all—both the press and the politicians.

Appendix C

A Postscript

Washington newsman David Kraslow's experiences with some of the major Latin American credibility crises of the 1960's are recounted in Chapter 3. When excerpts from Clifton Daniel's lecture on "The Press and National Security" were published in the New York *Times*, Kraslow rounded out the record with the following letter to Daniel.

Dear Mr. Daniel:

I am not sure about your conclusion, but I heartily endorse your view that every effort should be made to reconstruct the role of the American press in the pre-Bay of Pigs period. The same holds for the missile crisis.

Both events were indeed important in the history of relations between the press and the government.

The general outlines of what the New York *Times* did and did not do on both occasions have been known to many of us in Washington for a long time. The absorbing detail now supplied by you helps to flesh out important elements of the story.

As you suggest, however, the story is much broader than one dealing just with the involvement of the *Times*. You refer, for example, to a conversation with Don Shoemaker indicating just that.

I write, therefore, not only to applaud the effort to assemble a public record but also to offer additional first-hand information—another piece of the story—on both the Bay of Pigs episode and the missile crisis.

I don't think I could prove it, but I believe the Miami *Herald* was the first newspaper to become aware of what the CIA was up to—in fact, the *Herald* may have been several months ahead. An accident in a farming area near Homestead, some 30 miles south of Miami, and an alert *Herald* city desk led to the discovery.

In the summer of 1960, the CIA began to recruit and train Cuban exiles for some sort of effort against the Castro regime. One training camp was set up near Homestead, ostensibly run by a Cuban exile group but actually organized and fully backed by the CIA. Neighbors could hear drill orders over the camp loudspeaker and could see young Cubans in marching formation.

One day in August, some American youths bent on a practical joke tossed firecrackers into the camp. The Cubans, thinking they were being attacked by Castro agents, came out firing their carbines.

An American boy was wounded and a police case resulted, with several Cubans being charged. The city desk soon learned the case would not be prosecuted because of a confidential request from Federal authorities.

As the *Herald*'s Washington reporter, I was asked by the city desk to find out why. By mid or late September, after several weeks of checking at State, the White House, the FBI and elsewhere, I had the answer—and more.

Although troubled, I wrote a 1,500-word story revealing the CIA's involvement in the Homestead camp and in the broader effort to recruit Cuban exiles, the Justice Department's unhappiness over the brazen violation of the neutrality act by a government agency, and the pressure on Eisenhower from Bill Rogers and Hoover to force the CIA to move its training operation out of the country. I knew nothing, of course, at that time about any invasion of Cuba. That plan was not to jell until much later. My first information was that the exiles would be deposited in Cuba by the CIA after their training to undertake guerrilla warfare against Castro. Then I was advised the exiles would be employed in large-scale hit-and-run raids.

In any case, my story was killed by *Herald* management. What doubts I had about the story I resolved in favor of the basic principle of disclosure in a free society. My editors, because of a fear that the *Herald* might be tampering with national security, resolved their doubts in the other direction. I protested but, I must confess, not too strongly. I was not critical of management then, and am not critical now. Particularly under the circumstances, which I shall discuss, it was a very tough call to make.

I do not wish to indicate that the decision to kill the story was made quickly, or that once made the *Herald* forgot about it. Indeed, the *Herald* undertook an intensive effort to find out all it could about what the CIA was doing in Miami. It learned much.

I recall several lengthy conversations with Lee Hills and George Beebe in which we agonized over the proper course to follow. Our soul-searching reflected the murkiness and the magnitude of the problem before us. George Beebe, at one point, dispatched telegrams to Jim Hagerty and others high in government seeking guidance, but without success. In October, when a final decision on use of my story already had been pending for several weeks, I attempted—at the direction of my editors—to see Allen Dulles. I was advised he was out of the country, but that he probably would see me upon his return in November.

Ed Lahey, the Knight bureau chief, and I did see Dulles in his office in November. We spelled out for him what the *Herald* had uncovered in Miami and what I had learned earlier in Washington. Dulles replied that if the *Herald* published the kind of story Lahey and I had related to him, it would be most harmful to the national interest. That's about how he said it. He made no specific request that the story be suppressed. It was after this word was relayed to Miami that I was told definitely my story would not run. The *Herald*, however, continued to gather information, including photographs, and I contributed additional data, including facts on the airlift of exiles to Central America from Opa-locka field in Dade County.

This, in substance, is what I know first-hand of the Miami *Herald*'s coverage of the pre-Bay of Pigs story. . . . [This] is the only time I have tried to relate on paper the major facts within my knowledge.

A month after the Bay of Pigs I met with Louis Lyons and several editors considering my application for a Nieman Fellowship. Virtually the entire interview was devoted to a discussion of how the *Herald* had obtained its information and whether a newspaper's duty is to disclose what it knows about a questionable clandestine undertaking—no matter how firmly the government claims potential damage to national security. It seemed to me that the editors, even with the Bay of Pigs disaster fresh in their minds, were reluctant to render judgment.

At Harvard, I explored this matter at length with several people, including Oscar Handlin and the late Arthur Schlesinger. Their unanimous verdict was in line with your conclusion.

In the spring of 1963, it seemed ironic to me that the Kennedy administration would crack down on Cuban exile raiders for violating a law (the neutrality act) that the government had invited them to violate in 1960 and 1961. I wrote a piece disclosing the FBI-CIA conflict over neutrality act violations in the summer of 1960. The story appeared in the *Herald* and was distributed by the Chicago Daily News Service. . . .

I should like to discuss one incident in connection with the President's request to the *Times* on Oct. 21, 1962, that it withhold a story revealing the presence of Soviet missiles in Cuba.

On the morning of the 19th, a Friday, my editors in Miami advised me they had received [a] column containing the flat assertion that U. S. intelligence had established the presence of intermediate missiles and Il-28 bombers in Cuba. . . . [My] editors asked me to make a solid check on the column. I talked with Art Sylvester about 2 p.m. He said no one else had queried him on the column. I told him my editors were pressing for some kind of guidance on whether to use the column. He said he would see about it.

That evening a Pentagon news officer telephoned me at home with the answer (which Sylvester told me that weekend was cleared with McNamara). That answer was the lie that has rankled ever since—the one paragraph mimeographed statement that the Pentagon had no information on the presence of offensive Soviet weapons in Cuba. I wrote a story to that effect which ran on page one of the *Herald* the following morning—five days after the Pentagon had advised the President of the missiles and two days before the President went on television. The *Herald* and many other newspapers . . . were suckered by a lie. Within 48 hours, Scotty Reston had the facts to refute the lie so the President used the national security appeal.

I write not to argue what the *Times* and the *Herald* and other newspapers should or should not have done before the Bay of Pigs and the missile crisis. I think I could present a convincing case both for and against disclosure, particularly on the Bay of Pigs.

The point of the moment is that journalism has much to learn from these two events. . . .

Sincerely,
DAVID KRASLOW

Appendix D

John F. Kennedy Meets the Press

As a rule, President Kennedy enjoyed his encounters with the press. He had close friends in the press corps, and frequently he viewed his news conferences as challenges to match wits with the correspondents. More often than not, the President came out ahead in these exchanges.

There was no light banter, however, when Kennedy met the press on the morning of Friday, April 21, 1961. This was the first Presidential news conference since the Bay of Pigs disaster, and the mood was grim. As he faced hundreds of reporters—and the television cameras—in the State Department auditorium, the President announced that no "useful national purpose would be served by my going further into the Cuban question this morning." A few correspondents tried to raise the subject nonetheless, but with little success. Excerpts from the official transcript of that news conference follow.

PRESIDENT KENNEDY: I have several announcements to make. I know that many of you have further questions about Cuba. I made a statement on that subject yesterday afternoon. We are continuing consultations with other American republics. Active efforts are being made by ourselves and others on behalf of various individuals, including Americans, who may be in danger. I do not think that any useful national purpose would be served by my going further into the Cuban question this morning. I prefer to let my statement of yesterday suffice for the present.

*   *   *

Q: Mr. President, can you tell us anything about your talk with Vice President Nixon last night?

THE PRESIDENT: I brought—the Vice President came to the White House at my invitation, and I informed him or brought him up to date on the events of the past few days.

*   *   *

Q: Mr. President, quite respecting your feeling of not going beyond your statement of yesterday on Cuba, there still is in print this morning, quite widely distributed, a published report that you took the decision to continue training Cuban refugees with arms provided by this government and for releasing ships and fuel for launching the current operations in Cuba. Furthermore, this report says that you reached this decision against the advice of Secretary Rusk and Mr. [Chester] Bowles. Now, is this true?

THE PRESIDENT: I think that the facts of the matter involving Cuba will come out in due time. I am sure that an effort will be made to determine the facts accurately. As for me, I am confining myself to my statement for good reason.

Q: Mr. President, this is not a question about Cuba; it is a question about Castro. Could you tell us whether any intelligence that you have received can shed any light on the reports that the Prime Minister has been incapacitated, that he has not been heard from since Monday or Tuesday, or reports to that effect?

THE PRESIDENT: No, I cannot. I saw, I think, some reference on the ticker this morning that Mr. Castro was seeing some members of the press today, so I suppose we will have a better idea of that later on.

*   *   *

Q: Mr. President, at your last news conference you expressed hope that the Soviets would agree in a few days on a cease fire in Laos. More than a few days have gone by since then and they have not agreed. Can you tell us how long you will wait before you contemplate action?

THE PRESIDENT: I understand the Soviets and the British are conferring at the present time, using it in a general sense, and we are hopeful that a cease fire can be obtained in Laos. We continue to be hopeful.

Q: Mr. President, Mr. Nixon, on the Ev and Charlie Show yesterday, said that he was going to give you ten days' grace to produce on your campaign promises that certain things would be done by ninety days. Did he go into this or other domestic politics in your White House meeting?

THE PRESIDENT: No, there was nothing stated about—on politics. Mr. Nixon and I discussed matters of national concern, and it was done in a wholly non-political way, and Mr. Nixon's response was most helpful.

Q: Mr. President, sir, I wonder if you would tell us what your grounds, your investigations of the Major General [Edwin] Walker incident in Europe, if you will please tell us what grounds you found for relieving him of his command for allegedly teaching troops anti-Communist doctrine?

THE PRESIDENT: When I saw the stories in regard to the things which had been said, or at least alleged to have been said in regard to General Walker, I called Secretary McNamara and asked him to investigate. Secretary McNamara then, I believe, suspended General Walker, and my term may not be precise, "pending a completion of investigation," but no decision has been made in regard to General Walker until the investigation has been completed, to find out exactly what was going on.

I do not believe that Secretary McNamara took even that limited action, however, merely because he felt that General Walker was teaching—talking against the Communists. That was not the grounds for concern. But no final decision, to the best of my information, has been made on the matter of General Walker. He will be given every opportunity, and those who have been critical of him will be given every opportunity, to present their case, and a final decision will then be made by Mr. McNamara, who will then bring the matter to my attention, and I will then review it, without prejudice to General Walker.

Q: Mr. President, you don't seem to be pushing the space program nearly as energetically now as you suggested during the campaign that you thought it should be pushed. In view of the feeling of many people in this country that we must do everything we can to catch up with the Russians as soon as possible, do you anticipate applying any sort of crash program?

THE PRESIDENT: We have added, I think, $130 million to the budget on space several weeks ago, which provides some speedup for Saturn, and some speedup for Nova, and some speedup for

Rover. I will say that the budget for space next year will be around $2 billion. Now, we are now and have been for some time attempting to make a determination as to developing larger boosters, whether the emphasis should be put on chemical, nuclear rockets or liquid fuel, how much this would cost, and some of these programs have been estimated to be between twenty and forty billion dollars. We are attempting to make a determination as to which program offers the best hope before we embark on it, because you may commit a relatively small amount of money now for results in 1967, eight or nine, which will cost you billions of dollars, and therefore the Congress passed yesterday the bill providing for a Space Council which will be chaired by the Vice President, and we are attempting to make a determination as to which of these various proposals offers the best hope. When that determination is made we will then make a recommendation to the Congress.

In addition, we have to consider whether there is any program now regardless of its cost which offers us hopes of being pioneers in a project. It is possible to spend billions of dollars in these projects in space to the detriment of other programs and still not be successful. We are behind, as I said before, in large boosters. We have to make a determination whether there is any effort we could make in time or money which could put us first in any new area. Now, I don't want to start spending the kind of money that I am talking about without making a determination based on careful scientific judgments as to whether a real success can be achieved or whether we are so far behind now in this particular race we are going to be second in this decade.

So I would say to you it is a matter of great concern, but I think before we break through and begin a program which would not reach completion, as you know, until the end of this decade, for example, trips to the moon, may be ten years off, maybe a little less, but are quite far away and involve enormous sums, I don't think we ought to rush into it and begin them until we really know where we are going to end up. That study is now being undertaken under the direction of the Vice President.

Q: Mr. President, don't you agree that we should try to get to the moon before the Russians, if we can?

THE PRESIDENT: If we can get to the moon before the Russians, we should.

Q: Isn't it your responsibility to apply the vigorous leadership to spark up the program?

THE PRESIDENT: When you say "spark up the program," we have to make a judgment based on the best information we can get whether we can be ahead of the Russians to the moon. I am talking about a program which may be many years ahead.

Q: For instance, the Saturn is still on a forty-hour week, isn't it, Mr. President?

THE PRESIDENT: As I say, we have appropriated $126 million more for Saturn and we are attempting to find out what else we can do. Saturn is still going to put us well behind. Saturn does not offer any hope of being first to the moon. Saturn is several years behind the Soviet Union, and I can just say to you that regardless of how much money we spend on Saturn, we are still going to be second. The question is whether the nuclear rocket or other kinds of chemical rockets offer us a better hope of making a jump forward, but we are second, and Saturn will not put us first. I want, however, to speed up if we can on Saturn, and the Vice President is now leading a study to see what we ought to do in this area.

Q: Mr. President, do you anticipate that there will be a vote in both Houses of Congress this year on your medical care program?

THE PRESIDENT: I do not know. If we had a vote in the House it would depend, of course, on the action of the Ways and Means Committee. I haven't any information yet as to whether we will get a vote in the House. It is possible that there will be one in the Senate, which is not restricted by the same rules.

Q: There have been reports on Capitol Hill that this Administration has reconciled itself to no vote on medical care this year.

THE PRESIDENT: In either house?

Q: In either house; yes.

THE PRESIDENT: In either body; in either house?

Q: Yes, sir.

THE PRESIDENT: I have not seen the reports and I would not make that assumption. I am hopeful—we are dependent in the House on committee action. There cannot be a vote in the House without action by the committee and, of course, the rules of germaneness. In the Senate, however, there is a somewhat different situation, but there is no rule of germaneness. So it is possible that someone might offer a bill in the Senate with an amendment to the other bill. I do not know that yet. But it is very possible that you will get a vote in the Senate this year.

But the House is a different problem. You cannot get a vote unless the Ways and Means Committee acts.

Q: Your comment about General Walker suggests that you look askance at the John Birch Society. Can you tell us how you feel about that organization?

THE PRESIDENT: Well, I don't feel that their judgments are based on accurate information on the kinds of challenges that we face. I think we face an extremely serious and intensified struggle with the Communists. But I am not sure that the John Birch Society is wrestling with the real problems which are created by the Communist advance around the world.

I would hope that all those who are strongly concerned about it would address themselves to the kind of problems which are created by Laos, Vietnam, by internal subversion, by the desperate life lived by so many people in this hemisphere and so many other places which the Communists exploit.

These are the kinds of problems that we are dealing with. I said something about them yesterday. The use which the Communists make of democratic freedoms and the success which they are able to—once they have seized power—success with which they are able to maintain their power against dissent.

This, it seems to me, to be the problem. We have talked about and read stories of 7,000 to 15,000 guerrillas operating in Vietnam, killing 2,000 civil officers a year and 2,000 police officers a year, 4,000.

Now, there has been an election in Vietnam in which 75 percent of the people or 80 percent endorse the government, and yet we read how Vietnam is in danger because of guerrilla operations, carried on by this small, well disciplined, well supplied, across the border, group of guerrillas.

How we fight that kind of a problem which is going to be with us all through this decade seems to me to be one of the great problems now before the United States. I would hope all those who are concerned about the advance of Communism would face that problem and not concern themselves with the loyalty of President Eisenhower or President Truman or Mrs. Roosevelt or myself or someone else.

Q: Mr. President, was your speech yesterday before the editors intended to suggest another approach or a new departure in the Administration's dealing with the Russians?

THE PRESIDENT: No—I didn't—no.

Q: You have practiced what has been described as the quiet diplomacy approach, and your speech yesterday seemed to suggest that you have perhaps decided upon another approach.

THE PRESIDENT: No, I wouldn't attempt to make a judgment or response to that. I think that—I am concerned about these kinds of problems which I just described. I do not feel satisfied that we have an effective answer to it yet, and I think it is a matter of the greatest possible concern to all of us, because I think events have been moving with some speed.

The use which the Communists make of democracy, and then when they seize power, the effectiveness with which they manage the police apparatus so that dissent cannot arise, and so that the people can no longer express their will, liquidation by gunfire of the opposition or by forcing them out of the country to be refugees— this suggests the kind of a problem which we are going to have in this decade.

In my judgment, it is an extremely difficult matter for the free nations to deal with. But I must say that it is a matter to which we must address all of our energy and all of our attention.

Q: Mr. President, how would you evaluate the present state of your domestic program in Congress?

THE PRESIDENT: I think we have done better recently. Yesterday the Senate passed the $1.25 minimum wage, and there was action on aid to dependent children, and on social security. The vote in the Senate was very ample on the minimum wage. There were only twenty-eight votes against it, so I think that at least yesterday we made progress.

Q: How much more, sir, do you think needs to be done in order to give you a satisfactory score on your hoped-for legislative program?

THE PRESIDENT: Well, I am hopeful that we can move ahead on the various other parts of the program, including education and housing. We are making progress on Social Security, distressed areas and minimum wage. There may be other proposals which we might make to the Congress after we have considered or completed our review of the economy and made a judgment as to exactly what peak or plateau the economy is going to reach this year, and that is what we are attempting to do now, and to see whether any additional government programs may be necessary to encourage it.

Q: Mr. President, sir, since last Saturday a certain foreign policy decision has given rise to many conflicting stories. But during that time reporters in Washington have noticed that there has been a clamming up of information from formerly useful sources. To my knowledge the State Department and the White House has not attempted to take a representative group of reporters and say, "These are the facts as we know them," and this morning we are not permitted to ask any further questions about this foreign policy situation. In view of the fact we are taking a propaganda lambasting around the world, why is it not useful information, sir, for us to explore with you the real facts behind this, or our motivations?

THE PRESIDENT: Well, I think in answer to your question that we have to make a judgment as to how much we can usefully say that would aid the interest of the United States. One of the problems of a free society, a problem not met by a dictatorship, is the problem of information. A good deal has been printed in the paper and I wouldn't be surprised if those of you who are members of the press would be receiving a lot of background briefings in the next day or two by interested people or interested agencies.

There is an old saying that victory has a hundred fathers and defeat is an orphan. I wouldn't be surprised if information is poured into you in regard to all of the recent activities.

Now, I think we see some of the problems, to move from this particular case into the problem of space, where in the Soviet Union no reports were made in regard to any experiments that they carried out on "our man in space." And I saw in a national magazine where some student said the Americans talk a good deal about their man in space, and the Soviet Union says nothing and yet it wins. That is one of the problems of a democracy competing and carrying on a struggle for survival against a dictatorship.

But I will say to you, Mr. [Sander] Vanocur [of NBC News] that I have said as much as I feel can be usefully said by me in regard to the events of the past few days. Further statements and detailed discussions are not to conceal responsibility because I am the responsible officer of the government, but merely—and that is quite obvious—but merely because I do not believe that such a discussion would benefit us during the present difficult situation. I think you will be informed and some of the information, based on what I have seen, will not be accurate.

＊　　　　＊　　　　＊

Q: Mr. President, would you explain the reason for the dropping of espionage charges in Chicago recently against the Russian spy Melekh, and was that a part of the bargain for the RB-47 fliers?

THE PRESIDENT: In answer to the last part of the question, it was not. There was no connection. The dropping of the charges was made after an examination of the details of the case, and of the national interest, and it was felt that it would be useful to take the action we took. I am sorry I can't be more responsive. I will say it was not with regard to the RB-47 fliers.

Q: Mr. President, we have demonstrated a great capability in space in communications and meteorology. While these are not as dramatic as a man orbiting in space, there has been a strong feeling among scientists the world over that the country that would first develop a space telecommunications system to bring communications within the reach of every nation in the world at the price they could afford would make an even greater impact than the country that orbited man first in space. Are you considering putting more funds, because you have cut some, in both communications and meteorology, are you considering adding more funds to the budget?

THE PRESIDENT: Yes, I believe we have, or are about to, if we have not already done so, put an additional—I just have to go from memory now, of a decision made several weeks ago. I am under the impression that we decided to put another twenty-five to twenty-seven million dollars into a communication satellite, as part of this general program.

Q: Yes, but industry also has been interested in putting its funds in it, and there was a statement by Mr. [James] Webb that we were not going to at this point put any of this program into industry's hands until we had investigated further. Since they are willing to spend money, are you considering perhaps allowing them to share the cost in and advance this program?

THE PRESIDENT: Well, I don't know enough about the matter to give you a detailed answer, except I do know that we did put an additional sum of money for a communications satellite, amounting to the sum that I suggested there. If there are any other further things that can be done, or if anyone else wants to put their money into it, I am sure that Mr. Webb will be agreeable. But I must say from examining this and other programs, I find that the government puts most of the money into it.

Q: Mr. President, do you intend to send Vice President Johnson to Southeast Asia soon?

THE PRESIDENT: We have been considering the Vice President going to Southeast Asia, and I think a decision will be reached on that in the next—perhaps over the weekend or the next few days.

Q: Mr. President, given the stress that you have put this morning and in recent days on this problem of fighting the indirect Communist tactics, do you still—and also given the rather harsh language out of Moscow, including Mr. Khrushchev's note to you—do you still feel that it is useful to go ahead with efforts at the diplomatic level to negotiate formal agreements with the Soviet government?

THE PRESIDENT: Well, we still continue to hope that some agreement can be reached on the cessation of nuclear tests. We are, of course, very discouraged by the newest insistence of the Soviets on a veto. It is quite obvious that the Senate would not accept such a treaty nor would I send it to the Senate, because the inspection system then would not provide any guarantees at all. Now, I noticed the language used by Mr. Khrushchev, himself, not merely one of his representatives, in Mr. [Walter] Lippmann's article, that a strong insistence on the tripartite and on unanimous agreement in regard to the inspection system. I am hopeful that there may be a change in that. But if there is not a change in that position, it is going to be very hard to get an agreement. But I believe that Mr. [Arthur H.] Dean should continue because if these test conversations should break up, then of course our hopes of getting any agreement on disarmament would be substantially lessened, and we could look for a proliferation of atomic testing in other countries. So I feel that Mr. Dean should continue, though we have been discouraged by the Russian position.

Q: Do you feel, sir, that it is possible to have really a two-level operation here, an undeclared kind of warfare which you have been talking about, and yet a formalized effort not only in the test ban negotiations but in terms of exchanges and other types of negotiations? Are these two things compatible?

THE PRESIDENT: The incompatibility may rest in the fact that it is hard to get an agreement on any matter when there is suspicion between the two systems and when one of the systems are pressing their interest with great vigor around the world. It makes the chances of getting any agreement far less. I thought the best hope was the nuclear testing, even though it was always true that the obstacles were large. But if there is any chance at all of getting an agreement on a cessation of nuclear tests, regardless of what appears to be the obstacles, I think we should press on. So in answer to your question, I still believe that Mr. Dean should continue to work at Geneva.

THE PRESS: Thank you, Mr. President.

Appendix E

Lyndon B. Johnson Meets the Press

President Johnson has tried almost every conceivable style and setting for his news conferences. He has met with reporters in a hangar on his Texas ranch, on brisk strolls around the White House lawn, and in the decorous sitting room of the Executive Mansion. He has also experimented with a lavaliere microphone suspended around his neck to gain greater freedom of movement and gesture at a formal televised news conference. Johnson has an aversion to conferences of this type, which were favored by his two immediate predecessors, and has held them far less frequently than they did. His favorite format is the informal gathering of correspondents around the President's desk in the White House Oval Office.

Late in the afternoon of Wednesday, November 1, 1967, White House correspondents were summoned into the Cabinet Room for an impromptu news conference with the President. One reporter questioned the President about his 1964 statement that he would not "send American boys nine or ten thousand miles to do what Asian boys ought to be doing for themselves," and the President offered his explanation. The excerpts which follow were selected from the official transcript.

[President Johnson:] There were two or three developments in our Cabinet meeting that I thought you might be interested in. . . .

First of all, we have just entered our 81st month of prosperity. We had Gardner Ackley evaluate other periods in our history and the average periods of economic progress that have taken place.

Then we asked each Cabinet Member to give us his view and to give consideration to what this economic progress had meant in his jurisdiction. . . .

Second, we had a very excellent presentation on the report of a group I had asked to study the social and economic conditions of Negroes in the United States . . . I am hopeful all Americans can give serious study to it and make some contributions because I think probably our number one domestic problem is our urban problem, our city problem, the fact that Negroes and whites have left the rural areas and gone to the cities. There we have the problem of finding jobs, training, education, hospitals, and housing for these people.

We are doing our best to encourage and accelerate our efforts on every front toward finding the best solutions. We have had some disappointments.

We are greatly distressed at the action the Congress took in the Model Cities program. The program was very small beginning but it will necessarily be smaller now. . . .

We very much regret that the Congress saw fit to cut the rent supplements from $40 million to $10 million. That would have taken care of housing for many thousands of people. But the Congress did not see it that way. . . .

I will be glad to take your questions on these subjects or on any other subjects that you may want to take, subject only to your time limitation.

Q: Mr. President, what is your view of the likelihood of now getting a tax increase through the Congress?

THE PRESIDENT: The final decision will have to come from the Ways and Means Committee. We very much want it. We think it is very necessary in the national interest. We think that it will cost the American people much less by taking the tax route that we have suggested than by taking the inaction route that is now being followed.

As to prophesying or predicting what the Ways and Means Committee will do, even what the House will do when and if they act, I cannot be very accurate with you. All I can say is what we feel very strongly. We have informed the leadership and the Congress and the committees of both Houses of both Parties. I would be less than frank if I didn't tell you that we are disappointed at the results obtained thus far. . . .

As to whether Congress will act this session or not, you will have to wait and see.

*   *   *

Q: Secretary Rusk said the other day that Hanoi had been encouraged by the recent peace demonstrations. I wonder, sir, if you could give us your assessment of what damage you think has been done to the American cause by the peace demonstrations?

THE PRESIDENT: I would prefer not to be negative.

I would hope that every person, who has a plan, a program, or observation in connection with the war that our young men are fighting out there, would engage in some introspection and ask himself whether what he is about to say is going to make a contribution to solving the problem before he speaks.

If, in his judgment, it does, then he has that opportunity and that right.

So far as I am aware, there have been no great, unexpected developments that have flowed from the various suggestions and programs that have come from people on the outside who have busily engaged in finding out what is wrong.

I meet with Congressmen and Senators every day. I read every morning their statements.

We give consideration to them. But in considering them I must always bear in mind that most of those people, not even the intellectuals or the editorial writers or the columnists, pro or con, have had the benefit of the hundreds of cables that come from 110 countries, or from the men in charge, or men who really have the responsibility for the planning and execution of some of the most intricate, detailed, dangerous, and comprehensive steps that we have ever taken.

So while we want to be reasonable, keep an open mind, and take any suggestion that is designed to help—and will—I could not honestly tell you that the various plans, programs, phrases and key words that they use—like snow and phony—and the headline hunting phrases, I don't think they have really helped our Marines a whole lot up there on the DMZ.

I can't see that they have made any great contribution to solving the problem that we all are so earnestly seeking to solve.

I don't want to be critical of anyone. I think, though, that if the

American public could read Hanoi's cables and statements and could see their reaction to some of the things that are being said in the country, that they would agree with me that all their private proposals and statements have not contributed a great deal to the solution that we so eagerly seek.

Q: Who are Hanoi's cables to, Mr. President?

THE PRESIDENT: They are statements to people in this country. They are statements to people in other countries. They are statements on their radio. They are statements in their press. They are statements in their propaganda.

I use cables symbolically of what their expressions or statements are. I will substitute the word expression for you—or their statements—if it is better.

Q: Mr. President, sir, do you see any lessening of their determination to go on fighting?

THE PRESIDENT: I would not want to make a prediction as to their condition now. I have my views on it, but they involve a certain amount of speculation and judgments that I am making, so I couldn't underwrite and guarantee.

I would not want to pay the price of stating it and then back up later and say I misled you somewhere or made a mistake.

Q: Are you optimistic, sir?

THE PRESIDENT: Yes. I believe that we are making progress. I believe that we are doing what we ought to do. I think we are going to continue doing what we ought to do. I think that it is going to be exacting, difficult, and going to require the best that is in all of us—but not nearly as much from us as it is from the men fighting out there.

If we can manifest on the home front the same courage, the same stability, and the same good judgment they are manifesting out there, I have not the slightest doubt that we will find the solution—and find it much earlier united than we will divided.

Q: Mr. President, sir, one of the main points in the domestic arguments about the policy of the war has been the fact that in 1964, when you were campaigning, you spoke of not wishing to send American boys to fight a war that Asian boys should fight. Then a year later, the government did that. I wonder if you could give us your thinking on the change in policy?

THE PRESIDENT: There has not been a change of policy. You have quoted one sentence in a speech that contained many sentences and many paragraphs. We always have said—and we repeat now—that we do not want American boys to do the fighting that the South Vietnamese boys ought to do or that Asian boys ought to do.

We are asking them *all* to do *all* they can. But that did not imply then and does not imply now that we would not do what we needed to do to deter aggression.

As a matter of fact, before that statement was made, we began discussing at this table in May of that year the desirability of asking Congress to join with us in deterring aggression.

In presenting that resolution to Congress, we made clear to Congress some of the things that I would ask you not to overlook now; namely, that we had a vital security interest in Southeast Asia; that Asian security was important to our own American security.

Second, we intended to comply with what we believed to be our commitments under the SEATO Treaty signed by Senator Mansfield and others at Manila in September 1954.

Finally, that we ask the Congress not only to approve what we had already done in resisting aggression in the Tonkin Gulf, and elsewhere in that area, but to also authorize us to take whatever steps necessary to deter further aggression.

Q: Mr. President, you spoke of the urban problem as being our number one domestic problem. I would like to ask you a sort of double-barreled question.

THE PRESIDENT: I would say urban with all the other things related to it; jobs, housing, ghettos, etcetera—included.

Do you understand what I mean by that?

Q: Yes, sir.

Do you think now, sir, that that will be an issue in the next year's political campaign?

THE PRESIDENT: I can't tell what will be an issue. I am not thinking about what is going to happen in next year's campaign now. I am thinking about what we have to do right now—as quickly as we can.

If you are asking me whether it is a Democratic Party matter or whether it is a political matter, I do not think it ought to be. I would hope that most Democrats and a substantial number of Republicans would signify by their votes that they are willing to pay the price necessary to meet this problem.

*   *   *

Q: Mr. President, with the new government established in Saigon, do you think it would be useful or helpful or constructive if they could negotiate directly with the NLF?

THE PRESIDENT: I don't think it would be helpful for me to tell you to tell them what they ought to do. These people in South Vietnam have had five elections in a period of a little over three months.

We hope and we pray that as a result of this last election they will have a government that will be close to the people, that will provide good leadership and clean leadership, free of corruption, with a maximum of efficiency, and will get rid of incompetence wherever it appeared and corruption wherever it appeared.

We will have to see how these things develop as the government progresses.

This is their government selected by their people. We have made, I think, according to even our most embittered critics, a rather substantial political progress in the last 13 months.

I would ask all of you to remember that it took us 13 years to go from 1776 to 1789 when we finally got our own Constitution. They have come a long way from the time we met in Honolulu to the time they elected their President in something over 13 months. That is what we did in 13 years.

They selected a Constituent Assembly. They drafted their Constitution. They ratified their Constitution. They elected the Senate. They elected the House. They elected the President, and the Vice President.

Their elected leaders, in their judgment and in their wisdom, are there every day . . . trying to make progress and move forward.

A good many of the Vietnamese lost their brothers when they were trying to vote in one of these five elections. A great many people were killed. They died trying to vote.

Some were almost killed yesterday during the inauguration there— trying to get a President sworn in. That action ought to revolt the civilized world.

I do not know why people do not get worked up when they go to lobbing mortar shells into the city where the President is being inaugurated. But I think what they do is a matter for them to decide. Of course, we have our hopes and our desires.

I will be talking to Ambassador [Ellsworth] Bunker before very long. He will be coming here, I hope, before Ambassador [Carol]

Laise leaves. I will talk to him and get his judgments. I am sure if his counsel is sought it will be available.

Pardon me for including you out of this deal, but I am sure that he will respond when desirable.

Q: Mr. President, you talked about 81 months of stable economy. Yet the stock market appears very unstable. It has been going down for some days and it went down 13 points today. Does this suggest a loss of investor confidence in the economy?

THE PRESIDENT: First, I want to correct you before you get a credibility charge. I didn't say anything about a stable economy. I spoke of a prosperous economy.

The stock market goes up and it goes down. Last month they were talking about it going up and breaking 900 and this month it goes down.

I do think in fairness to your question our people are concerned and that concern may be reflected in the market. They do not know today what to expect from the Congress now or in the future so far as taxes are concerned.

I think when you have an uncertain future, you have uncertain markets and you have uncertain stock prices. Some of this uncertainty is being reflected in the market. I think it is being reflected in the bond market and in the interest rates. I think you are paying every day—more than you know, right this moment—for the inaction that is taking place and for the refusal of our people to stand up and take the action that responsibility requires.

. . . We are at a standstill. I would very much hope that the Congress could say, "Well, now, we want to cut appropriations so much—$5 billion, $6 billion or $7 billion." Whatever their judgment is. "And we are willing to give you $4 billion, or $5 billion, or $6 billion taxes." Whatever they are willing to do.

We will study the programs in the future and we will have a meeting of the minds. I think it is important to do this as soon as possible. Every day we are losing revenue. It costs us every day in increased prices and in increased uncertainty and greatly in increased interest.

It may have some bearing on the stocks that you are talking about.

Q: To follow that up, is it fair to say then you believe part of the reason for the downslide on the market is Congressional inaction on the Tax Bill?

THE PRESIDENT: No, I am not saying that. If you want to, you say that. If you don't know what I said, I hope you will read it. I didn't say that at all.

My job, as I have said to my press friends so many times, is to prevent a fight, not to provoke one. You have a different responsibility. I respect your position on the matter. I recognize it and I feel it.

Q: Mr. President, again, pressure is building up in the country and around the world to have another bombing pause. Will you discuss with us the pros and cons of that situation?

THE PRESIDENT: No. I don't think there is anything that I can contribute that would be helpful. We are doing what we believe and what we know to the best of our knowledge to be the right and proper thing to do. And we are going to continue to do what we believe is right.

I would admonish and caution all of you to avoid irresponsibility and quit grabbing out of the air these speculative future ventures about which we know very little and about which the folks that apparently are guessing for you know nothing.

Q: Mr. President, in that same vein, do you think that you, personally, can help to alleviate some of the uncertainty in the country over Vietnam?

THE PRESIDENT: I am doing my best to do that every day. I tried my best in San Antonio when I said to the American people on the televised networks—some live and some a little later that night delayed—and through all of the press, that we would go the last mile.

We were willing to, at that moment, stop our bombing and enter into prompt and productive discussions, assuming they would not take advantage of it. They have not given us any affirmative response to this point.

We will continue willing to negotiate now, to stop the bombing now, if they will talk promptly, productively, and not take advantage of us.

But the problem is not here with your country or with your government or with your soldiers. The problem is with the Communist enemy who insists on continuing the course that places us in Vietnam and that will keep us there until they decide might does not make right, and they cannot gobble up weaker people because they are stronger.

We are going to stand for limited objectives. We are going to try to keep from widening the war. We are going to try to deter aggression and to permit self-determination in South Vietnam.

And when that is done, we are going to be content. We do not want bases, domination, colonization. We do not practice colonialism.

We seek to do nothing except keep our commitments—try to help innocent people who want the right to live according to their own self-determination.

Q: Mr. President, in a general way, could you describe how you feel about how Administration programs are going in Congress and what you think the final score might look like?

THE PRESIDENT: They are not going as well as we would like. They are going better than most people would expect from the domestic standpoint when you look at the 47 new Republicans elected last November. Most of the 47 Democrats that supported measures like Model Cities were replaced . . . by 47 Republicans—a good many of whom oppose these bills. This is only the first half of this Congress.

The next half will begin next January. I do not know when the first half will be over, when the bell will ring. I hope it will not be until we have faced up to some of the compelling and immediate decisions that confront us. I do not recall precisely, but I believe that counting investment credit, tax bill, the draft, the Consular Treaty, and other matters of that nature—including some minor bills and treaties—that we have passed 76 measures.

We started out scheduling something over a hundred. I do not remember how many over a hundred. But I believe 76 of them have been finalized. Some of them are very minor. I *emphasize* minor. We do not want to overstate the case.

There are some 20 measures that have passed the House that we know the Senate is considering. Some of those will be passed, about 20 that have passed the Senate. Some will be considered by the House.

When you add what we expect the House to pass that the Senate has acted upon and what we expect the Senate to pass that the House has acted upon, that number will move up some. How much, I do not know.

But for the first half, I believe it will be a credible one. It will not be 90 percent as it has been in some sessions. But if you compare it to almost any other single session, you can form your judgment. I will leave that up to your opinion.

I looked at what we passed in 1935. I looked at the first hundred days in the New Deal. I looked at the first three years of the Kennedy-Johnson Administration, and I have reviewed the last three years of the Johnson-Humphrey Administration.

While this Session is not as good as the last Congress, this Session, I think, will stand reasonably well compared to the previous Congresses. That is a matter of judgment you can make by reviewing it all.

I am sure before we go home that if you desire we will review all of the achievements, accomplishments and failures.

THE PRESS: Thank you very much, sir.

Appendix F

A White House Briefing

Twice each day, at eleven in the morning and four in the afternoon, correspondents who cover the White House are briefed by the President's press secretary. At these sessions the President's on-the-record appointment list is announced, routine White House actions are made public, and reporters have an opportunity to seek comments and information.

The briefing recorded in the following transcript was somewhat longer than the average, running just over half an hour, but otherwise was fairly typical. It was conducted at the White House by Press Secretary George Christian on Monday morning, July 10, 1967, while Defense Secretary Robert S. McNamara was on one of his periodic visits to Vietnam. The transcript illustrates the broad range of correspondents' questions—from the President's affinity for bicycles to his appraisal of the latest Vietnam peace proposals—as well as the circumspection of Christian's replies.

MR. CHRISTIAN: On the President's schedule today: At 5:30, Mr. George Meany.

Otherwise the President will be working today mainly with staff members on action items.

Q: What is he going to talk to Meany about, George?

MR. CHRISTIAN: Mr. Meany asked for the appointment. The only matter I know of is the United Givers Campaign, which Mr. Meany is interested in.

Q: Do you think they might talk about anything else?

MR. CHRISTIAN: They sometimes exchange views, generally. This

234

is the only matter I know of specifically that he was interested in talking to the President about.

Q: George, the group of eight Republicans proposed a plan for scaling down the Vietnam war. They called it staged de-escalation. Is the White House familiar with it and does it have any comment on it?

MR. CHRISTIAN: I am sure that the President hasn't analyzed it and I certainly haven't. The President and Secretaries of State and Defense and the Joint Chiefs and others, of course, have heavy responsibilities in this field.

We do get suggestions from time to time from various individuals, including members of Congress. Unless Congress takes action on suggestions that come from their members, of course, it doesn't constitute official policies. They are in the category of suggestions. But I have not gone specifically into the report you mentioned.

I am just trying to make it clear that I wouldn't want to leave the impression this may be a policy that is about to be developed as far as the Executive Branch goes.

Q: There is a report from Norway that a group of Nobel Peace Prize winners have volunteered to act as mediators in the Vietnam War. Would the Administration welcome such a move?

MR. CHRISTIAN: The Administration has consistently encouraged every means that I can think of toward reaching a peaceful settlement of the Vietnam conflict. I am not familiar with the plans these people have in mind other than the report we saw.

Q: George, what is the outlook on the first meeting with Mc-Namara? Can you talk out loud a little about how that will work out this week?

MR. CHRISTIAN: Only to the extent that, as you know, just about every time Secretary McNamara goes to Vietnam the emphasis in the speculation is on troops, deployment of troops and numbers of troops and that sort of thing. Of course, this trip involves a great deal more than that.

General Wheeler is with the Secretary and Undersecretary Katzenbach and others are in the party who are also assessing the situation there. I am sure they are going into all facets of the present situation, including military activities, the pacification program, the coming election, how we are spending our dollars, and just about the whole gamut of activities there, in conjunction with the South Vietnamese and our allies.

I am sure that any reports, as such, that these gentlemen present will cover a great many things affecting the overall picture in Vietnam.

Q: When are they due back, George?

MR. CHRISTIAN: I am not sure.

Q: Will General Westmoreland see the President when he comes back this week?

MR. CHRISTIAN: I haven't talked to the President about it, but I know that the telegram the President sent to the General expressed sympathy on his loss. It indicated that the President expected him to rush home, of course, for the funeral and indicated that he did expect to see him before he returned.

Q: Do you have any idea, George, when that might be?

MR. CHRISTIAN: No, I do not.

Q: What can you tell us on the possibility of the President being in Boston tomorrow evening?

MR. CHRISTIAN: Only that this organization and many others invite the President regularly each year to attend their conventions. The invitation hasn't been accepted at this point and I don't have anything on it for you.

Q: What organization is it?

MR. CHRISTIAN: The NAACP.

Q: The NAACP has announced in Boston that he will be there.

MR. CHRISTIAN: I didn't see anything to that effect. I saw something in the Boston papers that they had invited the President.

Q: I got a call this morning from our Boston station saying the NAACP had announced that he was coming.

MR. CHRISTIAN: I haven't seen the stories.

Q: George, you say the invitation hasn't been accepted, but apparently he is giving it serious consideration; is that correct?

MR. CHRISTIAN: Really, all I know about it, Bob, at this point, is that the President was invited.

Q: George, there is a story in print to the effect that the United States has offered to exchange ten North Vietnamese sailors and survivors of the PT attack for ten American airmen. Can you confirm that?

MR. CHRISTIAN: Spencer, I have seen stories like that before. But I don't have any comment on them. I would refer you to the appropriate sources.

Q: George, do you have any idea when the final figures on the fiscal 1967 spending will be going up to the Hill?

MR. CHRISTIAN: No, I don't.

Q: George, there have been stories in print during this past week while the President was in Texas to the effect that he would be talking with the allied governments about their providing more manpower in South Vietnam and specifically there was a story over the weekend that this matter had been taken up in Seoul by the Vice President when he was out there. Can you tell us anything about that?

MR. CHRISTIAN: I can't really enlighten you on the accounts of this other than to remind you that the allied effort in South Vietnam does involve other countries; that other countries do have troop commitments along with this country; and that, of course, the commitments of those other countries are reviewed, I guess, from time to time, by those governments the same as we do here. There is frequently a consultation on these matters as there was in Manila last year.

Q: Is there such communication going on now?

MR. CHRISTIAN: Not that I know of specifically.

Q: You spoke of the communication between the countries that takes place when they review, as we do, their troop commitments and I was just picking up your suggestion there.

MR. CHRISTIAN: I don't know of anything specifically.

Tom just gave me a note that the President has received a reply from General Westmoreland. He was to depart July 10, Saigon time, to attend the funeral of his mother on Wednesday. General Westmoreland indicated he would contact the President about an appointment here.

Q: George, there have also been stories out of Texas by some of our colleagues which speak of the President bicycling. Has he taken up the bicycle?

MR. CHRISTIAN: Ray, I imagine the President, from time to time, has ridden a bicycle, for fifty years or so.

Q: Did he ride it last week?

MR. CHRISTIAN: I think he rides from time to time, yes.

Q: Does his Press Secretary?

MR. CHRISTIAN: Yes.

Q: With the President?

MR. CHRISTIAN: I have never ridden with the President.

Q: George, is this something he sort of returned to recently, though?

MR. CHRISTIAN: I honestly don't know.

Q: Was he riding around the ranch?

MR. CHRISTIAN: I think he has from time to time, yes. There are bicycles there which staff people use.

Q: Is this part of his personal fitness program?

MR. CHRISTIAN: I don't know.

Q: George, can I go back to your earlier answer on McNamara's mission. You said it involved a great deal more than numbers of troops and troop increases and so on. You don't mean to say that the question of troop increases is not under active consideration, do you?

MR. CHRISTIAN: No, I said that all of these matters are being looked at by the group headed by Secretary McNamara.

Q: George, is there any possibility that the President will go to the funeral of the General's mother?

MR. CHRISTIAN: I have heard of no plans.

Q: Do you think General Westmoreland would wait here until Secretary McNamara returns to have a big conference with the President and the Secretary?

MR. CHRISTIAN: Bob, I can't truthfully answer that now. I don't know. The first word I have had is to the date.

Q: George, could you tell us if the Prime Minister of Romania carried any message from the President on his current visit to China?

MR. CHRISTIAN: As I understand it, the Prime Minister told the President that he was going to Mainland China. I believe the President reviewed briefly his general feelings toward a peaceful Mainland China which he set out in some detail a year ago, July 12, 1966.

The President made a nation-wide radio-TV speech here directed to the American Alumni Council in White Sulphur Springs when he couldn't attend.

The President said then, for your information that "The fourth essential for peace in Asia which may seem the most difficult of all: reconciliation between nations that now call themselves enemies."

He said, "A hostile China must be discouraged from aggression. A misguided China must be encouraged toward understanding of the outside world and toward policies of peaceful cooperation."

The President went on to review his oft-stated belief that a peaceful Asia is essential to peace in the world.

I am just reviewing generally what the President has been saying on this subject in which I feel certain that he also—

Q: You said to [Romanian Prime Minister] Maurer. You are not now just summarizing as far as the speech?

MR. CHRISTIAN: This has been the President's general view and I feel certain that this was the same thing he expressed to the Prime Minister and other visitors—that with 700 million people in China and with 600 million people in India and Pakistan and 100 million in Indonesia added in, that that totals up to about half the world's population.

As the President said in this speech I referred to, hunger and disease and ignorance and poverty don't recognize national boundaries. As he said then, he referred to the fact that Communist China had rejected overtures to join in a peaceful society but we persist because we believe that even the most rigid societies will one day awaken to the rich possibilities of a diverse world.

This has been the President's general approach on the subject of Mainland China all along.

Q: But did he ask the Romanian Premier to convey these to the Chinese?

MR. CHRISTIAN: I think in general the President wanted the Prime Minister to know his attitude toward Mainland China so that the Prime Minister would understand what it was.

Q: There is a report on this. *Stern*, in its story about the interview with the President, said that he asked the Romanian Prime Minister to convey these views to the Red Chinese.

MR. CHRISTIAN: I didn't see the interview. But I am sure that in general the President would hope that the Prime Minister or any other visitor to Red China would understand his views and convey them in that sense in any discussions he might have, if he chose to do so.

Q: On the part of the Prime Minister visiting the President here, did the President know that he was going to Mainland China?

MR. CHRISTIAN: I understand the Prime Minister did tell him he was going.

Q: The *Stern* interview, which I have only seen a wire service story on, is that authentic as far as you have read? Did these people interview the President and do these represent his views?

MR. CHRISTIAN: Mr. Nannen, the editor of *Stern*, did see the

President, yes. There wasn't any transcript taken. I haven't seen the story. All I have seen is probably what you saw.

Q: But that is not inaccurate?

MR. CHRISTIAN: I don't recall everything precisely in the story. For your guidance, the only thing I noticed was that a statement was attributed to me. I didn't talk to the *Post*.

I would question that part of it since I didn't say anything about it to that extent.

Q: Wait a minute. You are not speaking now of the *Stern* story in itself?

MR. CHRISTIAN: No, I just saw an insert in the *Post* story attributing something to me.

Q: But as far as the *Stern* story is concerned from what you have seen of it you know of no error?

MR. CHRISTIAN: I don't know what is in context and what isn't. Just for your guidance on the story now, as I recall the President was asked to comment specifically on the recent Cabinet discussions in Germany on troops. He did not comment specifically on it. He said he didn't think it was proper to do it.

The President just expressed the general view that any troop questions like this involved problems, but he understood that other people had problems. That was about the general context of it.

Q: When was that interview?

MR. CHRISTIAN: It was Saturday.

Q: In that connection, one of these wire service stories said that President Johnson predicted in this interview that Red China would have a respected seat among the nations. Respected seat is in single quotes.

MR. CHRISTIAN: I think that is a little strong from what I heard, Spencer. Any discussion of China was pretty well in context of what I have given you in terms of people and population and reconciliation for a peaceful Asia.

Q: George, a bit earlier, you in effect took the spotlight away from the troop issue by making the point that there are large other areas in the team, that the team which has gone over to Vietnam is taking a look at.

Can you identify in terms of policy decisions any other decisions or range of decisions that could be made in Vietnam other than the decision of putting more money and more troops into the war?

MR. CHRISTIAN: Andy, I think I covered it about to the extent I can before Secretary McNamara and Mr. Katzenbach and others return.

Q: Maybe I can phrase that another way. In other words, what else is up for decision other than the troop issue, if you want to broaden it?

MR. CHRISTIAN: I think you have a general assessment from time to time on how effective your entire program is, your entire commitment is, how effective your tax dollars are being used in all of these things—pacification, military operations, everything, the whole war effort—and then plus the domestic situation there in South Vietnam.

They are in consultation with Ambassador Bunker, and Ambassador Locke, and Mr. Komer and others. They will get an on-the-ground assessment of the election process and how things are working out.

Q: George, in terms of decisions that may come out of this review, the only real decision can be in terms of the American commitment toward the war. Isn't that true?

MR. CHRISTIAN: I am not fully familiar with how many hard and fast decisions came out of Secretary McNamara's previous eight visits. I am sure there were some. But I don't know of anything specific that I can tell you about this morning.

THE PRESS: Thank you, sir.

Index